THE GOSPEL OF MATTHEW

THE IGNATIUS CATHOLIC STUDY BIBLE

REVISED STANDARD VERSION
SECOND CATHOLIC EDITION

THE GOSPEL OF MATTHEW

With Introduction, Commentary, and Notes

by

Scott Hahn and Curtis Mitch

and

with Study Questions by

Dennis Walters

IGNATIUS PRESS   SAN FRANCISCO

Published with ecclesiastical approval.

Original RSV Bible text:
Nihil Obstat: Thomas Hanlon, S.T.L., L.S.S, Ph. L.
Imprimatur: +Peter W. Bertholome, D.D.
Bishop of Saint Cloud, Minnesota,
May 11, 1966.

Second Catholic Edition approved under the same *imprimatur* by the
Secretariat for Doctrine and Pastoral Practices,
National Conference of Catholic Bishops,
February 29, 2000

Introduction, commentaries, and notes:
Imprimatur: + William J. Levada,
Archbishop of San Francisco,
November 29, 1999

Second Catholic Edition approved by the
National Council of the Churches of Christ in the USA.

Cover art: *Saint Matthew Inspired by an Angel*
Rembrandt van Rijn, Louvre, Paris
Scala/Art Resource, New York

Cover design by Riz Boncan Marsella

Published by Ignatius Press in 2000
Bible text: Revised Standard Version, Second Catholic Edition
© 2000 by the Division of Christian Education of the
National Council of the Churches of Christ in the United States of America
All rights reserved

Introductions, commentaries, notes, headings, and study questions
© 2000, Ignatius Press, San Francisco
All rights reserved
ISBN 978–0–89870–817–2
Printed in the United States of America ∞

CONTENTS

INTRODUCTION TO THE IGNATIUS STUDY BIBLE

You are approaching the "word of God". This is the title Christians most commonly give to the Bible, and the expression is rich in meaning. It is also the title given to the Second Person of the Blessed Trinity, God the Son. For Jesus Christ became flesh for our salvation, and "the name by which he is called is The Word of God" (Rev 19:13; cf. Jn 1:14).

The word of God is Scripture. The Word of God is Jesus. This close association between God's *written* word and his *eternal* Word is intentional and has been the custom of the Church since the first generation. "All Sacred Scripture is but one book, and this one book is Christ, 'because all divine Scripture speaks of Christ, and all divine Scripture is fulfilled in Christ'[1]" (CCC 134). This does not mean that the Scriptures are divine in the same way that Jesus is divine. They are, rather, divinely inspired and, as such, are unique in world literature, just as the Incarnation of the eternal Word is unique in human history.

Yet we can say that the inspired word resembles the incarnate Word in several important ways. Jesus Christ is the Word of God incarnate. In his humanity, he is like us in all things, except for sin. As a work of man, the Bible is like any other book, except without error. Both Christ and Scripture, says the Second Vatican Council, are given "for the sake of our salvation" (*Dei Verbum* 11), and both give us God's definitive revelation of himself. We cannot, therefore, conceive of one without the other: the Bible without Jesus, or Jesus without the Bible. Each is the interpretive key to the other. And because Christ is the subject of all the Scriptures, St. Jerome insists, "Ignorance of the Scriptures is ignorance of Christ"[2] (CCC 133).

When we approach the Bible, then, we approach Jesus, the Word of God; and in order to encounter Jesus, we must approach him in a prayerful study of the inspired word of God, the Sacred Scriptures.

Inspiration and Inerrancy The Catholic Church makes mighty claims for the Bible, and our acceptance of those claims is essential if we are to read the Scriptures and apply them to our lives as the Church intends. So it is not enough merely to nod at words like "inspired", "unique", or "inerrant". We have to understand what the Church means by these terms, and we have to make that understanding our own. After all, what we believe about the Bible will inevitably influence the way we read the Bible. The way we read the Bible, in turn, will determine what we "get out" of its sacred pages.

These principles hold true no matter what we read: a news report, a search warrant, an advertisement, a paycheck, a doctor's prescription, an eviction notice. How (or whether) we read these things depends largely upon our preconceived notions about the reliability and authority of their sources—and the potential they have for affecting our lives. In some cases, to misunderstand a document's authority can lead to dire consequences. In others, it can keep us from enjoying rewards that are rightfully ours. In the case of the Bible, both the rewards and the consequences involved take on an ultimate value.

What does the Church mean, then, when she affirms the words of St. Paul: "All scripture is inspired by God" (2 Tim 3:16)? Since the term "inspired" in this passage could be translated "God-breathed", it follows that God breathed forth his word in the Scriptures as you and I breathe forth air when we speak. This means that God is the primary author of the Bible. He certainly employed human authors in this task as well, but he did not merely assist them while they wrote or subsequently approve what they had written. God the Holy Spirit is the *principal* author of Scripture, while the human writers are *instrumental* authors. These human authors freely wrote everything, and only those things, that God wanted: the word of God in the very words of God. This miracle of dual authorship extends to the whole of Scripture, and to every one of its parts, so that whatever the human authors affirm, God likewise affirms through their words.

The principle of biblical inerrancy follows logically from this principle of divine authorship. After all, God cannot lie, and he cannot make mistakes. Since the Bible is divinely inspired, it must be without error in everything that its divine and human authors affirm to be true. This means that biblical inerrancy is a mystery even broader in scope than infallibility, which guarantees for us that the Church will always teach the truth concerning faith and morals. Of course the mantle of inerrancy likewise covers faith and morals, but it extends even farther to ensure that all the facts and events of salvation history are accurately presented for us in the Scriptures. Inerrancy is our guarantee that the words and deeds of God found in the Bible are unified and true, declaring with one voice the wonders of his saving love.

---

[1] Hugh of St. Victor, *De arca Noe* 2, 8: PL 176, 642: cf. ibid. 2, 9: PL 176, 642–43.
[2] *DV* 25; cf. Phil 3:8 and St. Jerome, *Commentariorum Isaiam libri xviii*, prol.: PL 24, 17b.

The guarantee of inerrancy does not mean, however, that the Bible is an all-purpose encyclopedia of information covering every field of study. The Bible is not, for example, a textbook in the empirical sciences, and it should not be treated as one. When biblical authors relate facts or events of the natural order, we can be sure they are speaking in a purely descriptive and "phenomenological" way, according to the way things appeared to their senses.

Biblical Authority Implicit in these doctrines is God's desire to make himself known to the world and to enter a loving relationship with every man, woman, and child he has created. God gave us the Scriptures not just to inform or motivate us; more than anything he wants to save us. This higher purpose underlies every page of the Bible, indeed every word of it.

In order to reveal himself, God used what theologians call "accommodation". Sometimes the Lord stoops down to communicate by "condescension"—that is, he speaks as humans speak, as if he had the same passions and weakness that we do (for example, God says he was "sorry" that he made man in Genesis 6:6). Other times he communicates by "elevation"—that is, by endowing human words with divine power (for example, through the prophets). The numerous examples of divine accommodation in the Bible are an expression of God's wise and fatherly ways. For a sensitive father can speak with his children either by condescension, as in baby talk, or by elevation, by bringing a child's understanding up to a more mature level.

God's word is thus saving, fatherly, and personal. Because it speaks directly to us, we must never be indifferent to its content; after all, the word of God is at once the object, cause, and support of our faith. It is, in fact, a test of our faith, since we see in the Scriptures only what faith disposes us to see. If we believe what the Church believes, we will see in Scripture the saving, inerrant, and divinely authored revelation of the Father. If we believe otherwise, we see another book altogether.

This test applies not only to rank-and-file believers but also to the Church's theologians and hierarchy, and even the Magisterium. Vatican II has stressed in recent times that Scripture must be "the very soul of sacred theology" (*Dei Verbum* 24). Joseph Cardinal Ratzinger echoes this powerful teaching with his own, insisting that, "The *normative theologians* are the authors of Holy Scripture" [emphasis added]. Elsewhere he reminds us that Scripture and the Church's dogmatic teaching are tied tightly together, to the point of being inseparable. He states: "Dogma is by definition nothing other than an interpretation of Scripture." The defined dogmas of our faith, then, encapsulate the Church's infallible interpretation of Scripture, and theology is a further reflection upon that work.

The Senses of Scripture Because the Bible has both divine and human authors, we are required to master a different sort of reading than we are used to. First, we must read Scripture according to its *literal* sense, as we read any other human literature. At this initial stage, we strive to discover the meaning of the words and expressions used by the biblical writers as they were understood in their original setting and by their original recipients. This means, among other things, that we do not interpret everything we read "literalistically", as though Scripture never speaks in a figurative or symbolic way (it often does!). Rather, we read it according to the rules that govern its different literary forms of writing, depending on whether we are reading a narrative, a poem, a letter, a parable, or an apocalyptic vision. The Church calls us to read the divine books in this way to ensure that we understand what the human authors were laboring to explain to God's people.

The literal sense, however, is not the only sense of Scripture, since we interpret its sacred pages according to the *spiritual* senses as well. In this way, we search out what the Holy Spirit is trying to tell us, beyond even what the human authors have consciously asserted. Whereas the literal sense of Scripture describes a historical reality—a fact, precept, or event—the spiritual senses disclose deeper mysteries revealed through the historical realities. What the soul is to the body, the spiritual senses are to the literal. You can distinguish them; but if you try to separate them, death immediately follows. St. Paul was the first to insist upon this and warn of its consequences: "God ... has qualified us to be ministers of a new covenant, not in a written code but in the Spirit; for the written code kills, but the Spirit gives life" (2 Cor 3:5–6).

Catholic tradition recognizes three spiritual senses that stand upon the foundation of the literal sense of Scripture (see CCC 115). (1) The first is the *allegorical* sense, which unveils the spiritual and prophetic meaning of biblical history. Allegorical interpretations thus reveal how persons, events, and institutions of Scripture can point beyond themselves toward greater mysteries yet to come (OT), or display the fruits of mysteries already revealed (NT). Christians have often read the Old Testament in this way to discover how the mystery of Christ in the New Covenant was once hidden in the Old, and how the full significance of the Old Covenant was finally made manifest in the New. Allegorical significance is likewise latent in the New Testament, especially in the life and deeds of Jesus recorded in the Gospels. Because Christ is the Head of the Church and the source of her spiritual life, what was accomplished in Christ the Head during his earthly life prefigures what he continually produces in his members through grace. The allegorical sense builds up the virtue of faith. (2) The second is the *tropological* or *moral* sense, which reveals how the actions of God's people in the Old Testament and the life of Jesus in the New Testament prompt us to form virtuous habits in our own lives. It therefore draws from Scripture warnings against sin and vice, as well as inspirations to pursue holiness and purity. The moral sense is intended to build up the virtue of charity. (3) The third is the *anagogical* sense, which points upward to heavenly glory. It shows us how countless events in the Bible prefigure our final union with God in eternity, and how things that are "seen" on earth are figures of things "unseen" in heaven. Because the anagogical sense leads us to contemplate our destiny, it is meant to build up the virtue of hope. Together with the literal sense, then, these spiritual senses draw out the fullness of what God wants to give us through his Word and as such comprise what ancient tradition has called the "full sense" of Sacred Scripture.

All of this means that the deeds and events of the Bible are charged with meaning beyond what is immediately apparent to the reader. In essence, that meaning is Jesus Christ and the salvation he died to give us. This is especially true of the books of the New Testament, which proclaim Jesus explicitly; but it is also true of the Old Testament, which speaks of Jesus in more hidden and symbolic ways. The human authors of the Old Testament told us as much as they were able, but they could not clearly discern the shape of all future events standing at such a distance. It is the Bible's divine Author, the Holy Spirit, who could and did foretell the saving work of Christ, from the first page of the Book of Genesis onward.

The New Testament did not, therefore, abolish the Old. Rather, the New fulfilled the Old, and in doing so, it lifted the veil that kept hidden the face of the Lord's bride. Once the veil is removed, we suddenly see the world of the Old Covenant charged with grandeur. Water, fire, clouds, gardens, trees, hills, doves, lambs—all of these things are memorable details in the history and poetry of Israel. But now, seen in the light of Jesus Christ, they are much more. For the Christian with eyes to see, water symbolizes the saving power of Baptism; fire, the Holy Spirit; the spotless lamb, Christ crucified; Jerusalem, the city of heavenly glory.

The spiritual reading of Scripture is nothing new. Indeed the very first Christians read the Bible this way. St. Paul describes Adam as a "type" that prefigured Jesus Christ (Rom 5:14). A "type" is a real person, place, thing, or event in the Old Testament that foreshadows something greater in the New. From this term we get the word "typology", referring to the study of how the Old Testament prefigures Christ (CCC 128–30). Elsewhere St. Paul draws deeper meanings out of the story of Abraham's sons, declaring, "This is an allegory" (Gal 4:24). He is not suggesting that these events of the distant past never really happened; he is saying that the events both happened *and* signified something more glorious yet to come.

The New Testament later describes the Tabernacle of ancient Israel as "a copy and shadow of the heavenly sanctuary" (Heb 8:5) and the Mosaic Law as a "shadow of the good things to come" (Heb 10:1). St. Peter, in turn, notes that Noah and his family were "saved through water" in a way that "corresponds" to sacramental Baptism, which "now saves you" (1 Pet 3:20–21). Interestingly, the expression that is translated "corresponds" in this verse is a Greek term that denotes the fulfillment or counterpart of an ancient "type".

We need not look to the apostles, however, to justify a spiritual reading of the Bible. After all, Jesus himself read the Old Testament this way. He referred to Jonah (Mt 12:39), Solomon (Mt 12:42), the Temple (Jn 2:19), and the brazen serpent (Jn 3:14) as "signs" that pointed forward to him. We see in Luke's Gospel, as Christ comforted the disciples on the road to Emmaus, that "beginning with Moses and all the prophets, he interpreted to them in all the scriptures the things concerning himself" (Lk 24:27). It was precisely this extensive spiritual interpretation of the Old Testament that made such an impact on these once-discouraged travelers, causing their hearts to "burn" within them (Lk 24:32).

Criteria for Biblical Interpretation. We too must learn to discern the "full sense" of Scripture as it includes both the literal and spiritual senses together. Still, this does not mean we should "read into" the Bible meanings that are not really there. Spiritual exegesis is not an unrestrained flight of the imagination. Rather, it is a sacred science that proceeds according to certain principles and stands accountable to sacred tradition, the Magisterium, and the wider community of biblical interpreters (both living and deceased).

In searching out the full sense of a text, we should always avoid the extreme tendency to "over-spiritualize" in a way that minimizes or denies the Bible's literal truth. St. Thomas Aquinas was well aware of this danger and asserted that "all other senses of Sacred Scripture are based on the literal" (*STh* I, 1, 10, ad 1, quoted in CCC 116). On the other hand, we should never confine the meaning of a text to the literal, intended sense of its human author, as if the divine Author did not intend the passage to be read in the light of Christ's coming.

Fortunately the Church has given us guidelines in our study of Scripture. The unique character and divine authorship of the Bible calls us to read it "in the Spirit" (*Dei Verbum* 12). Vatican II outlines this teaching in a practical way by directing us to read the Scriptures according to three specific criteria:

1. We must "[b]e especially attentive 'to the content and unity of the whole Scripture'" (CCC 112).

2. We must "[r]ead the Scripture within 'the living Tradition of the whole Church'" (CCC 113).

3. We must "[b]e attentive to the analogy of faith" (CCC 114; cf. Rom 12:6).

These criteria protect us from many of the dangers that ensnare readers of the Bible, from the newest inquirer to the most prestigious scholar. Reading Scripture out of context is one such pitfall, and probably the one most difficult to avoid. A memorable cartoon from the 1950s shows a young man poring over the pages of the Bible. He says to his sister: "Don't bother me now; I'm trying to find a Scripture verse to back up one of my preconceived notions." No doubt a biblical text pried from its context can be twisted to say something very different from what its author actually intended.

The Church's criteria guide us here by defining what constitutes the authentic "context" of a given biblical passage. The first criterion directs us to the literary context of every verse, including not only the words and paragraphs that surround it, but also the entire corpus of the biblical author's writings and, indeed, the span of the entire Bible. The *complete* literary context of any Scripture verse includes every text from Genesis to Revelation—because the Bible is a unified book, not just a library of different books. When the Church canonized the Book of Revelation, for example, she recognized it to be incomprehensible apart from the wider context of the entire Bible.

The second criterion places the Bible firmly within the context of a community that treasures a "living tradition". That community is the People of God down through the ages. Christians lived out their faith for well over a millennium before the printing press was invented. For centuries, few believers owned copies of the Gospels, and few people could read anyway. Yet they absorbed the gospel—through the sermons of their bishops and clergy, through prayer and meditation, through Christian art, through liturgical celebrations, and through oral tradition. These were expressions of the one "living tradition", a culture of living faith that stretches from ancient Israel to the contemporary Church. For the early Christians, the gospel could not be understood apart from that tradition. So it is with us. Reverence for the Church's tradition is what protects us from any sort of chronological or cultural provincialism, such as scholarly fads that arise and carry away a generation of interpreters before being dismissed by the next generation.

The third criterion places scriptural texts within the framework of faith. If we believe that the Scriptures are divinely inspired, we must also believe them to be internally coherent and consistent with all the doctrines that Christians believe. Remember, the Church's dogmas (such as the Real Presence, the papacy, the Immaculate Conception) are not something *added* to Scripture, but are the Church's infallible interpretation *of* Scripture.

Using This Study Guide This volume is designed to lead the reader through Scripture according to the Church's guidelines—faithful to the canon, to the tradition, and to the creeds. The Church's interpretive principles have thus shaped the component parts of this book, and they are designed to make the reader's study as effective and rewarding as possible.

Introductions: We have introduced the biblical book with an essay covering issues such as authorship, date of composition, purpose, and leading themes. This background information will assist readers to approach and understand the text on its own terms.

Annotations: The basic notes at the bottom of every page help the user to read the Scriptures with understanding. They by no means exhaust the meaning of the sacred text but provide background material to help the reader make sense of what he reads. Often these notes make explicit what the sacred writers assumed or held to be implicit. They also provide scores of historical, cultural, geographical, and theological information pertinent to the inspired narratives—information that can help the reader bridge the distance between the biblical world and his own.

Cross-References: Between the biblical text at the top of each page and the annotations at the bottom, numerous references are listed to point readers to other scriptural passages related to the one being studied. This follow-up is an essential part of any serious study. It is also an excellent way to discover how the content of Scripture "hangs together" in a providential unity. Along with biblical cross-references, the annotations refer to select paragraphs from the *Catechism of the Catholic Church*. These are not doctrinal "proof texts" but are designed to help the reader interpret the Bible in accordance with the mind of the Church. The *Catechism* references listed either handle the biblical text directly or treat a broader doctrinal theme that sheds significant light on that text.

Topical Essays, Word Studies, Charts: These features bring readers to a deeper understanding of select details. The *topical essays* take up major themes and explain them more thoroughly and theologically than the annotations, often relating them to the doctrines of the Church. Occasionally the annotations are supplemented by *word studies* that put readers in touch with the ancient languages of Scripture. These should help readers to understand better and appreciate the inspired terminology that runs throughout the sacred books. Also included are various *charts* that summarize biblical information "at a glance".

Icon Annotations: Three distinctive icons are

interspersed throughout the annotations, each one corresponding to one of the Church's three criteria for biblical interpretation. Bullets indicate the passage or passages to which these icons apply.

Notes marked by the book icon relate to the "content and unity" of Scripture, showing how particular passages of the Old Testament illuminate the mysteries of the New. Much of the information in these notes explains the original context of the citations and indicates how and why this has a direct bearing on Christ or the Church. Through these notes, the reader can develop a sensitivity to the beauty and unity of God's saving plan as it stretches across both Testaments.

Notes marked by the dove icon examine particular passages in light of the Church's "living tradition". Because the Holy Spirit both guides the Magisterium and inspires the spiritual senses of Scripture, these annotations supply information along both of these lines. On the one hand, they refer to the Church's doctrinal teaching as presented by various popes, creeds, and ecumenical councils; on the other, they draw from (and paraphrase) the spiritual interpretations of various Fathers, Doctors, and saints.

Notes marked by the key icon pertain to the "analogy of faith". Here we spell out how the mysteries of our faith "unlock" and explain one another. This type of comparison between Christian beliefs displays the coherence and unity of defined dogmas, which are the Church's infallible interpretations of Scripture.

Putting It All in Perspective Perhaps the most important context of all we have saved for last: the interior life of the individual reader. What we get out of the Bible will largely depend on how we approach the Bible. Unless we are living a sustained and disciplined life of prayer, we will never have the reverence, the profound humility, or the grace we need to see the Scriptures for what they really are.

You are approaching the "word of God". But for thousands of years, since before he knit you in your mother's womb, the Word of God has been approaching you.

One Final Note. The volume you hold in your hands is only a small part of a much larger work still in production. Study helps similar to those printed in this booklet are being prepared for *all* the books of the Bible and will appear gradually as they are finished. Our ultimate goal is to publish a single, one-volume Study Bible that will include the entire text of Scripture, along with all the annotations, charts, cross-references, maps, and other features found in the following pages. Individual booklets will be published in the meantime, with the hope that God's people can begin to benefit from this labor before its full completion.

We have included a long list of Study Questions in the back to make this format as useful as possible, not only for individual study but for group settings and discussions as well. The questions are designed to help readers both "understand" the Bible and "apply" it to their lives. We pray that God will make use of our efforts and yours to help renew the face of the earth! «

INTRODUCTION TO THE GOSPEL ACCORDING TO MATTHEW

Author As with Mark, Luke, and John, the first Gospel nowhere mentions its author. The attention of the Gospel is focused wholly on Jesus Christ and his inauguration of the kingdom of heaven. The title "According to Matthew" (Gk. *Kata Matthaion*) is thus not part of the original Gospel but was added at an early date to distinguish it from the other three Gospels. It bears witness to the unanimous consensus of the early Church that Matthew the Apostle, an eyewitness of Jesus, is its author. It was not until the eighteenth century that the tradition of Matthean authorship was questioned.

Little is known about the person and life of Matthew, also called "Levi" (Mk 2:14; Lk 5:27). He worked as a tax collector (9:9) and was called by Jesus to be a disciple. Soon afterward, Matthew hosted a "great feast" (Lk 5:29) for Jesus and his companions. He was later chosen as one of the twelve apostles (10:2–3). Some suggest that Matthew refers to himself in 13:52 as a "scribe who has been trained for the kingdom of heaven". The final appearance of Matthew in the NT occurs at Pentecost in Acts 1:13, where he is present with the Virgin Mary and the apostles praying in the upper room.

Date It is difficult to know exactly when the Gospel of Matthew was written. Dates ranging from A.D. 50 to 100 have been proposed. An early Church tradition is put forward by Papias (A.D. 130 and cited by Eusebius) and Irenaeus (A.D. 180). These Church Fathers give no specific dates but testify that Matthew wrote his Gospel—Papias refers to the "sayings" (Gk. *logia*) of Jesus—in either Hebrew or Aramaic. Since the version of Matthew we possess is written in Greek and is frequently cited in writings of the early Church, it is presumed that this Hebrew/Aramaic version, no longer in existence, predates the canonical Greek Gospel.

The Pontifical Biblical Commission, instituted by Pope Leo XIII to offer guidance to Catholic students of the Bible, concluded in 1911 that the original Hebrew/Aramaic version of Matthew was probably written before A.D. 70, when the Romans destroyed the city and Temple of Jerusalem. This conclusion finds support within the Gospel itself. For example, it is Matthew's normal procedure to point out how past events have enduring significance for the Church in his day (27:8; 28:15). Since Matthew records Jesus' Olivet Discourse foretelling the Temple's destruction (chap. 24; cf. 22:7), one might also expect references to the fulfillment of this pivotal event had his Gospel been written after the fact. As it is, Matthew is silent regarding the fulfillment of Jesus' prophecy (24:2); presumably the Temple was still standing and Jesus' words were unfulfilled at the time he wrote his Gospel. This suggests Matthew's Gospel can be reasonably dated before A.D. 70.

Destination Matthew probably wrote his Gospel for fellow Jewish Christians in and around Palestine. Unlike Mark, who wrote for a Roman audience, Matthew mentions Jewish customs without explanation or comment; he assumes that his readers are already familiar with the practices of Judaism in the first century A.D. (Mt 15:2; cf. Mk 7:2–4). More significantly, Matthew assumes his readers were intimately familiar with the OT. This explains why there are more than 100 references to the OT in his Gospel—many of which are direct quotations, while others are subtle allusions. At one level, Matthew cites OT passages with a keen awareness and sensitivity to their original contexts; at another, he reaches deep within the letter and surface meaning of the OT to draw out its spiritual meaning in light of Jesus Christ. Matthew's portrayal of Christ as the fulfillment of the OT Scriptures was thus to encourage Jewish believers in their faith and confirm for them that Jesus of Nazareth was the true Messiah from God.

Structure Matthew's Gospel is organized around five discourses (or sermons) that record Jesus' teaching about God and his heavenly kingdom. These discourses are set off by a pattern of similar concluding phrases that reveal the skeletal structure of the Gospel (7:28; 11:1; 13:53; 19:1; 26:1). In addition, each discourse is preceded by a short collection of stories or narratives that recount the deeds and miracles of Jesus' public life. The narrative-discourse units together comprise five "books", which are framed by a narrative prologue (chaps. 1–2) and the concluding Passion Week narratives (chaps. 26–28; see outline, page 7). Matthew's narrative-discourse arrangement highlights the complementarity of Jesus' works and words. It further suggests that the Gospel was organized to promote memorization and aid in the catechesis of early Christians.

Themes Several themes stand out in the first Gospel. Matthew emphasizes Jesus' establishment of the New Covenant as the fulfillment of God's covenant promises in salvation history. **(1)** *The Abrahamic Covenant*: As the "son of Abraham"

(1:1), Jesus fulfills God's covenant oath to bless "all the nations of the earth" through Abraham's descendants (Gen 22:18). It is in Jesus Christ that God's salvation spreads beyond the borders of Israel. Even Gentile nations are brought into Abraham's family by the Church's preaching and administration of the sacraments (8:10–12; 28:18–20). **(2)** *The Mosaic Covenant*: God's covenants with Israel at Mt. Sinai (Ex 19—Lev 26) and on the plains of Moab (Deut) were fulfilled in Jesus Christ in two ways. Negatively, Jesus highlights the temporary nature of Mosaic ceremonial laws; the sacrificial and juridical dimensions of the Old Law were scheduled to expire with the arrival of God's New Covenant. Jesus initiates this new era by offering forgiveness apart from Israel's Temple and priesthood (9:1–8). He erects a new standard of covenant righteousness that penetrates deeper than the Law of Moses and advocates holiness that is interior and personal (5:20; 9:13; 23:23). Jesus also revokes Moses' permission of divorce (19:1–9; Deut 24:1–4) and foretells the destruction of Jerusalem's Temple, the architectural symbol of the Old Covenant (chap. 24; cf. 27:51). Positively, Jesus is cast as the new Moses who ascends a new mountain to give the New Covenant Law in the Beatitudes (5:3–12). He perfects and intensifies the moral codes of the Old Law (5:17–48) and binds the Church to himself by his "blood of the covenant" in the Eucharist (26:28). As the Deuteronomic covenant was fulfilled in Israel's possession of the Promised Land, so the New Covenant promises heaven as the inheritance of God's children (25:34, 46). **(3)** *The Davidic Covenant*: Matthew's Gospel most prominently features Jesus as the "son of David" (1:1). It is Christ who fulfills God's covenant oath to establish David's empire forever (2 Sam 7:12–13; Ps 89; Acts 2:29–30). God's covenant appeared threatened when David's dynasty collapsed in 586 B.C. (1:11). Jesus, however, stands amidst the wreckage of David's kingdom to announce its restoration. He is born "king of the Jews" (2:2) and the Father's designated heir to David's throne (Lk 1:32–33). The old kingdom, governed by David and Solomon, was thus an earthly prototype awaiting perfection in the kingdom of heaven. It is now Christ who rules "at the right hand of Power" (26:64) and who reconstitutes the old kingdom in a new and spiritual way (cf. Acts 15:15–18).

Against this backdrop of the Davidic kingdom, Matthew presents the Church as the kingdom of heaven on earth. Of all four Gospels, only Matthew explicitly mentions the "church" (16:18; 18:17). He is particularly concerned to preserve Jesus' teaching on the government of the Church. The apostles are given unique roles in the kingdom as Jesus' cabinet of royal ministers—those who "sit on twelve thrones, judging the twelve tribes of Israel" (19:28). Peter is given a primacy over the Church in matters of authority and teaching as the king's prime minister and guardian of the "keys of the kingdom of heaven" (16:19). Peter is also the foundational "rock" (16:18) upon which the new Temple of the Church is built. The other apostles are invested with royal authority to "bind" and "loose" (18:18) as teachers and administrators of Church discipline. As the reigning Davidic king and Temple builder, it is Jesus himself who guarantees the Church's stability throughout history (16:18). «

OUTLINE OF THE GOSPEL ACCORDING TO MATTHEW

1. **Prologue Narrative: The Ancestry and Infancy of Jesus (1:1—2:23)**
   A. Genealogy of Jesus (1:1–17)
   B. Birth of Jesus in Bethlehem (1:18–25)
   C. Visit of the Wise Men (2:1–12)
   D. Flight of the Holy Family into Egypt (2:13–15)
   E. Slaughter of the Holy Innocents (2:16–18)
   F. Return of the Holy Family to Nazareth (2:19–23)

2. **Book One: John the Baptist and the Early Ministry of Jesus (3:1—7:29)**
   A. *Narrative*: Ministry of John and Jesus (chaps. 3–4)
   B. *Discourse*: Sermon on the Mount (chaps. 5–7)

3. **Book Two: Jesus' Miracles and the Commission of the Twelve (8:1—10:42)**
   A. *Narrative*: Miracle Stories of Jesus (chaps. 8–9)
   B. *Discourse*: Missionary Sermon for the Apostles (chap. 10)

4. **Book Three: Growing Controversy and the New Kingdom (11:1—13:58)**
   A. *Narrative*: Jesus Confronts an Evil Generation (chaps. 11–12)
   B. *Discourse*: Parables of the Kingdom (chap. 13)

5. **Book Four: Jesus Instructs Peter and the Twelve (14:1—18:35)**
   A. *Narrative*: Various Travels and Miracles of Jesus (chaps. 14–17)
   B. *Discourse*: Sermon on Life in the Church (chap. 18)

6. **Book Five: Jesus Travels to Judea and Enters Jerusalem (19:1—25:46)**
   A. *Narrative*: Events in Judea and Jesus' Teaching in the Temple (chaps. 19–23)
   B. *Discourse*: The Olivet Discourse—Judgment on Jerusalem (chaps. 24–25)

7. **Passion Week Narratives: The Suffering and Resurrection of Jesus (26:1—28:20)**
   A. Anointing at Bethany (26:1–16)
   B. The Last Supper (26:17–29)
   C. Betrayal and Trials of Jesus (26:30—27:26)
   D. Crucifixion and Burial of Jesus (27:27–66)
   E. Resurrection of Jesus (28:1–15)
   F. The Great Commission (28:16–20)

THE GOSPEL ACCORDING TO
MATTHEW

The Genealogy of Jesus Christ

The book of the genealogy of Jesus Christ, the son of David, the son of Abraham.

²Abraham was the father of Isaac, and Isaac the father of Jacob, and Jacob the father of Judah and his brothers, ³and Judah the father of Perez and Zerah by Tamar, and Perez the father of Hezron, and Hezron the father of Ram,ᵃ ⁴and Ramᵃ the father of Ammin'adab, and Ammin'adab the father of Nahshon, and Nahshon the father of Salmon, ⁵and Salmon the father of Bo'az by Rahab, and Bo'az the father of Obed by Ruth, and Obed the father of Jesse, ⁶and Jesse the father of David the king.

And David was the father of Solomon by the wife of Uri'ah, ⁷and Solomon the father of Rehobo'am, and Rehobo'am the father of Abi'jah, and Abi'jah the father of Asa,ᵇ ⁸and Asaᵇ the father of Jehosh'aphat, and Jehosh'aphat the father of Joram, and Joram the father of Uzzi'ah, ⁹and Uzzi'ah the father of Jotham, and Jotham the father of Ahaz, and Ahaz the father of Hezeki'ah,

¹⁰and Hezeki'ah the father of Manas'seh, and Manas'seh the father of Amos,ᶜ and Amosᶜ the father of Josi'ah, ¹¹and Josi'ah the father of Jechoniah and his brothers, at the time of the deportation to Babylon.

12 And after the deportation to Babylon: Jechoni'ah was the father of She-al'ti-el,ᵈ and She-al'ti-elᵈ the father of Zerub'babel, ¹³and Zerub'babel the father of Abi'ud, and Abi'ud the father of Eli'akim, and Eli'akim the father of Azor, ¹⁴and Azor the father of Zadok, and Zadok the father of Achim, and Achim the father of Eli'ud, ¹⁵and Eli'ud the father of Elea'zar, and Elea'zar the father of Matthan, and Matthan the father of Jacob, ¹⁶and Jacob the father of Joseph the husband of Mary, of whom Jesus was born, who is called Christ.

17 So all the generations from Abraham to David were fourteen generations, and from David to the deportation to Babylon fourteen generations, and from the deportation to Babylon to the Christ fourteen generations.

1:1–17: Lk 3:23–38.   **1:3–6:** Ruth 4:18–22; 1 Chron 2:1–15.   **1:11:** 2 Kings 24:14; Jer 27:20.

1:1 book of the genealogy: A title for the following ancestry (1:2–16) and the entire Gospel. The opening words recall the Greek OT in Gen 2:4 and 5:1. **Christ:** A title (Gk. *Christos*) meaning the "Anointed One". It is the Greek rendering of the OT word for "Messiah". According to Lk 4:18–19, Jesus is anointed by the Holy Spirit (cf. Acts 10:36–38). It is this title for Jesus that Matthew elucidates throughout his Gospel. See word study: *Christ* at Mk 14 (CCC 436).

1:2–17 The Abrahamic and Davidic ancestry of Jesus establishes his credentials to be the royal Messiah of Israel (1:1, 16). God long ago promised that "kings" would stem from Abraham's line (Gen 17:6) and later swore a covenant oath that David would always have a dynastic heir (2 Sam 7:16; Ps 89:3–4). Note that Matthew's genealogy reaches back to Abraham, the forefather of Israel, whereas Luke's genealogy of Jesus stretches back to Adam, the father of all nations (Lk 3:23–38). This difference is heightened by numerous discrepancies between the two genealogies, especially in the generations spanning from David to Jesus. More than a dozen solutions have been proposed to harmonize them. At the very least, it should be recognized that gaps are a common feature in genealogical registries from antiquity. There are also many examples in Scripture of one person having more than one name—a fact that must be considered when attempting to identify the ancestors of Jesus (e.g., Solomon/Jedidiah, 2 Sam 12:24–25). As one early Christian writer (Julius Africanus) reminds us, neither Matthew nor Luke is in error, for both record Jesus' genealogy intricately and yet accurately.

1:3-6 The inclusion of women (**Tamar, Rahab, Ruth,** and the **wife of Uriah**) in a Jewish genealogy is unusual, but not unprecedented (1 Chron 1:32, 39, 50; 2:4). All are Gentiles (Canaanite, Canaanite, Moabite, and Hittite, respectively), and three (all but Ruth) are associated with sexual immorality (Gen 38:12-26; Josh 2:1; 2 Sam 11:2-5). These irregularities may reflect an apologetic strategy. **(1)** Gentile blood within Jesus' lineage anticipates the international scope of the gospel for men and women of "all nations" (28:19). **(2)** Matthew defuses Jewish accusations that the women in Jesus' genealogy undermine his messianic credentials. By listing the immoral women in the generations before Solomon, Matthew implies that if these women did not disqualify Solomon as the royal son of David, then neither do they disqualify Jesus, who assumes that same title as the Messiah (1:1). Indeed, Solomon's birth through the immorally arranged marriage of David and Uriah's wife (2 Sam 11) stands in vivid contrast to Mary's virginal conception of Jesus by the Spirit (1:18).

1:16 the husband of: The final link in the genealogy breaks with the preceding pattern. Joseph is not called the father of Jesus but only the spouse of Mary. This prepares for the virginal conception of Jesus in 1:18–25. Joseph is, however, the legal foster-father of Jesus and exercises his paternal duty by naming the Child (1:25) and protecting the Holy Family (2:13–22). Following Jewish custom, Jesus received full hereditary rights through Joseph, even though he was adopted (CCC 437, 496). ● In Catholic tradition, the fatherhood of Joseph is also held to be spiritual and real, albeit virginal, just as the Fatherhood of God is spiritual and non-physical.

1:17 fourteen generations: Matthew divides the genealogy into three units of 14. It is not exhaustive, since several OT names are omitted and the divisions cover unequal periods of time. Matthew stresses the number 14 to show Jesus as the new Davidic king: **(1)** David and Jesus are the only names listed with their respective titles (**king**, 1:6; **Christ**, 1:16);

ᵃ Greek *Aram*.   ᵇ Greek *Asaph*.
ᶜ Other authorities read *Amon*.   ᵈ Greek *Salathiel*.

The Birth of Jesus the Messiah

18 Now the birth of Jesus Christ *f* took place in this way. When his mother Mary had been betrothed to Joseph, before they came together she was found to be with child of the Holy Spirit; [19]and her husband Joseph, being a just man and unwilling to put her to shame, resolved to send her away quietly. [20]But as he considered this, behold, an angel of the Lord appeared to him in a dream, saying, "Joseph, son of David, do not fear to take Mary your wife, for that which is conceived in her is of the Holy Spirit; [21]she will bear a son, and you shall call his name Jesus, for he will save his people from their sins." [22]All this took place to fulfil what the Lord had spoken by the prophet:

[23] "Behold, a virgin shall conceive and bear a son, and his name shall be called Emma'nuel"

(which means, God with us). [24]When Joseph woke from sleep, he did as the angel of the Lord commanded him; he took his wife, [25]but knew her not until she had borne a son; and he called his name Jesus.

The Visit of the Wise Men

2 Now when Jesus was born in Bethlehem of Judea in the days of Herod the king, behold, wise men from the East came to Jerusalem, saying, [2]"Where is he who has been born king of the Jews? For we have seen his star in the East, and have come to worship him." [3] When Herod the king heard

---

1:18: Lk 1:26–38. **1:21:** Lk 2:21; Jn 1:29; Acts 13:23. **1:23:** Is 7:14. **2:1:** Lk 2:4–7; 1:5.
2:2: Jer 23:5; Zech 9:9; Mk 15:2; Jn 1:49; Nb 24:17.

---

(2) David is the 14th name in the list; **(3)** the numerical value of David's name (three consonants) in Hebrew equals 14 (D = 4 + V = 6 + D = 4). ● *Allegorically* (St. Jerome, *Epist. ad Fabiolam*, 42), Jesus' 42 total generations signify the 42 encampments of the Israelites between the Exodus and their entry into the Promised Land (Num 33). The generations from Abraham (1:2) to Jesus Christ (1:16) are thus successive steps between the world's deliverance from spiritual slavery and the inheritance of heaven (11:28; 25:34). **deportation to Babylon:** The Exile of the Jews starting in 586 B.C. under the Babylonian king Nebuchadnezzar. After that time, Israel's Davidic kingdom collapsed, and no legitimate heir assumed David's throne. Jesus comes as the awaited Messiah-king (21:4–5; Jn 1:49) to fulfill God's covenant oath to perfect and establish the Davidic dynasty for all time (cf. Ps 132:11–12; Lk 1:32–33).

1:18 betrothed to Joseph: Betrothal in ancient Judaism was unlike modern-day engagements. It was a temporary period (up to one year) between the covenant of marriage itself and the time when spouses lived together. Because couples were legally married during this intervening phase, a betrothal could be terminated only by death or divorce (Deut 24:1–4). **of the Holy Spirit:** Although many view this as an editorial comment that Matthew inserts to inform the *reader* of Jesus' virginal conception, it more likely indicates that *Joseph* and possibly others discovered that Mary's pregnancy was the result of a divine miracle.

1:19 just man: Or "righteous man". The expression highlights Joseph's moral character in the following narrative (1:18–25). **send her away:** Two interpretations attempt to explain why Joseph decided to separate from Mary. They give opposite answers to the question: Who did Joseph think was the unworthy partner in the betrothal? **(1)** *The Suspicion Theory*. This view holds that Joseph suspected Mary of adultery when he discovered she was pregnant. The troubling news led him to seek a divorce in accordance with Deut 24:1–4, although he wished to do this secretly to avoid subjecting Mary to the rigorous law of Deut 22:23–24, which mandates capital punishment for adulterers. Joseph was a just man inasmuch as he resolved to act (divorce) in accordance with the Mosaic Law. This common interpretation suffers from a serious weakness: Joseph's desire to follow the law for divorce (Deut 24) does not square with his willingness to sidestep the law prescribed for adulterers (Deut 22). A truly righteous man would keep God's Law completely, not selectively. **(2)** *The Reverence Theory*. This view holds that Joseph, already informed of the divine miracle within Mary (1:18), considered himself unworthy to be part of God's work in this unusual situation (cf. Lk 5:8; 7:6). His resolve to separate quietly from Mary is thus viewed as a reverent and discretionary measure to keep secret the mystery within

her. Notably, the expression **to put her to shame** is weaker in Greek than in the translation: it means that Joseph did not wish to "exhibit" Mary in a public way. The angelic announcement in 1:20, then, directs Joseph to set aside pious fears that would lead him away from his vocation to be the legal father of the Davidic Messiah. This view more aptly aligns Joseph's righteousness with his intentions.

1:20 Joseph: The angel's message is urgent: Joseph must maintain his marriage in order to be the foster-father of Jesus. As a descendant of King **David**, he imparts to Jesus Davidic (royal) rights of inheritance. ● Matthew's portrait of Joseph recalls the OT patriarch Joseph. **(1)** Both share the same name (1:18; Gen 30:24); **(2)** both have fathers named Jacob (1:16; Gen 30:19–24); **(3)** God spoke to both of them through dreams (1:20–21; 2:13, 19–20, 22; Gen 37:5–11); **(4)** both were righteous and chaste (1:19; Gen 39:7–18); **(5)** both saved their families by bringing them to Egypt (2:13; Gen 45:16–20).

1:21 Jesus: The Greek name *Iēsous* is equivalent to the Hebrew name Joshua (*Yehoshua*'), meaning "Yahweh saves". It was a popular name among first-century Jews. ● Even greater than Joshua, who led Israel into the Promised Land (Sir 46:1), Jesus leads God's people into the eternal land of heaven (25:34; cf. Heb 4:1–11). Greater also than David (2 Sam 3:18), Jesus will **save his people from their sins**, not from their national enemies (i.e., the Romans) (CCC 430–32, 2666).

1:23 Behold, a virgin: The first of several "formula-quotations" in Matthew (2:6, 15, 18, 23). Here the citation is from Is 7:14 of the Greek OT. Matthew interprets it with reference to Mary (**virgin**) and Jesus (**son**). ● Isaiah 7:14 initially prophesied the birth of King Hezekiah, who rescued Israel from many evils (2 Kings 18:1–6). Matthew sees a deeper level of fulfillment here, where the absence of a human father in the prophecy points to the virginal conception of the Messiah (CCC 497). The name **God with us** is most perfectly fulfilled in Jesus' Incarnation, where his ongoing presence in the world is both ecclesial (18:20; 28:20) and eucharistic (26:26).

1:25 until: The Greek *heōs* does not imply that Joseph and Mary had marital relations following Jesus' birth. This conjunction is often used (translated "to" or "till") to indicate a select period of time, without implying change in the future (2 Sam 6:23 [LXX]; Jn 9:18; 1 Tim 4:13). Here Matthew emphasizes only that Joseph had no involvement in Mary's pregnancy *before* Jesus' birth. ● Mary's perpetual virginity is firmly established in Church tradition. Its doctrinal formulation is traced to the Lateran Synod of A.D. 649 and was reaffirmed in 1968 by Pope Paul VI (*The* Credo *of the People of God*, 14; CCC 499–501).

2:1 Bethlehem: A small village south of Jerusalem. Its Hebrew name means "house of bread", and it came to be known as the "city of David" (Lk 2:4). As the new Davidic king, Jesus is born in the hometown of David and his family (1 Sam

---

f Other ancient authorities read *of the Christ.*

this, he was troubled, and all Jerusalem with him; [4]and assembling all the chief priests and scribes of the people, he inquired of them where the Christ was to be born. [5]They told him, "In Bethlehem of Judea; for so it is written by the prophet:

[6] 'And you, O Bethlehem, in the land of Judah,
   are by no means least among the rulers of
      Judah;
   for from you shall come a ruler
   who will govern my people Israel.' "

7 Then Herod summoned the wise men secretly and ascertained from them what time the star appeared; [8]and he sent them to Bethlehem, saying, "Go and search diligently for the child, and when you have found him bring me word, that I too may come and worship him." [9]When they had heard the king they went their way; and behold, the star which they had seen in the East went before them, till it came to rest over the place where the child

was. [10]When they saw the star, they rejoiced exceedingly with great joy; [11]and going into the house they saw the child with Mary his mother, and they fell down and worshiped him. Then, opening their treasures, they offered him gifts, gold and frankincense and myrrh. [12]And being warned in a dream not to return to Herod, they departed to their own country by another way.

The Escape to Egypt

13 Now when they had departed, behold, an angel of the Lord appeared to Joseph in a dream and said, "Rise, take the child and his mother, and flee to Egypt, and remain there till I tell you; for Herod is about to search for the child, to destroy him." [14]And he rose and took the child and his mother by night, and departed to Egypt, [15]and remained there until the death of Herod. This was to fulfil what the Lord had spoken by the prophet, "Out of Egypt have I called my son."

16 Then Herod, when he saw that he had been

2:5: Jn 7:42.　**2:6:** Mic 5:2.　**2:11:** Mt 1:18; 12:46.　**2:12:** Mt 2:22; Acts 10:22; Heb 11:7.　**2:15:** Hos 11:1; Ex 4:22.

16:1). It is also the site where David was anointed king (1 Sam 16:4–13). **Herod the king:** Herod the Great, ruler of Palestine. He was part of a non-Jewish (Edomite) family that held political favor with Rome. Herod was appointed "King of the Jews" by the Roman Senate in 40 B.C. to replace the collapsing dynasty of Jewish priestly rulers. He took power in Jerusalem in 37 B.C. and reigned until his death. He is famous for extensive building projects, especially his renovation of the Jerusalem Temple. As a ruler, he was extremely harsh and inflexible. He enjoyed little favor with the Jews since he remained loyal to the Roman emperor and was not a rightful Davidic leader. According to our current calendar, Jesus was born near the end of Herod's reign, either between 6 and 4 B.C. or 3 and 2 B.C.(cf. 2:16). **wise men from the East:** Probably astrologers from Persia—this would explain their interest in an extraordinary "star" (2:2). In Matthew, the Magi are the first Gentiles to recognize the kingship of Jesus (CCC 528). ● The star recalls OT prophecy about the Messiah. In Num 24:17, Balaam predicted: "a star shall come forth out of Jacob, and a scepter shall rise out of Israel." Herod the Edomite was "troubled" (2:3), knowing that the same oracle foretold disaster for his family: "Edom shall be dispossessed" (Num 24:18). ▯ **2:6 And you, O Bethlehem:** A combined citation of Mic 5:2 and 2 Sam 5:2. Both the birthplace and the kingship of the Messiah are central. ● According to Mic 5:2, the greatness of Bethlehem will far outweigh its small size because of the great king who will arise there. The reference to 2 Sam 5:2 also has a royal context, narrating David's covenant of kingship with the 12 tribes of Israel. The mention of these OT texts by the "chief priests and scribes" (2:4) indicates their close association with messianic expectations during NT times. ▯▯▯ **2:11 into the house:** This setting suggests the event took place after Jesus' presence in the "manger" (Lk 2:7) and the earlier visit of the shepherds (Lk 2:15–17). ● A similar time lapse is reflected in the Roman liturgy: the Feast of the Epiphany is celebrated on January 6, almost two weeks after Christmas, on December 25. **their treasures:** It was customary in the ancient Near East to offer gifts to a king. ● The episode evokes Is 60:3, 6, where Gentile nations bring gifts of **gold** and **frankincense** to the God of Israel (cf. Tob 13:11; Ps 72:10–15). **myrrh:** An anointing oil used to consecrate Levitical priests and the wilderness Tabernacle (Ex 30:23–33). It was also a burial ointment (Jn 19:39–40). ● *Allegorically* (St. Irenaeus, *AH* 3, 9, 2), the gifts of the Magi signify the mystery of Christ incarnate. Gold, a symbol of royalty, represents the kingship of Jesus. Frankincense, used in the worship

of God, points to his divinity. Myrrh, a burial ointment, signifies the humanity of Christ, especially in his Passion and death. *Morally* (St. Gregory the Great, *Hom. in Evan.* 10), the treasures signify the gifts we present to Christ in our daily lives. Gold is Christ's wisdom, which shines in us, frankincense is the prayer and adoration we give him (cf. Rev 8:3–4), and myrrh is our daily self-sacrifices (10:39; cf. Rom 12:1).
2:13 Rise, take the child: God works within the structures of the family: Joseph is instructed by the angel because he is the head of the Holy Family and the one most responsible for their well-being (cf. Eph 5:21–6:3). **Egypt:** A frequent place of refuge in the OT (Gen 12:10; 46:4; 1 Kings 11:40; Jer 26:21) and the location of large Jewish colonies (Alexandria and Elephantine) during NT times.
▯ **2:15 Out of Egypt:** A quotation from Hos 11:1. Matthew anticipates its fulfillment in 2:21. ● Hosea 11:1

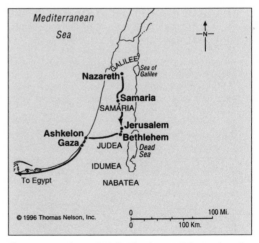

Mediterranean Sea

GALILEE

Nazareth · Sea of Galilee

Samaria

SAMARIA

Jerusalem

Ashkelon · Bethlehem
Gaza · JUDEA · Dead Sea

To Egypt · IDUMEA

NABATEA

—N—

© 1996 Thomas Nelson, Inc.

0 · 100 Mi.
0 · 100 Km.

The Journeys of Jesus' Birth. The decree of Caesar Augustus required Mary and Joseph, who were from Nazareth, to register for the census in the Judean city of Bethlehem (Lk 2:1–5). After the wise men from the East had visited to worship the Child, Joseph heeded the warning of the angel of the Lord and took his family to Egypt, where they remained until the death of Herod the Great.

Is Matthew's Infancy Narrative Historical?

THE historical trustworthiness of the Christian Gospels is an important issue for the Church. Vatican II restated (1965) the Church's enduring conviction: the NT Gospels faithfully transmit the historical truth about Jesus, his teaching, and his mighty works (*Dei Verbum*, 19). Nevertheless, scholars sometimes question whether the Gospel writers intended to record history at all. Some claim that Matthew's Infancy Narrative (chaps. 1–2) is a prime example of this. Matthew, it is said, did not recount the events of Jesus' birth in the strict sense—he instead composed a *midrash* on the OT.

The word *midrash* is a Hebrew noun meaning "interpretation" or "commentary". The term has various meanings today. Sometimes it denotes ancient Jewish writings—common after A.D. 200—that use OT stories to teach religious truths. It can also describe the methods of OT interpretation found in these writings. Most notably, *midrash* is notorious for retelling biblical stories and embellishing them with fictional details. One *midrash* on the birth of Moses imaginatively expands the story found in Ex 2, describing how Moses' father had a dream predicting his birth, an Egyptian scribe informed Pharaoh of his birth, and the scribe himself later sought to kill the young Moses. These details add color to Moses' earliest years, but no such detail is found in the Bible. Matthew 1–2 is thought to fit in a similar category of pious reflection; the evangelist is thus charged with fabricating events related to OT passages but having no real basis in history. A response to this claim may be outlined in several points.

1. Matthew 1–2 is stylistically different from *midrash*. Unlike *midrash*, the evangelist's story of Jesus is not founded on an OT text. Whereas *midrash* seeks to mine deeper meanings of the OT, Matthew does not seek to interpret the OT for its own sake. More to the point, Matthew is not retelling OT episodes but is telling an entirely new story! It is a story with new characters and events; it is a story that could stand on its own apart from his OT citations. Matthew employs the OT to illuminate the significance of Jesus' birth, not to determine in advance its plot and outcome.

2. Matthew sees Jesus as the fulfillment of OT promises. He draws from Scripture to support Jesus' qualifications as Israel's Messiah by linking important episodes (virginal conception, flight to Egypt, massacre of the Innocents, etc.) with ancient oracles. Unless these *events* are anchored in history in the first place, it seems unlikely that Matthew would fabricate stories *as if* Jesus fulfilled the OT. Scripture was never really fulfilled if the events Matthew narrates never happened. In this case, Matthew's exegesis of the OT would amount to little more than an exercise in self-delusion. Besides, were it Matthew's tendency to invent stories out of OT texts, it is likely his narrative would have turned out differently. For example, Ps 72:10 and Is 60:3–6 clearly stand behind Matthew's story of the wise men in Mt 2. Were Matthew writing *midrash*, these OT verses would probably exert greater control in shaping his story: Jesus would then receive only "two gifts" (gold and frankincense) instead of three, and "kings", instead of Persian astrologers, would pay him homage.

3. Matthew does not regard the OT as a simple, pre-written script of Jesus' life. With the exception of Mic 5:2 (Mt 2:6), Matthew's OT citations appear to be unlikely candidates for messianic prophesies, were he not peering at deeper mysteries within their literal meaning. For example, Is 7:14 (Mt 1:23) was first spoken about the birth of king Hezekiah; Hosea 11:1 (Mt 2:15) was originally looking backward to Israel's Exodus from Egypt; Jer 31:15 (Mt 2:18) describes the tragedy of the Jewish Exile in 586 B.C.; and Matthew's reference to the "Nazarene" (Mt 2:23) is difficult even to locate. Thus Matthew is not assembling the most obvious OT prophesies about the Messiah and neatly attaching them to Jesus. His use of the OT is legitimate and spiritual but not artificial. That Matthew gathers obscure texts to interpret Jesus' infancy suggests that history is controlling his story, not the OT.

4. Matthew 1–2 coheres well with our knowledge of history from extrabiblical sources. First, the Holy Family's flight to Egypt (2:13) squares with known historical circumstances: Egypt at this time was the home of large Jewish colonies (e.g., Alexandria, Elephantine). Second, the role of the wise men in Mt 2 corresponds with our knowledge of Persian sages from the ancient East. Their interests in astrology naturally link them with stellar phenomena (i.e., the star of Bethlehem). Third, the moral character of Herod the Great known from other sources is consistent with his actions in Mt 2. Having murdered many suspected adversaries—and even family members—it is reasonable to think Herod would execute young Bethlehemites (2:16) as a preemptive strike against future threats to his crown.

5. Of some relevance: the Pontifical Biblical Commission addressed the issue of historicity in Matthew's Infancy Narrative at the turn of the twentieth century. This commission was instituted by Pope Leo XIII (1902) to examine select biblical questions related to the Catholic faith. The decisions and decrees of this commission are not necessarily infallible, but they may be taken as authoritative guidance. After careful study of this issue, weighing both ancient and modern interpretive traditions, the commission concluded on June 19, 1911, that contemporary challenges to the historical authenticity of Mt 1—2 are devoid of solid foundation.

In summary, Matthew's Infancy Narrative is both theological and historical. Matthew cites the OT as *confirmation* of his story, not as its *foundation*. He intends readers to view Jesus' early life as real events with real characters. For Matthew, Jesus himself holds the key to the OT, and his coming marks a new era in salvation history that gathers up all of God's promises and brings them to fulfillment. The historical reliability of Mt 1–2, then, is consistent with Catholic tradition and the sound principles of biblical and historical study. «

tricked by the wise men, was in a furious rage, and he sent and killed all the male children in Bethlehem and in all that region who were two years old or under, according to the time which he had ascertained from the wise men. [17]Then was fulfilled what was spoken by the prophet Jeremiah:

[18] "A voice was heard in Ramah,
wailing and loud lamentation,
Rachel weeping for her children;
she refused to be consoled,
because they were no more."

The Return from Egypt

19 But when Herod died, behold, an angel of the Lord appeared in a dream to Joseph in Egypt, saying, [20]"Rise, take the child and his mother, and go to the land of Israel, for those who sought the child's life are dead." [21]And he rose and took the child and his mother, and went to the land of Is-rael. [22]But when he heard that Archelaus reigned over Judea in place of his father Herod, he was afraid to go there, and being warned in a dream he withdrew to the district of Galilee. [23]And he went and dwelt in a city called Nazareth, that what was spoken by the prophets might be fulfilled, "He shall be called a Nazarene."

The Proclamation of John the Baptist

3 In those days came John the Baptist, preaching in the wilderness of Judea, [2]"Repent, for the kingdom of heaven is at hand." [3]For this is he who was spoken of by the prophet Isaiah when he said,

" The voice of one crying in the wilderness:
Prepare the way of the Lord,
make his paths straight."

[4]Now John wore a garment of camel's hair, and a leather belt around his waist; and his food was locusts and wild honey. [5]Then went out to him Jerusalem and all Judea and all the region about

---

2:18: Jer 31:15.   **2:19:** Mt 1:20; 2:13.   **2:23:** Lk 1:26; Is 11:1; Mk 1:24.   **3:1–12:** Mk 1:3–8; Lk 3:2–17; Jn 1:6–8, 19–28.
3:2: Mt 4:17; Dan 2:44; 4:17; Mt 10:7.   **3:3:** Is 40:3.   **3:4:** 2 Kings 1:8; Zech 13:4; Lev 11:22.

---

points back to the Exodus, where God's "first-born son" (Ex 4:22), Israel, was delivered from slavery under the oppressive Pharaoh. Matthew sees this text also pointing forward, when Jesus, the eternal first-born Son (Rom 8:29), is delivered from the tyrant Herod and later brought out of Egypt (2:21) (CCC 530).

2:16 a furious rage: Extrabiblical history paints a similar portrait of Herod: he murdered his favorite wife, three of his sons, and others who threatened his throne. • The Church considers these children from Bethlehem the first Christian martyrs. Their feast is celebrated December 28. • Matthew begins here to portray Jesus as a new and greater Moses: (1) The lives of both Jesus and Moses are threatened in their infancy by an imperial edict to kill Hebrew male children (Ex 1:15–16); (2) both were saved from the decree by the intervention of a family member (2:13; Ex 2:1–10); (3) both found protection for a time within Egypt (2:14–15; Ex 2:5–10); (4) both were called back to their respective birthplaces after a time of flight and exile (2:20; Ex 4:19); (5) both spent 40 days and nights fasting alone in the wilderness (4:2; Ex 34:28); (6) both were commissioned by God to promulgate his covenant Law (chaps. 5–7; Deut 5:1–21). See chart: *Jesus and the Old Testament* at Mt 12.

2:18 A voice was heard: A citation from Jer 31:15. • Jeremiah looks to **Ramah**, a city five miles north of Jerusalem, as a place of sorrow and exile. The Assyrians first devastated northern Israel in the eighth century B.C. by sweeping through the land and engulfing the city (Is 10:29; Hos 5:8); later the Babylonians conquered the southern tribes in the sixth century B.C., and Ramah became the assembly point for hauling away captives (Jer 40:1). In both cases, some Israelites were killed, and others were carried into exile. Matthew sees Bethlehem as a new city of sorrow where many are killed and the young Jesus, representing Israel, is carried away. These two sites are linked with the burial place of **Rachel:** one tradition puts her tomb on the outskirts of Bethlehem, where she gave birth to Benjamin in sorrow (Gen 35:17-19), while another locates it in the tribal territory of Ramah (1 Sam 10:2; cf. Josh 18:25).

2:22 Archelaus: Son of Herod the Great. After Herod's death, the Roman emperor Augustus divided his kingdom among his three sons. Archelaus was given the title "ethnarch" of Judea, Idumea, and Samaria. He quickly acquired a reputation like his father's, governing with a ruthless and heavy hand. He was eventually banished by Augustus to Gaul in A.D. 6.

Joseph took Mary and the Child north to the **district of Galilee,** where Archelaus' younger brother, Herod Antipas, ruled as "tetrarch" until A.D. 39.

2:23 Nazareth: An obscure Galilean village nowhere mentioned in the OT. It was insignificant in the eyes of many Jews (cf. Jn 1:46). **He shall be called a Nazarene:** No OT prophecy corresponds to this exact wording. Matthew apparently paraphrases the message of several **prophets** into a summary statement about the Messiah. • The paraphrase is based on a word association between Jesus' home of Nazareth and the Hebrew word *netser*, translated as "branch" in Is 11:1. Isaiah used the image of a branch growing from a stump to signify hope for the kingdom of David. The great Davidic tree (dynasty) had been cut off since the Exile, but the sprouting branch indicated that God would raise up another king from the hopeless situation. Later prophets used this same image to signify the Messiah-king (Jer 23:5, 33:14–16) who would build the Temple (Zech 3:8, 6:11–13). See notes on 1:17 and 16:18.

3:1 John the Baptist: The forerunner to the Messiah. A Levite (Lk 1:5) and relative of Jesus (Lk 1:36), John was considered a prophet by many Jews (21:26) and even by Jesus himself (11:9). His message was accompanied by an austere life of penance and self-denial (CCC 523). • John's clothing (3:4) recalls the OT prophet Elijah who "wore a garment of haircloth, with a belt of leather about his loins" (2 Kings 1:8). A figure like Elijah was expected to return before the Messiah (Mal 4:5) to begin restoring the tribes of Israel (Sir 48:10).

3:2 kingdom: A word used more than 50 times in Matthew. It is closely related to God's covenant oath to establish David's royal kingdom (2 Sam 7:12–17; Ps 89:3, 4). John announces the spiritual restoration of David's empire by Jesus the Messiah (cf. Mk 11:10; Lk 1:32–33). While the phrase "kingdom of God" occasionally appears (four times), "kingdom of heaven" (32 times) is the dominant motif in Matthew for two reasons: (1) It undercuts the political and military expectations surrounding the Messiah; many Jews hoped for an earthly kingdom (cf. Jn 6:15). (2) While Christ's kingdom begins on earth, it will reach its full perfection in heaven (CCC 541, 669, 671). See note on Lk 4:43.

3:3 The voice of one crying: A quotation from Is 40:3. • Isaiah's oracle outlines John's mission: he is the important figure who prepares the **way of the Lord.** All four Gospels connect Isaiah's words with John's ministry (Mk 1:3; Lk 3:4; Jn 1:23). See note on Lk 3:4–6.

the Jordan, [6]and they were baptized by him in the river Jordan, confessing their sins.

7 But when he saw many of the Pharisees and Sad'ducees coming for baptism, he said to them, "You brood of vipers! Who warned you to flee from the wrath to come? [8]Bear fruit that befits repentance, [9]and do not presume to say to yourselves, 'We have Abraham as our father'; for I tell you, God is able from these stones to raise up children to Abraham. [10]Even now the axe is laid to the root of the trees; every tree therefore that does not bear good fruit is cut down and thrown into the fire.

11 "I baptize you with water for repentance, but he who is coming after me is mightier than I, whose sandals I am not worthy to carry; he will baptize you with the Holy Spirit and with fire. [12]His winnowing fork is in his hand, and he will clear his threshing floor and gather his wheat into the gra-nary, but the chaff he will burn with unquenchable fire."

The Baptism of Jesus

13 Then Jesus came from Galilee to the Jordan to John, to be baptized by him. [14]John would have prevented him, saying, "I need to be baptized by you, and do you come to me?" [15]But Jesus answered him, "Let it be so now; for thus it is fitting for us to fulfil all righteousness." Then he consented. [16]And when Jesus was baptized, he went up immediately from the water, and behold, the heavens were opened[g] and he saw the Spirit of God descending like a dove, and alighting on him; [17]and behold, a voice from heaven, saying, "This is my beloved Son,[h] with whom I am well pleased."

The Temptation of Jesus

4 Then Jesus was led up by the Spirit into the wilderness to be tempted by the devil. [2]And he

---

3:7: Mt 12:34; 23:33; 1 Thess 1:10. **3:9:** Jn 8:33; Rom 4:16. **3:10:** Mt 7:19. **3:12:** Mt 13:30.
3:13–17: Mk 1:9–11; Lk 3:21–22; Jn 1:31–34. **3:17:** Mt 12:18; 17:5; Mk 9:7; Lk 9:35; Ps 2:7; Is 42:1.
4:1–11: Mk 1:12–13; Lk 4:1–13; Heb 2:18; 4:15. **4:2:** Ex 34:28; 1 Kings 19:8.

3:6 the river Jordan: Runs along the eastern side of Palestine. Its headwaters begin north of the Sea of Galilee, and it flows southward into the Dead Sea. ● In the OT, the Jordan is associated with God's deliverance. Like the Red Sea, it parted so that the Israelites could cross over on dry ground and inherit the Promised Land (Josh 3:14–17). Naaman the Syrian was cleansed from leprosy at this location when he "dipped" (LXX: *ebaptisato*) seven times in the river at the command of Elisha (2 Kings 5:14). Both OT events prefigure the saving power of the Sacrament of Baptism (CCC 1222).

3:11 I baptize you: John's baptism differed from sacramental Baptism, which confers forgiveness and the regenerating grace of justifying faith (Acts 2:38). His was a visible token of repentance and preparation for the Messiah (cf. Is 1:16; Heb 9:10; CCC 718). **with water:** John administered a baptism by water alone as a sign of purification. But as was shown in Noah's day, water alone cannot cleanse the soul; the sinfulness of man's heart remained unchanged even after the flood (Gen 6:5; 8:21). Only the Sacrament of Baptism infuses the **Holy Spirit** (Jn 3:5) and marks one's adoption into God's family (28:19) (CCC 1265). **with fire:** A symbol of God and his purifying judgment (Deut 4:24; Sir 2:5; Is 4:3–5; Acts 2:3–4; CCC 696).

3:15 it is fitting: Jesus is sinless and has no need for John's baptism (Heb 4:15; 1 Pet 2:22). He nevertheless submits to the rite to identify with sinners and align himself with God's plan. Jesus performs Old Covenant regulations to fulfill and perfect them in the New (5:17; cf. Lk 2:21–28; CCC 536). ● *Mystically* (St. Thomas Aquinas, *ST* 3, 39, 8), Jesus' baptism prefigures the Christian sacrament. The water, Spirit, and divine voice signify the effects of Baptism whereby the soul is cleansed (Acts 22:16), the grace of the Holy Spirit is imparted (3:11; 1 Cor 12:13), and the recipient is adopted as a beloved child of God (3:17; Gal 3:26–27; CCC 537).

3:16 the heavens: The episode reveals the Blessed Trinity: the Father speaks, the Son is baptized, and the Holy Spirit descends as a dove.

4:1–11 Matthew's temptation narrative recounts Jesus' spiritual preparation for ministry. ● The event contrasts the disobedience of ancient Israel with the obedience of Jesus, representative of the new Israel: **(1)** Israel and Jesus are both called God's son (3:17; Ex 4:22); **(2)** the temptations of both Israel and Jesus are preceded by a baptism (3:13–17; 1 Cor 10:1–5); **(3)** Israel was tested for 40 years, Jesus is tempted for **forty days and forty nights** (4:2); **(4)** Israel failed its wilderness testing, while Jesus triumphs over Satan through obedience and self-abasement (4:11). These parallels are supported by Jesus' three responses (4:4, 7, 10) to the devil taken from Deut 6–8. These texts (Deut 8:3; 6:16; 6:13) warned the Israelites against disobedience and reminded them of God's provisions in the wilderness (CCC 538–39). ● *Morally* (St. John Chrysostom, *Hom. in Matt.* 8), Jesus' victory sets an example for Christian obedience. Earthly life is a wilderness trial for God's people en route to the land of heaven. Through this probationary period, God wills the faithful to overcome temptations from the world, the flesh, and the devil. Triumph is possible through penance and obedience to God's word. Rather than earthly bread and power, the faithful must desire the food of God's will and the humility of Christ (11:29; Jn 4:34). The battle successfully won merits heavenly comfort in the company of angels (4:11). The Church annually reminds us of this life-long vocation during the 40 days of Lent (CCC 540, 2849).

---

[g] Other ancient authorities add *to him*.
[h] Or *my Son, my* (or *the*) *Beloved*.

WORD STUDY

Righteousness (3:15)

Dikaiosunē (Gk.): denotes the uprightness and faithfulness of God and his people (Deut 6:25; Is 48:18). The word is part of a distinctive covenant vocabulary found throughout the Bible. It is used seven times in Matthew and 85 times in the rest of the NT. **(1)** God's *righteousness* is characteristic of his being (holy) and revealed through his saving deeds and care of Israel (Deut 32:4; Is 5:16; 42:6). God is righteous because he perfectly fulfills his covenant with Israel as a divine Father. The NT builds on this foundation: God now demonstrates his *righteousness* through the saving work of Jesus Christ. The New Covenant is ratified by Jesus' obedience to the Father (Mt 3:15; Rom 3:21–26) and is proclaimed in the gospel (Rom 1:16–17). **(2)** For God's people, *righteousness* is a New Covenant gift from Christ. It is first given in Baptism and received by faith (Rom 5:17). It denotes one's restored relationship with God as an adopted son or daughter. This gift of *righteousness* can increase through love and obedience to God's covenant Law (Mt 5:6; 6:33; Rom 6:16; Eph 4:24; 1 Pet 2:24; 1 Jn 3:7).

fasted forty days and forty nights, and afterward he was hungry. [3]And the tempter came and said to him, "If you are the Son of God, command these stones to become loaves of bread." [4]But he answered, "It is written,

'Man shall not live by bread alone,
but by every word that proceeds from the
mouth of God.'"

[5]Then the devil took him to the holy city, and set him on the pinnacle of the temple, [6]and said to him, "If you are the Son of God, throw yourself down; for it is written,

'He will give his angels charge of you,'

and

'On their hands they will bear you up,
lest you strike your foot against a stone.'"

[7]Jesus said to him, "Again it is written, 'You shall not tempt the Lord your God.'" [8]Again, the devil took him to a very high mountain, and showed him all the kingdoms of the world and the glory of them; [9]and he said to him, "All these I will give you, if you will fall down and worship me." [10]Then Jesus said to him, "Begone, Satan! for it is written,

'You shall worship the Lord your God
and him only shall you serve.'"

[11]Then the devil left him, and behold, angels came and ministered to him.

Jesus Begins His Ministry in Galilee

12 Now when he heard that John had been arrested, he withdrew into Galilee; [13]and leaving Nazareth he went and dwelt in Caper'na-um by the sea, in the territory of Zeb'ulun and Naph'tali, [14]that what was spoken by the prophet Isaiah might be fulfilled:

[15] "The land of Zeb'ulun and the land of
Naph'tali,
toward the sea, across the Jordan,
Galilee of the Gentiles—
[16] the people who sat in darkness
have seen a great light,
and for those who sat in the region and shadow
of death
light has dawned."

[17]From that time Jesus began to preach, saying, "Repent, for the kingdom of heaven is at hand."

Jesus Calls the First Disciples

18 As he walked by the Sea of Galilee, he saw two brothers, Simon who is called Peter and Andrew his brother, casting a net into the sea; for they were fishermen. [19]And he said to them, "Follow me, and I will make you fishers of men." [20]Immediately they left their nets and followed him. [21]And going on from there he saw two other brothers, James the son of Zeb'edee and John his brother, in the boat with Zeb'edee their father, mending their nets, and he called them. [22]Immediately they left the boat and their father, and followed him.

4:4: Deut 8:3. **4:5:** Mt 27:53; Neh 11:1; Dan 9:24; Rev 21:10. **4:6:** Ps 91:11–12. **4:7:** Deut 6:16. **4:10:** Deut 6:13; Mk 8:33. **4:11:** Mt 26:53; Lk 22:43. **4:12:** Mk 1:14; Lk 4:14; Mt 14:3; Jn 1:43. **4:13:** Jn 2:12; Mk 1:21; Lk 4:23. **4:15:** Is 9:1–2. **4:17:** Mk 1:15; Mt 3:2; 10:7. **4:18–22:** Mk 1:16–20; Lk 5:1–11; Jn *1:35–42.*

4:1 tempted: Having witnessed the Father's declaration (3:17), Satan tests Jesus' identity as the Son of God. He tempts Jesus to embrace an earthly and political mission (4:8–9) and seeks to divert him from suffering and death. Peter is later rebuked as "Satan" (16:23) when he refuses to accept Jesus' path of suffering (16:21). • The Second Council of Constantinople (A.D. 553) condemned the view that Jesus was impeccable only after his Resurrection (can. 12). On the contrary, Christ is a divine Person and so could not have sinned at any time during his earthly life (Jas 1:13; 1 Jn 3:5). Furthermore, his temptations came entirely from the suggestions of the devil and had nothing to do with the inner struggles and disordered desires of fallen human nature that we experience (Jas 1:14–15).

4:6 it is written: Both Jesus (4:4, 7, 10) and Satan (4:6) quote from Scripture. Whereas Jesus handles Scripture with reverence and sensitivity, Satan misconstrues its meaning. • Satan's use of Ps 91:11–12 violates its original meaning. The psalm encourages trust and faith in God's protection; it does not advocate testing him. Jesus' proper interpretation of Deut 6:16 (4:7) excludes the possibility of twisting Ps 91 to justify testing God.

4:12 Galilee: The uppermost region of Palestine, north of Judea and Samaria. In ancient Israel, Galilee was home to several of the nation's 12 tribes. After military devastations by the Assyrians in the eighth century B.C. (2 Kings 15:29), Galilee was ruled separately from Judea and Samaria for most of its history extending into NT times. While some Jews resided in Galilee when Jesus lived there, many were descendants of the northern tribes of Israel who lived alongside Gentile immigrants.

Even after the NT period, the Jewish Mishnah (A.D. 200) consistently refers to Galileans as "Israelites", as distinct from southern "Jews" or "Judeans" (cf. 10:5–6; Jn 1:47). Jesus chose Galilee as the place to restore the "lost sheep of the house of Israel" (15:24), regather his scattered disciples (26:31–32), and send them on a worldwide mission (28:7, 10, 16–20).

4:15–16 The land of Zebulun . . . dawned: A citation from Is 9:1–2 concerning the land allotments of two Israelite tribes, Zebulun and Naphtali. Since these Galilean regions were the first to be ravaged by Assyrian invasions from 733 to 732 B.C. (2 Kings 15:29), Jesus targets Galilee as the place to begin reversing the tragedies of Israel's history by restoring the 12 tribes in the New Covenant (cf. 15:24; 19:28; Rev 7:4–8). • Isaiah foresees a "latter time" (Is 9:1), when God will restore hope to Galilee. Matthew links this with Jesus' residence in "Capernaum" (4:13), a town north of the Sea of Galilee where the tribal territories of Zebulun and Naphtali intersect. Matthew's sustained interest in the Davidic kingship of Jesus suggests that the fuller context of this oracle is also significant. Isaiah 9:1–2 prefaces an Immanuel prophecy of the birth of a new king who will sit "upon the throne of David" (Is 9:7) and restore this land of hope to Galilee (cf. Lk 1:32–33).

4:18–22 fishermen: A common Galilean occupation. Matthew emphasizes the promptness of the disciples' response to Jesus (**Immediately** 4:20, 22). Three of them—Peter, James, and John—enjoyed a special relationship with him (17:1; 26:37). • God's New Covenant grace builds upon, perfects, and elevates our human nature. The natural skills of these fishermen are thus raised to a new and spiritual level by grace, enabling them to gather souls for the kingdom as missionaries in the Church.

Jesus Ministers to Crowds of People

23 And he went about all Galilee, teaching in their synagogues and preaching the gospel of the kingdom and healing every disease and every infirmity among the people. ²⁴So his fame spread throughout all Syria, and they brought him all the sick, those afflicted with various diseases and pains, demoniacs, epileptics, and paralytics, and he healed them. ²⁵And great crowds followed him from Galilee and the Decap´olis and Jerusalem and Judea and from beyond the Jordan.

The Beatitudes

5 Seeing the crowds, he went up on the mountain, and when he sat down his disciples came to him. ²And he opened his mouth and taught them, saying:

3 "Blessed are the poor in spirit, for theirs is the kingdom of heaven.

4 "Blessed are those who mourn, for they shall be comforted.

5 "Blessed are the meek, for they shall inherit the earth.

4:23–25: Mk 1:39; Lk 4:15, 44; Mt 9:35; Mk 3:7–8; Lk 6:17.   **5:1–12:** Lk &17, 20–23; Mk 3:13; Jn 6:3.
5:3: Mk 10:14; Lk 22:29.   **5:4:** Is 61:2; Jn 16:20, Rev 7:17.   **5:5:** Ps 37:11.

4:23 synagogues: Buildings for Jewish worship, prayer, and instruction in the Scriptures. They also served a more general function as community centers within rural villages. Assemblies were normally held on the Sabbath (in the evening) and the liturgy centered on the proclamation and explanation of the Hebrew Bible. Since these are unmentioned in the OT, the origin of the synagogue is uncertain. Their beginning may be linked with teaching centers in the 48 Levitical cities (Num 35:1–8) or to the return of the Jewish exiles from Babylon in the sixth century B.C. Since Jewish males were required to travel to the Jerusalem Temple only three times annually (Deut 16:16), the synagogue was a complementary site for non-sacrificial worship and education during the remainder of the year.

4:25 Decapolis: Literally, the "ten cities". These were predominantly Gentile cities in Palestine, and most were located east of the river Jordan. They are known for their distinctive Hellenistic (Greek) architecture.

5:1–7:29 The Sermon on the Mount encapsulates the Law of the New Covenant. It is a collection of Jesus' teachings on Christian living and his perfection of Old Covenant moral laws (5:17). As the first of five discourses in Matthew (see outline), the sermon envisions our heavenly destiny based on acceptance or rejection of Jesus and his teaching (CCC 1965–68).

5:1 on the mountain: The setting of Jesus' promulgation of the Law of the New Covenant parallels Moses' experience on Mt. Sinai delivering God's Old Covenant Law to Israel (Ex 24:12–18). See note on 2:16. • *Symbolically* (St. Augustine, *De serm. Dom.* 1, 1, 2), the mountain signifies the high standards of the New Covenant. The tablets of the Mosaic Law were brought down Mt. Sinai and promulgated at the foot of the mountain as a concession to the Israelites—they were yet weak and unfit to ascend into God's presence (Ex 19:23; 32:15–19). The Old Covenant Law was thus a lower and less-perfect Law (cf. Ezek 20:25; Mt 19:8). The New Law, however, introduces higher standards of holiness; Christ thus brings disciples up the mountain to receive his teaching. Jesus himself fulfills the New Law perfectly and empowers the Church to live it faithfully through the Holy Spirit (cf. 11:29; Rom 5:5; 8:3–4). **he sat down:** A traditional posture for Jewish rabbis speaking with authority (cf. 23:1–2; Lk 4:20; Jn 8:2).

5:3–12 The Beatitudes follow a distinctive pattern and logic. Each blessing builds upon the one before it; the beatitude of spiritual poverty is thus the foundation for all of them. • *Morally* (St. Augustine, *De Serm. Dom.* 1, 4, 11), the first seven Beatitudes correspond to the seven gifts of the Holy Spirit (Is 11:2). These gifts are possessed in their fullness by Christ and are given also to the baptized (CCC 1831). According to this arrangement, the eighth beatitude (5:10) summarizes the first seven. **(1)** The "poor in spirit" (5:3) exercise the fear of the Lord, a gift of reverence for God that awakens the soul to its weaknesses and fosters a childlike fear of the Father. **(2)** Those who "mourn" (5:4) exercise knowledge, the gift that imparts a correct estimation of created things and their relative value before God. **(3)** The "meek" (5:5) exercise piety, the gift of filial love for God that moves the soul to worship and protects against the hardening of one's heart in the midst of trials. **(4)** Those who "hunger and thirst for righteousness" (5:6) exercise might (or fortitude), the gift of firm resolution to pursue holiness despite obstacles. **(5)** The "merciful" (5:7) exercise counsel, the gift that assists decision making and helps to guard against rashness; as an interior guide, it assists one to counsel others and to extend compassion to them. **(6)** The "pure in heart" (5:8) exercise understanding, the gift of insight into the mysteries of faith. It is not mere intellectual understanding but the spiritual perceptions of the heart. **(7)** The "peacemakers" (5:9) exercise wisdom, the gift of contemplative reflection on—and love for—divine things. It enables one to assess the world by revealed truths and instills peace in the soul.

5:3 poor in spirit: Those keenly aware of their spiritual poverty and need for God's mercy. They are like the lowly of the OT, seeking only the riches of heaven (Ps 34:6; Is 61:1; Zeph 2:3). While this includes the powerless and the materially poor, it refers primarily to those who recognize their moral weakness. With a humble spirit, they live inwardly detached from earthly goods (CCC 544, 2546).

5:4 those who mourn: Being "poor in spirit" (5:3), these lament mankind's earthly plight. They recognize that one cannot, with human effort alone, reach the blessedness of heaven. Disciples who *mourn* are likewise troubled by the injustices of the world and grieve over their sins (cf. Ps 51:17; Is 61:2).

5:5 the meek: Meekness is not weakness, but humility and faith in God especially during trials (cf. Jas 1:12). The *meek* maintain serenity and self-control through difficult circumstances. Moses exemplified this virtue more than any other in

---

WORD STUDY

Blessed (5:3–10)

Makarios (Gk.): a favorable standing in the grace of God's covenant. The word is found 13 times in Matthew and 37 times in the rest of the NT. It does not primarily mean "happy" as a subjective experience but denotes one's righteousness before God. Covenant blessings are gifts that the Father bestows on his children. The *blessed* are those whose sins are forgiven (Ps 32:1–2), who have faith in God (Ps 2:12; Jn 20:29), and who receive God's life as their family inheritance (1 Jn 5:11). *Blessed* too are those who love God and obey his covenant from the heart (cf. Deut 30:19–20; Ps 1:1; 119:1). In Matthew, the eight Beatitudes (Mt 5:3–10) announce the blessings of the New Covenant. These blessings are introduced on earth but fully realized in heaven (cf. 1 Jn 2:15–17; Jas 1:12; 1 Pet 3:14). Opposite God's blessings are covenant curses or woes that befall faithless sinners who prefer worldly comfort and esteem above holiness and humility (cf. Deut 30:19; Mt 23:13–29; Lk 6:24–26).

6 "Blessed are those who hunger and thirst for righteousness, for they shall be satisfied.

7 "Blessed are the merciful, for they shall obtain mercy.

8 "Blessed are the pure in heart, for they shall see God.

9 "Blessed are the peacemakers, for they shall be called sons of God.

10 "Blessed are those who are persecuted for righteousness' sake, for theirs is the kingdom of heaven.

11 "Blessed are you when men revile you and persecute you and utter all kinds of evil against you falsely on my account. 12Rejoice and be glad, for your reward is great in heaven, for so men persecuted the prophets who were before you.

Salt and Light

13 "You are the salt of the earth; but if salt has lost its taste, how shall its saltiness be restored? It is no longer good for anything except to be thrown out and trodden under foot by men.

14 "You are the light of the world. A city set on a hill cannot be hidden. 15Nor do men light a lamp and put it under a bushel, but on a stand, and it gives light to all in the house. 16Let your light so shine before men, that they may see your good works and give glory to your Father who is in heaven.

The Law and the Prophets

17 "Do not think that I have come to abolish the law and the prophets; I have come not to abolish them but to fulfil them. 18For truly, I say to you, till heaven and earth pass away, not an iota, not a dot, will pass from the law until all is accomplished. 19Whoever then relaxes one of the least of these commandments and teaches men so, shall be called least in the kingdom of heaven; but he who does them and teaches them shall be called great in the kingdom of heaven. 20For I tell you, unless your

5:6: Is 55:1–2; Jn 4:14; 6:48–51. **5:8:** Ps 24:4; Heb 12:14; 1 Jn 3:2; Rev 22:4. **5:10:** 1 Pet 3:14; 4:14. **5:12:** 2 Chron 36:16; Mt 23:37; Acts 7:52; 1 Thess 2:15; Jas 5:10. **5:13:** Mk 9:49–50; Lk 14:34–35. **5:14:** Eph 5:8; Philemon 2:15; Jn 8:12. **5:15–16:** Lk 11:33; Mk 4:21; 1 Pet 2:12. **5:18:** Lk 16:17; Mk 13:31. **5:19:** Jas 2:10.

the OT (Num 12:3; Sir 45:4). It is preeminently characteristic of Jesus (11:29), who obeyed the Father's will unto death (Phil 2:8). **shall inherit the earth:** A blessing similar to Ps 37:11, which offered the Promised Land to the meek of ancient Israel. Jesus' words encompass the whole earth, which God can safely entrust to "those who mourn" (5:4), and correctly estimate the world's value in light of eternity.

5:6 hunger and thirst: The "meek" (5:5) are not satisfied with earth but long for a heavenly inheritance. They strive to secure it through holiness and obedience to God (cf. Heb 12:14). **righteousness:** The gift of sonship and inheritance in God's covenant family. Those adopted by God desire his will to be known and fulfilled in their lives. See word study: *Righteousness* at Mt 3. **shall be satisfied:** Those who seek and desire God's *righteousness* receive it as a heavenly gift (cf. 6:33; 7:7; Rom 5:17).

5:7 the merciful: Those "satisfied" (5:6) with God's righteousness and mercy long to extend that gift to others (cf. Lk 6:36). They imitate God by forgiving their neighbor (18:21–22) and seek to remedy material and spiritual injustices in the world (CCC 2447).

5:8 the pure in heart: For ancient Hebrews, the heart signified the center of the person and the source of love and obedience—it was the origin of every act and decision. Having obtained "mercy" (5:7), the pure are given clear spiritual vision for single-minded devotion. **they shall see God:** The inwardly pure behold God in the simplicity of faith. They will see him "face to face" in heaven (1 Cor 13:12; 1 Jn 3:2; CCC 2517–19).

5:9 the peacemakers: In the Bible, God's peace (Heb. *shalom*) is the interpersonal harmony established by covenant relationships. More than a mere absence of conflict, true peace stems from reconciliation with God (cf. 2 Cor 5:18–20). The "pure in heart" (5:8) already stand in God's peace as his children (Rom 5:1). They seek to extend this gift to others by advancing the gospel (CCC 2305).

5:10 those who are persecuted: The "peacemakers" (5:9) who spread the gospel inevitably encounter persecution. Jesus envisions New Covenant disciples in line with the Old Covenant prophets, many of whom were abused and killed by their kinsmen (5:12; 23:37; Heb 11:32–38). They suffered maltreatment for their unwavering fidelity to God and their denunciation of personal and social evil.

5:14 the light of the world: Christians are called to fulfill the vocation of Israel (Gal 6:16). • God adopted OT Israel to be a "light to the nations" (Is 42:6; 49:6). By their obedience to God's Law—itself a light (Is 51:4; Bar 4:2)—the

Israelites were called to live exemplary lives that would attract other nations. Jesus now calls us to shed the light of the New Covenant by doing "good works" (5:16) and influencing the world around us. **A city set on a hill:** An allusion to Jerusalem, built atop Mt. Zion in Judea. According to the NT, the New Covenant Church is a spiritual "Mount Zion" and "heavenly Jerusalem" (Heb 12:22).

5:16 your Father: Earlier chapters make no mention of the Fatherhood of God. In the Sermon on the Mount, however, Jesus calls God "Father" a total of 17 times (chaps. 5–7). • God's Fatherhood is the deepest mystery of his identity; from eternity he fathers a divine Son (Jn 1:1), and throughout history he adopts us as his children in Christ (Jn 1:12; Gal 4:4–7).

5:17 the law and the prophets: A shorthand expression for the entire OT. **to fulfil them:** Jesus completely fulfilled the Mosaic Law and OT prophecies (1:23; 2:6, 15; 4:15–16; Lk 24:44–47). The Greek word translated *fulfil* means "to make complete". The New Covenant thus includes and concludes the Old Covenant; it both perfects it and transforms it. While sacrificial laws of the OT expired with the sacrifice of Jesus, the moral Law (Ten Commandments, etc.) was retained and refined (5:21, 27, 43; 19:17). In the Christian life, the power of God's Spirit is necessary if we are to obey the Law and grow in holiness (cf. Rom 8:4; CCC 577–81, 1967).

5:18 an iota: Corresponds to the smallest letter of the Hebrew alphabet (*yod*). **a dot:** Tiny extensions that distinguish similar-looking Hebrew letters from one another.

5:20 your righteousness: Jesus inaugurates a new and climactic phase in salvation history. He introduces a New Covenant standard of righteousness that surpasses the real, but insufficient, righteousness of the Old Covenant (cf. Deut 6:25; Is 48:18). The Old Covenant governed the temporal affairs of the earthly kingdom of Israel. The Mosaic Law (especially Deuteronomy) was designed to establish and maintain Israel as a nation-state in the land of Canaan. Its laws regulated public behavior to maintain civil order; it thus erected an outward standard of righteousness that defined God's people as a nation. Jesus invites **the scribes and Pharisees** to recognize the Mosaic Law as God's temporary arrangement for Israel (cf. Mt 19:8). It was a means of drawing them closer to God by separating them from the sins of the Gentiles (Lev 15:31; 20:26). Eventually, the Israelites expected a day when God would write his Law on their hearts (Jer 31:31–34; cf. Deut 30:6; Ezek 36:25–27). Christ's New Covenant signals the dawning of this great day when he perfects the moral laws of the Old Covenant

Matthew 5

righteousness exceeds that of the scribes and Pharisees, you will never enter the kingdom of heaven.

Concerning Anger

21 "You have heard that it was said to the men of old, 'You shall not kill; and whoever kills shall be liable to judgment.' [22]But I say to you that every one who is angry with his brother[i] shall be liable to judgment; whoever insults[j] his brother shall be liable to the council, and whoever says, 'You fool!' shall be liable to the hell[k] of fire. [23]So if you are offering your gift at the altar, and there remember that your brother has something against you, [24]leave your gift there before the altar and go; first be reconciled to your brother, and then come and offer your gift. [25]Make friends quickly with your accuser, while you are going with him to court, lest your accuser hand you over to the judge, and the judge to the guard, and you be put in prison; [26]truly, I say to you, you will never get out till you have paid the last penny.

Concerning Adultery

27 "You have heard that it was said, 'You shall not commit adultery.' [28]But I say to you that every one who looks at a woman lustfully has already committed adultery with her in his heart. [29]If your right eye causes you to sin, pluck it out and throw it away; it is better that you lose one of your mem-

bers than that your whole body be thrown into hell.[k] [30]And if your right hand causes you to sin, cut it off and throw it away; it is better that you lose one of your members than that your whole body go into hell.[k]

Concerning Divorce

31 "It was also said, 'Whoever divorces his wife, let him give her a certificate of divorce.' [32]But I say to you that every one who divorces his wife, except on the ground of unchastity, makes her an adulteress; and whoever marries a divorced woman commits adultery.

Concerning Oaths

33 "Again you have heard that it was said to the men of old, 'You shall not swear falsely, but shall perform to the Lord what you have sworn.' [34]But I say to you, Do not swear at all, either by heaven, for it is the throne of God, [35]or by the earth, for it is his footstool, or by Jerusalem, for it is the city of the great King. [36]And do not swear by your head, for you cannot make one hair white or black. [37]Let what you say be simply 'Yes' or 'No'; anything more than this comes from evil.[l]

Concerning Retaliation

38 "You have heard that it was said, 'An eye for an eye and a tooth for a tooth.' [39]But I say to you,

---

5:21: Ex 20:13; Deut 5:17; 16:18. **5:25–26:** Lk 12:57–59. **5:27:** Ex 20:14; Deut 5:18.
5:29–30: Mk 9:43–48; Mt 18:8–9. **5:31–32:** Lk 16:18; Mk 10:11–12; Mt 19:9; 1 Cor 7:10–11; Deut 24:1–4.
5:33–37: Mt 23:16–22; Jas 5:12; Lev 19:12; Nb 30:2; Deut 23:21.

---

and brings that covenant's temporary and national phase to a close. He implements a new level of covenant *righteousness* that stretches beyond the boundaries of the Old Law in two directions. **(1)** Outwardly, the scope of the New Covenant is wider than the one nation of Israel; it encompasses an international **kingdom** in the Church. All nations can now share in God's blessing and become his covenant people. **(2)** Inwardly, the New Covenant penetrates to the heart; it reaches within to govern personal and private life by a maximal standard of holiness. As the Old Covenant formed virtuous citizens in Israel, so the New Covenant generates saints in the Church (CCC 1963–68). See also word study: *Righteousness* at Mt 3.
5:21–48 Sometimes called the "Six Antitheses". Jesus acts with divine authority to perfect and deepen the moral codes of the Mosaic Law (cf. 7:29). Each antithesis follows a similar format: Jesus cites the Old Law, saying, **you have heard that it was said** (5:21, 27, 31, 33, 38, 43), and responds with the refrain, **but I say to you** (5:22, 28, 32, 34, 39, 44). The pattern underscores Jesus' authority as a new Moses and the lawgiver of the New Covenant. See notes on 2:16 and 17:5.
5:21 You shall not kill: Jesus reaffirms that murder is unlawful (Ex 20:13; Deut 5:17) but introduces a new dimension to the civil law. Not only acts of murder but even personal anger (5:22) and private slander (5:22) constitute a violation of the New Law. Degrees of personal guilt are illustrated (5:22) by an escalating movement from a local court verdict ("judgment"), to the Jewish Sanhedrin ("council"), to eternal punishment ("hell"). At each step, the judgment corresponds to the severity of the sin (CCC 2302).
5:22 You fool!: The ancient use of this term was more insulting than today. A fool was someone who refused to honor and obey God (Ps 14:1; 53:1). **the hell of fire:** The Greek expression (also in 5:29–30) denotes the Valley of Gehenna south of Jerusalem. It served as a large dump where garbage was

burned continually. Jesus uses the image to illustrate the frightful reality of damnation (CCC 1034–35). See word study: *Hell* at Mk 9.
5:27 adultery: Like the Mosaic Law, Jesus forbids acts of adultery (Ex 20:14; Deut 5:18). Yet he extends the prohibition to forbid even personal lust and interior thoughts of impurity. Looking and thinking "lustfully" (5:28) already violate the New Law, even if the exterior act of adultery is not committed (CCC 2380).
5:29 pluck it out: A figurative overstatement, not a literal command of self-mutilation. Jesus uses alarming images to underscore the severity of sexual sins (cf. 18:7–9); extreme measures are needed to avoid occasions of sin, the sins themselves, and the eternal punishment they lead to.
5:31 a certificate of divorce: Divorce and remarriage were permitted under the Old Covenant only because of Israel's sinfulness (19:8; cf. Deut 24:1–4). In the New Covenant, remarriage leads to adultery (CCC 2382). **except on the ground of unchastity:** Matthew alone records this added "exception clause" (cf. 19:9). For the meaning of this clause, see topical essay: *Jesus on Marriage and Divorce* at Mt 19.
5:33 not swear falsely: Jesus forbids oath swearing for private purposes. Oaths are important, however, in the public sector for the good of society. Judges, doctors, soldiers, politicians, and other professionals swear oaths for public service. Oaths are also sworn to make or renew covenants (cf. Heb 6:13–18). In every context, God's holy name is invoked to bring divine assistance (blessing) to the upright and divine punishment (curse) to those who violate their oaths. In Jesus' day, the practice of oath swearing was sometimes mishandled; people would swear private oaths for personal advantage. By invoking something other than God's name (heaven/earth/Jerusalem; 5:34–35), oaths were taken lightly or even disregarded (23:16–22). Jesus denounces this, teaching that truthfulness and integrity should govern private life. Matthew recounts three episodes where such illicit oaths are sworn for personal purposes (14:7; 26:72, 74; 27:25) (CCC 2153–54).
5:38 An eye for an eye: Jesus forbids the misuse of Mosaic

---

[i] Other ancient authorities insert *without cause.*
[j] Greek *says Raca to* (an obscure term of abuse).
[k] Greek *Gehenna.* [l] Or *the evil one.*

Do not resist one who is evil. But if any one strikes you on the right cheek, turn to him the other also; [40]and if any one would sue you and take your coat, let him have your cloak as well; [41]and if any one forces you to go one mile, go with him two miles. [42]Give to him who begs from you, and do not refuse him who would borrow from you.

Love for Enemies

43 "You have heard that it was said, 'You shall love your neighbor and hate your enemy.' [44]But I say to you, Love your enemies and pray for those who persecute you, [45]so that you may be sons of your Father who is in heaven; for he makes his sun rise on the evil and on the good, and sends rain on the just and on the unjust. [46]For if you love those who love you, what reward have you? Do not even the tax collectors do the same? [47]And if you salute only your brethren, what more are you doing than others? Do not even the Gentiles do the same? [48]You, therefore, must be perfect, as your heavenly Father is perfect.

Concerning Almsgiving

6 "Beware of practicing your piety before men in order to be seen by them; for then you will have no reward from your Father who is in heaven.

2 "Thus, when you give alms, sound no trumpet before you, as the hypocrites do in the synagogues and in the streets, that they may be praised by men. Truly, I say to you, they have received their reward. [3]But when you give alms, do not let your left hand know what your right hand is doing, [4]so that your alms may be in secret; and your Father who sees in secret will reward you.

Concerning Prayer

5 "And when you pray, you must not be like the hypocrites; for they love to stand and pray in the synagogues and at the street corners, that they may be seen by men. Truly, I say to you, they have their reward. [6]But when you pray, go into your room and shut the door and pray to your Father who is in secret; and your Father who sees in secret will reward you.

7 "And in praying do not heap up empty phrases as the Gentiles do; for they think that they will be heard for their many words. [8]Do not be like them, for your Father knows what you need before you ask him. [9]Pray then like this:

Our Father in heaven,
Hallowed be your name.
[10] Your kingdom come.

5:35: Is 66:1; Acts 7:49; Ps 48:2. **5:38:** Ex 21:24; Lev 24:20; Deut 19:21.
5:39–42: Lk 6:29–30; 1 Cor 6:7; Rom 12:17; 1 Pet 2:19; 3:9; Prov 24:29. **5:43–48:** Lk 6:27–28, 32–36; Lev 19:18; Prov 25:21–22.
5:48: Lev 19:2. **6:1:** Mt 23:5. **6:4:** Col 3:23–24. **6:5:** Mk 11:25; Lk 18:10–14. **6:7:** 1 Kings 18:25–29.
6:8: Mt 6:32; Lk 12:30. **6:9–13:** Lk 11:2–4.

---

civil law to justify private vengeance. Exodus 21:24 was meant to limit retribution; it was never an invitation to inflict punishment for personal injuries or extend personal vengeance beyond the injury suffered (cf. Lev 24:20; Deut 19:21). The punishment had to fit the crime but not exceed it. Jesus eliminates such a policy of retaliation from personal life (cf. Rom 12:17).

5:41 if anyone forces you: Roman soldiers in NT Palestine reserved the right to recruit and compel Jews into temporary service. Simon of Cyrene was forced under this custom to carry Jesus' Cross in 27:32. Jesus calls for ungrudging generosity beyond the required call of duty.

5:43 love your neighbor: A reference to Lev 19:18. Jesus considers it one of the two great commandments of the Mosaic Law (22:39). Unlike Jesus, however, some Jews held a narrow interpretation of *neighbor*, restricting it only to one's fellow Israelite (cf. Lk 10:29–37) (CCC 1933). **hate your enemy:** Probably a reference to Israel's warfare laws in Deut 20. Because Gentiles in Canaan worshiped false gods, they were enemies of God. Moses thus called Israel to exterminate them under Joshua and the Judges, lest Israel imitate their idolatry (cf. Ex 23:32–33; Ps 139:19–22). Against this background, Jesus counters Jewish disdain for Gentiles who continue to live in Palestine. He broadens the meaning of *neighbor* to include Gentiles, even their Roman persecutors. The Father's impartial treatment of all people is a model for Christian mercy (5:45).

5:48 You . . . must be perfect: Jesus advocates moral righteousness higher than the Old Covenant—it is a standard of mercy. Just as Israel was to imitate God in being "holy" (Lev 19:2), so Jesus calls the Church to imitate God's perfect compassion (Lk 6:36). The Father is kind and merciful to the good and evil alike, so his children must extend mercy even to their enemies (5:7; Lk 10:29–37; Jas 2:13). See note on Lk 6:36 (CCC 1968, 2842).

6:1–18 Jesus reaffirms three traditional works of mercy honored by Jews (cf. Tob 12:8–10): almsgiving (6:2–4), prayer (6:5–15), and fasting (6:16–18) (CCC 1434, 1969). **piety:** Literally "righteousness", as in 3:15; 5:6, 20; 6:33. See word study: *Righteousness* at Mt 3. Jesus does not challenge these prac-

tices in themselves; he warns against performing them for public esteem (CCC 1430).

6:2 give alms: Charitable gifts given to the poor (Sir 17:22; Lk 3:11; CCC 2447). **hypocrites:** Refers to "actors" or "stage players". Jesus may have certain scribes and Pharisees in mind (cf. 23:5, 27–28) who perform outward devotions to be seen and **praised by men**. The exercise of one's faith can be public, so long as it flows from proper intentions (5:16).

6:6 in secret: Private prayer stands in contrast to the false piety of hypocrites. It was Jesus' own custom to withdraw from the public and pray alone to the Father (14:23; Mk 1:35; Lk 9:18). Private prayer is a complement to communal prayer, not a rejection of it (cf. 18:20; Acts 1:12–14; CCC 2602, 2655).

6:7 empty phrases . . . many words: Jesus briefly considers the false religiosity of **Gentiles**. Pagans would recite long litanies of divine names to gain the attention of gods. This was meant to ensure that the deity was addressed properly. Jesus considers the practice empty—i.e., devoid of faith and of love for the deity. Note that his warning is not aimed at repetitious or lengthy prayer in itself. With a pure heart, such prayer can be fruitful and intimate. Jesus himself prayed to the Father in Gethsemane three times "saying the same words" (26:44) and "all night" (Lk 6:12) before choosing the apostles (CCC 2668).

6:9–13 The Our Father is a model of prayer. Given by God's Son, it is part of the family inheritance of God's children. It has seven petitions and can be divided into two parts: the first section (6:9–10) glorifies God, while the second half (6:11–13) petitions God about human needs (CCC 2765, 2781).

6:9 Our: The first person plural (our, us, we) is prominent in the Our Father. It is thus a prayer for the Church (CCC 2768). **Father:** Jesus may have taught this prayer in Aramaic, a language related to ancient Hebrew and in common usage among first-century Jews. In this case, Jesus would have addressed the Father as "Abba", an affectionate title preserved elsewhere in the NT (Mk 14:36; Rom 8:15; Gal 4:6). While Jesus alone is the Father's Son by nature, we too become his children by the grace of divine adoption (Rom 8:14–16; Gal 4:4–7). As God's children in Christ (Jn 1:12), Christians now regard God as their

Your will be done,
  On earth as it is in heaven.
[11] Give us this day our daily bread;[m]
[12] And forgive us our trespasses,
  As we also have forgiven those who trespass
    against us;
[13] And lead us not into temptation,
  But deliver us from evil.[n]
[14]For if you forgive men their trespasses, your heavenly Father also will forgive you; [15]but if you do not forgive men their trespasses, neither will your Father forgive your trespasses.

Concerning Fasting

16 "And when you fast, do not look dismal, like the hypocrites, for they disfigure their faces that their fasting may be seen by men. Truly, I say to you, they have received their reward. [17]But when you fast, anoint your head and wash your face, [18]that your fasting may not be seen by men but by your Father who is in secret; and your Father who sees in secret will reward you.

Concerning Treasures

19 "Do not lay up for yourselves treasures on earth, where moth and rust[o] consume and where thieves break in and steal, [20]but lay up for yourselves treasures in heaven, where neither moth nor rust[o] consumes and where thieves do not break in and steal. [21]For where your treasure is, there will your heart be also.

The Sound Eye

22 "The eye is the lamp of the body. So, if your eye is sound, your whole body will be full of light; [23]but if your eye is not sound, your whole body will be full of darkness. If then the light in you is darkness, how great is the darkness!

Serving Two Masters

24 "No one can serve two masters; for either he will hate the one and love the other, or he will be devoted to the one and despise the other. You cannot serve God and mammon.

Do Not Worry

25 "Therefore I tell you, do not be anxious about your life, what you shall eat or what you shall drink, nor about your body, what you shall put on. Is not life more than food, and the body more than clothing? [26]Look at the birds of the air: they neither sow nor reap nor gather into barns, and yet your heavenly Father feeds them. Are you not of more value than they? [27]And which of you by being anxious can add one cubit to his span of life?[p] [28]And why are you anxious about clothing? Consider the lilies of the field, how they grow; they neither toil nor spin; [29]yet I tell you, even Solomon in all his glory was not clothed like one of these. [30]But if God so clothes the grass of the field, which today is alive and tomorrow is thrown into the oven, will he not much more clothe you, O men of little faith? [31]Therefore do not be anxious, saying, 'What shall we eat?' or 'What shall we drink?' or 'What shall we wear?' [32]For the Gentiles seek all these things; and your heavenly Father knows that you need them all. [33]But seek first his kingdom and his righteousness, and all these things shall be yours as well.

6:13: 2 Thess 3:3; Jn 17:15; Jas 1:13.   **6:14–15:** Mt 18:35; Mk 11:25; Eph 4:32; Col 3:13.   **6:16:** Is 58:5.   **6:18:** Mt 6:4, 6
6:19–21: Lk 12:33–34; Mk 10:21; 1 Tim 6:17–19; Jas 5:1–3.   **6:22–23:** Lk 11:34–36; Mt 20:15; Mk 7:22.   **6:24:** Lk 16:13.
6:25–33: Lk 12:22–31; 10:41; 12:11; Philemon 4:6; 1 Pet 5:7.   **6:26:** Mt 10:29.   **6:27:** Ps 39:5.   **6:29:** 1 Kings 10:4–7
6:30: Mt 8:26; 14:31; 16:8.   **6:33:** Mt 19:28; Mk 10:29–30; Lk 18:29–30.

Father in a more profound way than OT Israel had (Deut 32:6): they participate in God's divine life (2 Pet 1:4; 1 Jn 3:1; CCC 2766, 2780). **Hallowed be your name:** A petition that all would recognize God's name as holy (Ps 111:9; Lk 1:49). To call upon God's name is an ancient form of worship (Gen 4:26; Ps 116:17; Joel 2:32), and the Law warns against taking his name "in vain" (Ex 20:7) (CCC 2807).

6:11 our daily bread: The Greek *epiousios* (translated *daily*) is used only here and in Lk 11:3 in the NT. It probably means "for tomorrow" or "for the future". The petition thus concerns food for the body and soul: (1) The necessities of life that fathers give their children is a form of daily bread. This may recall the manna that God provided each day for the Israelites in the wilderness (Ex 16:13–17). (2) Several Church Fathers interpret *daily bread* as a reference to the Holy Eucharist—a form of supernatural sustenance (Acts 2:46). The two connotations are connected, since Jesus advocates dependence on the Father for daily living (6:25–34) and later associates the manna with the Eucharist (Jn 6:30–40; CCC 2837).

6:13 evil: Also translated "the evil one", as in 13:19 (cf. Jn 17:15; 2 Thess 3:3). As such, it designates Satan, fallen angel and adversary of God. The petition is projected into the future: Christians pray for God's deliverance in the final days, when the devil and evil will be destroyed (Rev 20:10).

6:17 anoint your head: Fasting was often a public practice accompanied by wearing sackcloth and putting ashes on one's head (Esther 4:3; Dan 9:3). While it was intended to express inner repentance, hypocrites utilized it to appear devout. Washing and anointing outwardly symbolize happiness and disguise one's inner commitment to God (Ruth 3:3; Ps 23:5; Is 61:3; CCC 1438).

6:22 The eye is the lamp: An ancient metaphor (Tob 10:5; Prov 15:30; Sir 23:19). Jesus uses it to advocate generosity. Those with evil or unsound eyes are stingy with their belongings (Deut 15:9; Sir 14:8–10; cf. Mt 20:15); they are full of darkness (6:23). Those with sound eyes share their goods with the needy (4:7); they are filled with **light**.

6:24 mammon: An Aramaic word meaning "wealth" or "property". Jesus warns that earthly possessions can threaten an undivided love for God. The NT elsewhere exposes the dangers surrounding money and the accumulation of temporal goods (13:22; Lk 12:13–21; 1 Tim 6:10; Heb 13:5; CCC 2113).

6:28–30 Jesus teaches with the logic of Jewish rabbis: the lesser fact of God's care for **lilies** (6:28) implies God's greater concern for **men** (6:30; CCC 2830). • *Anagogically*, God supplies our physical needs to signify his greater concern for our spiritual needs. As his care for the lilies and the grass is outmatched by his provision of clothing for us, so the garments we receive prefigure God's desire to clothe us with glory and immortality in heaven (cf. 1 Cor 15:51-55; Rev 19:7-8).

6:33 seek first his kingdom: Christians must prioritize the pursuit of holiness in their lives. This is not an excuse for lazi-

---

[m] Or *our bread for the morrow.*
[n] Or *the evil one.* Other authorities, some ancient, add, in some form, *For yours is the kingdom and the power and the glory, for ever. Amen.*
[o] Or *worm.*   [p] Or *to his stature.*

34 "Therefore do not be anxious about tomorrow, for tomorrow will be anxious for itself. Let the day's own trouble be sufficient for the day.

Judging Others

7 "Judge not, that you be not judged. [2]For with the judgment you pronounce you will be judged, and the measure you give will be the measure you get. [3]Why do you see the speck that is in your brother's eye, but do not notice the log that is in your own eye? [4]Or how can you say to your brother, 'Let me take the speck out of your eye,' when there is the log in your own eye? [5]You hypocrite, first take the log out of your own eye, and then you will see clearly to take the speck out of your brother's eye.

Profaning the Holy

6 "Do not give dogs what is holy; and do not throw your pearls before swine, lest they trample them under foot and turn to attack you.

Ask, Search, Knock

7 "Ask, and it will be given you; seek, and you will find; knock, and it will be opened to you. [8]For every one who asks receives, and he who seeks finds, and to him who knocks it will be opened. [9]Or what man of you, if his son asks him for bread, will give him a stone? [10]Or if he asks for a fish, will give him a serpent? [11]If you then, who are evil, know how to give good gifts to your children, how much more will your Father who is in heaven give good things to those who ask him! [12]So whatever you wish that men would do to you, do so to them; for this is the law and the prophets.

The Narrow Gate

13 "Enter by the narrow gate; for the gate is wide and the way is easy,[q] that leads to destruction, and those who enter by it are many. [14]For the gate is narrow and the way is hard, that leads to life, and those who find it are few.

False Prophets

15 "Beware of false prophets, who come to you in sheep's clothing but inwardly are ravenous wolves. [16]You will know them by their fruits. Are grapes gathered from thorns, or figs from thistles? [17]So, every sound tree bears good fruit, but the bad tree bears evil fruit. [18]A sound tree cannot bear evil fruit, nor can a bad tree bear good fruit. [19]Every tree that does not bear good fruit is cut down and thrown into the fire. [20]Thus you will know them by their fruits.

Concerning Self-Deception

21 "Not every one who says to me, 'Lord, Lord,' shall enter the kingdom of heaven, but he who does the will of my Father who is in heaven. [22]On that day many will say to me, 'Lord, Lord, did we not prophesy in your name, and cast out demons in your name, and do many mighty works in your name?' [23]And then will I declare to them, 'I never knew you; depart from me, you evildoers.'

7:1–2: Lk 6:37–38; Mk 4:24; Rom 2:1; 14:10.   **7:3–5:** Lk 6:41–42.
7:7–11: Lk 11:9–13; Mk 11:24; Jn 15:7; 1&23–24; Jas 4:3; 1 Jn 3:22; 5:14.   **7:12:** Lk 6:31.
7:13–14: Lk 13:23–24; Jer 21:8; Deut 30:19; Jn 14:6; 10:7.   **7:15:** Mt 24:11, 24; Ezek 22:27; 1 Jn 4:1; Jn 10:12.
7:16–20: Lk 6:43–44; Mt 12:33–35; Mt 3:10; Jas 3:12; Lk 13:7.   **7:21:** Lk 6:46.   **7:22–23:** Lk 13:26–27; Mt 25:12; Ps 6:8.

---

ness in practical matters (2 Thess 3:6-13) but a call to trust in the Father's care (Phil 4:6; CCC 2608).

7:1–6 Jesus' teaching on judgment is two-sided. **(1)** He condemns judging other's faults (7:1-2; Lk 6:37). We are incapable of judging with fairness and accuracy since God alone knows the heart (Prov 21:2; Lk 16:15). **(2)** However, Jesus commands us to exercise critical discernment (7:6, 15–19; 1 Thess 5:21). Examination is necessary to avoid profaning what is holy (7:6) and embracing what is false (7:15).

7:2 you will be judged: i.e., by God (theological passive). We set the standards of our personal judgment by our own conduct toward others (cf. 18:35).

7:6 dogs . . . swine: Derogatory Jewish epithets for pagans (15:26–28). Dogs were generally undomesticated in Jewish culture, and most were stray scavengers. Swine were especially contemptible to Jews; they were unclean and could not be eaten (Lev 11:7-8; cf. Is 66:3). Jesus redirects these insulting labels to anyone inhospitable to the gospel, Jew or Gentile (cf. Phil 3:2; Rev 22:15). **what is holy:** In Judaism, holiness characterized anything consecrated for covenant worship. To treat holy articles in a common manner would profane them (Ex 29:37; Lev 22:10-16). Jesus carries this same notion into the New Covenant. The early Church applied this statement to the Holy Eucharist, a sacrament rightly withheld from the unbaptized (*Didache* 9:5).

7:7 Ask . . . given you: Jesus advocates perseverance in prayer (cf. Lk 18:1; Col 4:2; 1 Thess 5:17). Answered prayers stem from upright and faith-filled intentions (Jas 1:5-8; CCC 2609).

7:11 you then, who are evil: Indicates the pervasive sinfulness of man. **how much more:** A rhetorical device familiar to Jewish rabbis and used also by the Apostle Paul (Rom 5:15–17). See note on 6:28-30. **good things:** the material necessities of life, as well as the grace to live as God's children. The Lk 11:13 parallel identifies the gift as the "Holy Spirit".

7:12 do so to them: The "Golden Rule". It is similar to statements in the OT (Tob 4:15; Sir 31:15) and other world religions. While normally a negative statement (based upon *not* doing to others), Jesus states it positively (CCC 1970).

7:13 the narrow gate: An image with various associations. **(1)** Cities surrounded by a fortified wall had gates to permit access. Main gates were wide and tall enough for caravans of people and animals; smaller gates permitted only pedestrian traffic. Jesus envisions the **many** passing with ease through a main gate. The **few** must exert greater effort to enter a narrow pedestrian gate (cf. 22:14). **(2)** The Jerusalem Temple had a series of gates that prohibited entry for the unqualified; only a privileged few had close access to God. This teaching of the "two ways" is common in the OT (cf. Deut 30:15-20; Ps 1; Wis 5:6-7; CCC 1696).

7:15 false prophets: These so-called prophets appear harmless, yet their ministry breeds error, division, and immorality (cf. 24:24; 2 Pet 2:1-3). The distinction between true and false prophets is rooted in the OT (Deut 18:20-22; Jer 14:13-16).

7:22 On that day: The Day of Judgment. Jesus is portrayed as the divine Judge (cf. 25:31-46; Jn 5:25-29; 2 Cor 5:10; CCC 678, 682). • God's sanctifying grace enlivens the soul, making it fit for heaven; it is the grace of divine Sonship. It is manifested through conformity with the Father's will by knowing and obeying Jesus (7:23; cf. Jn 17:3; 1 Jn 2:3-6). In Catholic tradition, sanctifying grace is distinct from graces that are manifest through miraculous works such as prophecy

---

[q] Other ancient authorities read *for the way is wide and easy.*

Hearers and Doers

24 "Every one then who hears these words of mine and does them will be like a wise man who built his house upon the rock; ²⁵and the rain fell, and the floods came, and the winds blew and beat upon that house, but it did not fall, because it had been founded on the rock. ²⁶And every one who hears these words of mine and does not do them will be like a foolish man who built his house upon the sand; ²⁷and the rain fell, and the floods came, and the winds blew and beat against that house, and it fell; and great was the fall of it."

28 And when Jesus finished these sayings, the crowds were astonished at his teaching, ²⁹for he taught them as one who had authority, and not as their scribes.

Jesus Cleanses a Leper

8 When he came down from the mountain, great crowds followed him; ²and behold, a leper came to him and knelt before him, saying, "Lord, if you will, you can make me clean." ³And he stretched out his hand and touched him, saying, "I will; be clean." And immediately his leprosy was cleansed. ⁴And Jesus said to him, "See that you say nothing to any one; but go, show yourself to the priest, and offer the gift that Moses commanded, for a proof to the people." ʳ

Jesus Heals a Centurion's Servant

5 As he entered Caper′na-um, a centurion came forward to him, begging him ⁶and saying, "Lord, my servant is lying paralyzed at home, in terrible distress." ⁷And he said to him, "I will come and heal him." ⁸But the centurion answered him, "Lord, I am not worthy to have you come under my roof; but only say the word, and my servant will be healed. ⁹For I am a man under authority, with soldiers under me; and I say to one, 'Go,' and he goes, and to another, 'Come,' and he comes, and to my slave, 'Do this,' and he does it." ¹⁰When Jesus heard him, he marveled, and said to those who followed him, "Truly, I say to you, not even ˢ in Israel have I found such faith. ¹¹I tell you, many will come from

---

7:24–27: Lk 6:47–49; Jas 1:22–25.   **7:28–29:** Mk 1:22; Lk 4:32; Mt 11:1; 13:53; 19:1; 26:1.   **8:2–4:** Mk 1:40–44; Lk 5:12–14.
8:2: Mt 9:18; 15:25; 18:26; 20:20; Jn 9:38.   **8:4:** Mk 3:12; 5:43; 7:36; 8:30; 9:9; Lev 14:2.   **8:5–13:** Lk 7:1–10; Jn 4:46–53.
8:11–12: Lk 13:28–29; Is 49:12; 59:19; Mal 1:11; Ps 107:3.

---

and exorcism. These charismatic graces are also heavenly gifts but are not conclusive evidence of one's personal sanctity or membership in the family of God (CCC 2003).

7:24 like a wise man: True wisdom puts Jesus' teaching into practice and prepares for the future (cf. 25:1–13; Jas 2:14–26). **his house:** The parable reflects building conditions in NT Palestine. Houses made of mud brick were generally built during the dry season. When torrential rains arrived, only the house with a solid foundation resisted erosion and ultimate destruction (cf. Prov 14:11). • Jesus' reference to the wise man and his house alludes to King Solomon. He was known for his wisdom (1 Kings 3:10–12) and built the Lord's house (i.e., Temple; 1 Kings 8:27) upon a great foundation stone (1 Kings 5:17; 7:10; cf. Is 28:16). See note on 16:18. • *Morally*, the enduring house (7:25) is like the soul; it is maintained only through labor and the materials of prayer and virtue grounded on Christ (Ps 127:1; 1 Cor 3:11). The foolish man neglects sound construction and maintenance, building on a weak foundation of wealth and earthly success. The Day of Judgment will expose the foundation and destiny of every spiritual builder (Prov 10:25; 1 Tim 6:17–19).

7:29 one who had authority: Jesus' teaching differs from that of the **scribes**, who taught the already-existing traditions of Judaism. Jesus, cast as a new Moses, delivered "new teaching" (Mk 1:27) that excelled even the Mosaic Law in perfection (5:21–48). Jesus later denounced traditions that were incompatible with God's word (15:3–6) (CCC 581).

8:1—9:38 Matthew assembles ten miracle stories. They portray Jesus bringing into the world a divine holiness that overpowers the causes of defilement: sin, disease, demons, and even death. The Jews, especially the Pharisees, considered those defiled by these things to be unclean and untouchable; Jesus, however, takes an offensive stance against evil and by his mighty words (8:13, 16, 26, 32; 9:6) and physical touch (8:3, 15; 9:21, 25, 29) heals the effects of sin. He was not only immune to uncleanness, but the superior power of his holiness went forth to purify others in his midst. These episodes also reveal Jesus' favor with the crowds (8:1, 16, 18; 9:8, 31, 33) as well as mounting opposition by skeptical authorities (9:3, 34).

8:2 a leper: Leprosy infects human skin, garments, and homes (Lev 13—14). The skin disease was to be diagnosed by a Levitical priest. If the infection spread, the victim was pronounced ritually unclean and was excluded from the social and religious life of Israel. The Law required lepers to live in isolation and maintain a ragged appearance (Lev 13:45–46). Since contact with lepers rendered others unclean, it was shocking by Jewish standards for Jesus to cure the man by touching him (7:3). His ability is later recalled as a messianic credential (11:5).

8:4 the gift that Moses commanded: The Law required anyone healed of leprosy to be examined by a Levitical priest (Lev 13:1–3). Upon approval, the individual would undertake procedures for cleansing and reinstatement into the covenant life of Israel. This entailed a sacrifice tailored to his ability to pay (Lev 14:1–32). • *Symbolically* (St. Augustine, *Quaest. Evan.* 2, 40), Jesus' cleansing of the leper signifies the Sacrament of Reconciliation. Leprosy represents mortal sin, the spiritual disease that extinguishes grace from the soul and impedes one's full participation in the Church. This condition can also be contagious and influence others through scandal and false contrition. The Levitical priest typifies New Covenant priests, who are instrumental in reconciling sinners with God and restoring them to spiritual health through the sacrament.

8:5 centurion: A Roman military commander of 100 soldiers. Emphasis falls on his ethnic identity as a Gentile who has faith in Jesus (8:10). According to Luke, he was favorable to the Jewish nation and responsible for building a synagogue in Capernaum (Lk 7:5).

8:8 Lord, I am not worthy: Demonstrates great faith and humility. Jesus "marveled" (8:10) that such virtue was displayed by a Gentile. • These words are adapted for use in the Roman liturgy. Unworthy to receive the Eucharist, Christians ask to be cleansed of personal faults and place their faith in the healing power of God's word (CCC 1386).

8:11 sit at table: Alludes to an OT promise of a great feast to accompany the messianic age (Is 25:6–9). See note on 22:2. **Abraham, Isaac, and Jacob:** Jesus hints at the universal spread of the gospel to all nations in the Church (28:19). • These OT patriarchs are linked with God's covenant oath to Abraham that all nations would eventually share his blessings (Gen 22:18; CCC 543). The covenant was renewed with Isaac (Gen 26:3–5) and Jacob (Gen 28:14).

ʳ Greek *to them.*
ˢ Other ancient authorities read *with no one.*

east and west and sit at table with Abraham, Isaac, and Jacob in the kingdom of heaven, [12]while the sons of the kingdom will be thrown into the outer darkness; there men will weep and gnash their teeth." [13]And to the centurion Jesus said, "Go; let it be done for you as you have believed." And the servant was healed at that very moment.

Jesus Heals Many at Peter's House

14 And when Jesus entered Peter's house, he saw his mother-in-law lying sick with a fever; [15]he touched her hand, and the fever left her, and she rose and served him. [16]That evening they brought to him many who were possessed with demons; and he cast out the spirits with a word, and healed all who were sick. [17]This was to fulfil what was spoken by the prophet Isaiah, "He took our infirmities and bore our diseases."

Would-Be Followers of Jesus

18 Now when Jesus saw great crowds around him, he gave orders to go over to the other side. [19]And a scribe came up and said to him, "Teacher, I will follow you wherever you go." [20]And Jesus said to him, "Foxes have holes, and birds of the air have nests; but the Son of man has nowhere to lay his head." [21]Another of the disciples said to him, "Lord,

let me first go and bury my father." [22]But Jesus said to him, "Follow me, and leave the dead to bury their own dead."

Jesus Stills the Storm

23 And when he got into the boat, his disciples followed him. [24]And behold, there arose a great storm on the sea, so that the boat was being swamped by the waves; but he was asleep. [25]And they went and woke him, saying, "Save us, Lord; we are perishing." [26]And he said to them, "Why are you afraid, O men of little faith?" Then he rose and rebuked the winds and the sea; and there was a great calm. [27]And the men marveled, saying, "What sort of man is this, that even winds and sea obey him?"

Jesus Heals the Gadarene Demoniacs

28 And when he came to the other side, to the country of the Gadarenes,[t] two demoniacs met him, coming out of the tombs, so fierce that no one could pass that way. [29]And behold, they cried out, "What have you to do with us, O Son of God? Have you come here to torment us before the time?" [30]Now a herd of many swine was feeding at some distance from them. [31]And the demons begged him, "If you cast us out, send us away into the

---

8:12: Mt 13:42, 50; 22:13; 24:51; 25:30; Lk 13:28.   **8:14–16:** Mk 1:29–34; Lk 4:38–41; Mt 4:23–24.   **8:17:** Is 53:4..
8:18–22: Lk 9:57–60; Mk 4435; Lk 8:22.   **8:22:** Mt 9:9; Jn 1:43; 21:19.   **8:23–27:** Mk 4:36–41; Lk 8:22–25.
8:26: Mt 6:30; 14:31; 16:8.   **8:28–34:** Mk 5:1–17; Lk 8:26–37.   **8:29:** Judg 11:12; 2 Sam 16:10; Mk 1:24; Jn *2:4*.

8:12 weep and gnash their teeth: Describes the pangs of the damned excluded from the heavenly banquet (22:13). ● Similar language in the OT portrays the wicked who slander the righteous with hatred and disgust (Job 16:9; Ps 37:12; 112:10).

8:17 He took our infirmities: A formula quotation from Is 53:4. Jesus fulfills this role by physical healings. Matthew evokes the same OT context to speak also of Jesus' spiritual healing of sinners (1 Pet 2:24–25; cf. Is 53:5–6). ● Isaiah foretold of a Servant figure who would take Israel's sins upon himself and heal God's people (Is 52:13–53:12). This Servant would inaugurate the restoration of the tribes of Israel and bring the Gentiles to the family of God (Is 49:6). Matthew sees Jesus in this role, ushering in the kingdom by expelling demons and healing diseases. The close relationship between sin and physical affliction is assumed (cf. Ps 107:17; Is 33:24; CCC 1505).

8:22 Follow me: Discipleship is based on the imitation of Christ (11:29). Unlike the apostles, who left their occupations and families (4:19, 22; 9:9), this would-be follower of Jesus is hesitant to embrace the demanding call (8:21). **bury their own dead:** Burial was a sacred duty in ancient Judaism (Gen 50:5; Tob 4:3–4). Jesus singles out the custom to emphasize the greater importance of discipleship. Allegiance to Jesus must outweigh even family commitments (10:37; 19:29; Lk 14:26). Those who are spiritually dead (i.e., clinging to worldly concerns) can bury the physically dead. Jesus does not thereby undermine the propriety of burial but uses it as a stepping-stone to illustrate the higher demands of the Christian life. ● The episode resembles Elijah's call of Elisha to be his follower (1 Kings 19:19–21). Unlike Elijah, however, Jesus denies the request to fulfill parental duties, showing that discipleship in the New Covenant has higher demands than in the Old. ● Following Jesus, the Church considers burial a corporal work of mercy (CCC 2447).

8:23–27 Here Jesus reveals his divine authority over creation. See note on 8:27. ● Jesus' stilling of the storm parallels the experience of Jonah in the OT (Jon 1:1–16). **(1)** Both set sail on a **boat** (8:23; Jon 1:3); **(2)** both are caught in a **storm on the sea** (8:24; Jon 1:4, 11); **(3)** both are found **asleep** (8:24; Jon 1:5); **(4)** both are accompanied by frightened sailors (8:24–26; Jon 1:5); **(5)** both groups of sailors call upon the Lord for deliverance (8:25; Jon 1:14); **(6)** both are instrumental in bringing about a **great calm** (8:26; Jon 1:12, 15); **(7)** and the sailors in both episodes **marveled** at the outcome (8:27; Jon 1:16). Jesus' identity as a new Jonah is mentioned elsewhere, in 12:39–41 and 16:4. See note on Mk 4:35–41. ● *Morally* (St. John Chrysostom, *Hom. in Matt.* 28), the wave-tossed boat signifies the struggles of the Christian life. Endangered by the wind and fierce waves, God's people are awakened by spiritual assaults and become aware of their helplessness. They call upon the Lord for salvation and inner peace. The near presence of Christ assures their deliverance, and his swiftness strengthens their wavering faith.

8:24 storm: The Greek term *seismos* literally means "earthquake", as in 24:7, 27:54, and 28:2. It here describes the violent conditions of the sea.

8:26 rebuked: The verb (Gk. *epitimaō*) is elsewhere used in connection with exorcisms and the rebuking of Satan himself (17:18; Mk 1:25; Lk 4:41; Jude 1:9).

8:27 winds and sea obey him: The OT credits God alone with authority over the sea (Job 26:11–14; Ps 89:8–10; 93:4; 107:28–31). Aware of this, the disciples marvel and question Jesus' identity. Their uncertainty indicates that Jesus manifested his divinity gradually; it was not until later that they worshiped him as the "Son of God" (14:33).

8:28 the Gadarenes: The city of Gadara was about six miles southeast of the Sea of Galilee. It was one of the Decapolis cities (cf. 4:25), and its population was predominantly Gentile. This non-Jewish setting is reinforced by the presence and herding of swine in 8:30, animals considered unclean by the Mosaic Law (Lev 11:7–8).

---

[t] Other ancient authorities read *Gergesenes*; some, *Gerasenes*.

herd of swine." ³²And he said to them, "Go." So they came out and went into the swine; and behold, the whole herd rushed down the steep bank into the sea, and perished in the waters. ³³The herdsmen fled, and going into the city they told everything, and what had happened to the demoniacs. ³⁴And behold, all the city came out to meet Jesus; and when they saw him, they begged him to leave their neighborhood.

Jesus Heals a Paralytic

9 And getting into a boat he crossed over and came to his own city. ²And behold, they brought to him a paralytic, lying on his bed; and when Jesus saw their faith, he said to the paralytic, "Take heart, my son; your sins are forgiven." ³And behold, some of the scribes said to themselves, "This man is blaspheming." ⁴But Jesus, knowing ᵘ their thoughts, said, "Why do you think evil in your hearts? ⁵For which is easier, to say, 'Your sins are forgiven,' or to say, 'Rise and walk'? ⁶But that you may know that the Son of man has authority on earth to forgive sins"—he then said to the paralytic—"Rise, take up your bed and go home." ⁷And he rose and went

home. ⁸When the crowds saw it, they were afraid, and they glorified God, who had given such authority to men.

The Call of Matthew

9 As Jesus passed on from there, he saw a man called Matthew sitting at the tax office; and he said to him, "Follow me." And he rose and followed him.

10 And as he sat at table ᵛ in the house, behold, many tax collectors and sinners came and sat down with Jesus and his disciples. ¹¹And when the Pharisees saw this, they said to his disciples, "Why does your teacher eat with tax collectors and sinners?" ¹²But when he heard it, he said, "Those who are well have no need of a physician, but those who are sick. ¹³Go and learn what this means, 'I desire mercy, and not sacrifice.' For I came not to call the righteous, but sinners."

The Question about Fasting

14 Then the disciples of John came to him, saying, "Why do we and the Pharisees fast,ʷ but your disciples do not fast?" ¹⁵And Jesus said to them, "Can the wedding guests mourn as long as the bridegroom is with them? The days will come,

---

9:1–8: Mk 2:1–12, Lk 5:17–26. **9:2**: Mt 9:22; Mk 6:50; 10:49; Jn 16:33; Acts 23:11; Lk 7:48. **9:9–13**: Mk 2:13–17; Lk 5:27–32; 15:1–2; 7:34. **9:13**: Hos 6:6; Mt 12:7; 1 Tim 1:15. **9:14–17**: Mk 2:18–22; Lk 5:33–39; 18:12.

8:32 into the sea: Jesus manifests divine power by his control over demons. • In the OT, waters represent hostile forces (Ps 69:1-4) that are sometimes personified as beasts that rise out of the sea (Dan 7:1-3; cf. Rev 13:1). By driving the demon-possessed beasts back into the sea, Jesus symbolically demonstrates his triumph over the legions of Satan's kingdom.

9:1 his own city: Capernaum in Galilee (cf. 4:13; Mk 2:1).

9:3 the scribes: Jewish leaders and experts in the Mosaic Law. The episode marks the beginning of a growing resistance to Jesus, which culminates in his death (16:21; 20:18; 27:41-43). **blaspheming:** A charge leveled at Jesus for his claim to absolve sins (cf. Lev 24:16; Jn 10:33). From the scribes' perspective, only God can rightly forgive (Ps 103:12; Is 43:25; Mk 2:7). Moreover, this forgiveness was available only through the sacrificial system of the Temple. Jesus' actions hence prove scandalous: he not only claims to forgive, but he does so apart from the Old Covenant system. In the end, the scribes remain unaware that Jesus has divine authority to inaugurate the New Covenant (Jer 31:31–34; CCC 589).

9:6 that you may know: Since forgiveness cannot be verified by his audience, Jesus demonstrates his power by healing the man. His authority over paralysis points beyond the body—it signifies his ability to cure the soul. The OT indicates that bodily sickness is sometimes tangible evidence of sin (Ps 107:17; Is 33:24; cf. Jn 5:14; 9:2). • *Anagogically* (St. Ambrose, *In Luc.*), the healing of the paralytic signifies the future resurrection of the faithful. The paralytic is the Christian whose sins are forgiven and who stands before God as son (9:2). When the Lord raises him (9:7), he will take up the bed of his body (9:7) and proceed to his heavenly home with God (9:6; cf. Jn 14:2-3).

9:8 authority to men: The crowd links Jesus' authority with his power to forgive. • Matthew's description points forward to the Sacrament of Reconciliation. After his Resurrection, Jesus invests other men (apostles) with this same power to forgive sins in his name (Jn 20:23; cf. Mt 18:18; CCC 1441, 1444).

9:9 the tax office: Collecting taxes in the territory of Herod

Antipas (Galilee) involved frequent contact with Gentiles. Many religious Jews thus despised the occupation, considering tax collectors socially equivalent to "sinners" (9:10; 11:19) and Gentiles (18:17). Undeterred by this religious and cultural convention, Jesus invites Matthew to break with his livelihood and **follow** him. Matthew's former life as a sinner only increased his need to be a disciple.

9:13 I desire mercy: Jesus challenges the Pharisees with Hos 6:6 (12:7). Understanding the prophet's message will explain Jesus' fellowship with "those who are sick" (9:12). • Hosea addressed the Northern Kingdom of Israel and declared them sick and wounded by sin (Hos 5:13). Their rebellion against Yahweh (Hos 4:1–2), their rejection of the Jerusalem Temple, and their preference for idolatrous sacrifices (Hos 4:13–14; 8:11–13; 13:2) made this sickness deadly. The real tragedy is that Yahweh appointed Israel to be a physician to the nations, yet Israel acted irresponsibly and so contracted the very illness (idolatry) they were supposed to eradicate. Jesus cites Hosea to make an implied comparison between the prophet's sinful contemporaries and his own critical opponents, the Pharisees. Just as the Northern Kingdom of Israel rejected the royal son of David (the Judean king) to sacrifice to idols, so the Pharisees have rejected the messianic Son of David (Jesus) in preference to the sacrificial and purity regulations of the Mosaic Law. By eating with sinners and tax collectors—whom the Pharisees considered unclean and untouchable—Jesus claims to fulfill Israel's original vocation by reaching out to the sick with divine mercy. See note on 5:20. **not to call the righteous:** Jesus came, not to perpetuate the Old Covenant, but to inaugurate the New Covenant of forgiveness (Jer 31:31-34). His frequent fellowship with sinners was central to this healing work (9:12).

9:15 the bridegroom: A depiction of Jesus found elsewhere in Matthew (25:1-13). See note on Mk 2:19. • Similar OT imagery depicts Yahweh as the husband of Old Covenant Israel (Is 54:5; Jer 3:20; Hos 2:14–20). Jesus takes this role upon himself and is now the divine spouse of the New Covenant Church (Jn 3:29; Eph 5:25; Rev 19:7-9; CCC 796). **The days will come:** Only after Jesus' departure (Passion and Ascension) is fasting appropriate (cf. 6:16).

ᵘ Other ancient authorities read *seeing.* ᵛ Greek *reclined.*
ʷ Other ancient authorities read *much* or *often.*

when the bridegroom is taken away from them, and then they will fast. [16]And no one puts a piece of unshrunk cloth on an old garment, for the patch tears away from the garment, and a worse tear is made. [17]Neither is new wine put into old wineskins; if it is, the skins burst, and the wine is spilled, and the skins are destroyed; but new wine is put into fresh wineskins, and so both are preserved."

A Girl Restored to Life and a Woman Healed

18 While he was thus speaking to them, behold, a ruler came in and knelt before him, saying, "My daughter has just died; but come and lay your hand on her, and she will live." [19]And Jesus rose and followed him, with his disciples. [20]And behold, a woman who had suffered from a hemorrhage for twelve years came up behind him and touched the fringe of his garment; [21]for she said to herself, "If I only touch his garment, I shall be made well." [22]Jesus turned, and seeing her he said, "Take heart, daughter; your faith has made you well." And instantly the woman was made well. [23]And when Jesus came to the ruler's house, and saw the flute players, and the crowd making a tumult, [24]he said, "Depart; for the girl is not dead but sleeping." And they laughed at him. [25]But when the crowd had been put outside, he went in and took her by the hand, and the girl arose. [26]And the report of this went through all that district.

Jesus Heals Two Blind Men

27 And as Jesus passed on from there, two blind men followed him, crying aloud, "Have mercy on us, Son of David." [28]When he entered the house, the blind men came to him; and Jesus said to them, "Do you believe that I am able to do this?" They said to him, "Yes, Lord." [29]Then he touched their eyes, saying, "According to your faith let it be done to you." [30]And their eyes were opened. And Jesus sternly charged them, "See that no one knows it." [31]But they went away and spread his fame through all that district.

Jesus Heals a Man Who Was Mute

32 As they were going away, behold, a mute demoniac was brought to him. [33]And when the demon had been cast out, the mute man spoke; and the crowds marveled, saying, "Never was anything like this seen in Israel." [34]But the Pharisees said, "He casts out demons by the prince of demons."

The Harvest Is Plentiful, the Laborers Are Few

35 And Jesus went about all the cities and villages, teaching in their synagogues and preaching the gospel of the kingdom, and healing every disease and every infirmity. [36]When he saw the crowds, he had compassion for them, because they were harassed and helpless, like sheep without a shepherd. [37]Then he said to his disciples, "The harvest is plentiful, but the laborers are few; [38]pray therefore the Lord of the harvest to send out laborers into his harvest."

The Twelve Apostles

10 And he called to him his twelve disciples and gave them authority over unclean spirits, to cast them out, and to heal every disease and every infirmity. [2]The names of the twelve apostles are

---

9:18–26: Mk 5:21–43; Lk 8:40–56. 9:18: Mt 8:2; 15:25; 18:26; 20:20; Jn 9:38. 9:20: Nb 15:38; Deut 22,12; Mt 14:36; Mk 3:10. 9:22: Mk 10:52; Lk 7:50; 17:19; Mt 15:28; 9:29. 9:27–31: Mt 20:29–34 9:32–34: Lk 11.;14–15; Mt 12:22–24; Mk 3:22; Jn 7:20 9:35: Mt 4:23; Mk 6:6. 9:36: Mk 6:34; Mt 14:14; 15:32; Nb 27:17; Zech 10:2. 9:37–38: Lk 10:2; Jn 4:35. 10:1–4: Mk 6:7; 3:16–19; Lk 9:1; 6:14–16; Acts 1:13.

9:16 an old garment: An image of the Old Covenant. It suggests that Jesus viewed it as a "worn out" piece of clothing ready to be cast off. • According to Ps 102:26, the Old Covenant world was scheduled to "wear out like a garment" (Heb 1:10–12; cf. Is 65:17; Rev 21:1).

9:17 new wine . . . old wineskins: Fermenting wine is accompanied by a build-up of pressure. If kept in skins already used and dried out, the wine would certainly **burst** them. Jesus thus illustrates the impossibility of inaugurating the New Covenant while maintaining the Old. The abundance of New Covenant grace cannot be contained within the structures of the Old Covenant (cf. Jn 1:16). A new kingdom is needed to contain it—one fashioned to endure for ever.

9:18 a ruler: Mark 5:22 and Lk 8:41 refer to him as "Jairus", head of the local Capernaum synagogue.

9:20 fringe of his garment: According to the Mosaic Law, Israelites were instructed to wear "tassels on the corners of their garments" (Num 15:38; cf. Mt 14:36; 23:5). These were outward reminders to follow God's commandments.

9:27 Son of David: A messianic title for Jesus, used eight times in Matthew. It is sometimes linked with Jesus' healings and exorcisms (20:30–34; CCC 439). See note on 12:23.

9:36 compassion: Those needing spiritual and physical healing lie close to Jesus' heart (14:14; 15:32; 20:34). **like sheep without a shepherd:** A familiar OT simile. • Sheep often represent the people of Israel (1 Kings 22:17; Jud 11:19; Jer 23:1–3; Zech 10:2). Shepherd imagery is used for Israel's spiritual leaders. **(1)** Joshua was Moses' successor and the "shepherd" of Israel (Num 27:17). **(2)** David was elected to "shepherd" Israel as its king (2 Sam 5:2–3). **(3)** In Ezek 34, God himself promised to set "one shepherd" (Ezek 34:23) over his people to feed and protect them as a new Davidic king (Ezek 34:23–24; cf. Jer 23:1–6). Jesus draws on these to illustrate his own role as the Shepherd and King of the restored Israel, the Church (25:31–34; Jn 10:16; 1 Pet 2:25).

9:37 the laborers are few: Anticipates the following narrative, where Jesus chooses the apostles as laborers to shepherd the "lost sheep" of Israel (10:6; cf. Jer 23:4; Mt 15:24).

10:1–11:1 The second major discourse in Matthew (see outline). Jesus selects twelve apostles and delivers a "missionary sermon" before sending them to the surrounding Galilean villages and charging them to preach that "the kingdom of heaven is at hand" (v. 7; cf. 3:2; 4:17). Jesus confers on the apostles the same authority of healing and exorcism displayed during his early ministry (v. 1, 8; cf. 4:23, 24; 9:35).

10:2 the twelve: Jesus chooses 12 patriarchs, like the 12 sons of Israel in the OT, to carry out his mission (Gen 35:22–26). In doing so, he designates the Church as the restored Israel (cf. 19:28; Gal 6:16). **apostles:** The Greek term *apostolos* means "one who is sent forth" (cf. 10:5) and invested with the authority of the sender (cf. 10:40). See chart: *The Twelve Apostles* at Mk 3.

---

x Other ancient authorities read *Lebbaeus* or *Labbaeus called Thaddaeus.*

Matthew 10

these: first, Simon, who is called Peter, and Andrew his brother; James the son of Zeb′edee, and John his brother; ³Philip and Bartholomew; Thomas and Matthew the tax collector; James the son of Alphaeus, and Thaddaeus;ˣ ⁴Simon the Cananaean, and Judas Iscariot, who betrayed him.

The Mission of the Twelve

5 These twelve Jesus sent out, charging them, "Go nowhere among the Gentiles, and enter no town of the Samaritans, ⁶but go rather to the lost sheep of the house of Israel. ⁷And preach as you go, saying, 'The kingdom of heaven is at hand.' ⁸Heal the sick, raise the dead, cleanse lepers, cast out demons. You received without paying, give without pay. ⁹Take no gold, nor silver, nor copper in your belts, ¹⁰no bag for your journey, nor two tunics, nor sandals, nor a staff; for the laborer deserves his food. ¹¹And whatever town or village you enter, find out who is worthy in it, and stay with him until you depart. ¹²As you enter the house, salute it. ¹³And if the house is worthy, let your peace come upon it; but if it is not worthy, let your peace return to you. ¹⁴And if any one will not receive you or listen to your words, shake off the dust from your feet as you leave that house or town. ¹⁵Truly, I say to you, it shall be more tolerable on the day of judgment for the land of Sodom and Gomor′rah than for that town.

Coming Persecutions

16 "Behold, I send you out as sheep in the midst of wolves; so be wise as serpents and innocent as doves. ¹⁷Beware of men; for they will deliver you up to councils, and flog you in their synagogues, ¹⁸and you will be dragged before governors and kings for my sake, to bear testimony before them and the Gentiles. ¹⁹When they deliver you up, do not be anxious about how you are to speak or what you are to say; for what you are to say will be given to you in that hour; ²⁰for it is not you who speak, but the Spirit of your Father speaking through you. ²¹Brother will deliver up brother to death, and the father his child, and children will rise against parents and have them put to death; ²²and you will be hated by all for my name's sake. But he who endures to the end will be saved. ²³When they persecute you in one town, flee to the next; for truly, I say to you, you will not have gone through all the towns of Israel, before the Son of man comes.

24 "A disciple is not above his teacher, nor a servantʸ above his master; ²⁵it is enough for the disciple to be like his teacher, and the servant ʸ like his master. If they have called the master of the house Be-el′zebul, how much more will they malign those of his household.

Whom to Fear

26 "So have no fear of them; for nothing is covered that will not be revealed, or hidden that will not be known. ²⁷What I tell you in the dark, utter in the light; and what you hear whispered, proclaim upon the housetops. ²⁸And do not fear those who kill the body but cannot kill the soul; rather fear him who can destroy both soul and body in hell.ᶻ ²⁹Are not two sparrows sold for a penny? And not one of them will fall to the ground without your Father's will. ³⁰But even the hairs of your head are all numbered. ³¹Fear not, therefore; you are of more value than many sparrows. ³²So every one who acknowledges me before men, I also will acknowledge before my Father who is in heaven; ³³but whoever denies me before men, I also will deny before my Father who is in heaven.

10:5: Lk 9:52; Jn 4:9; Acts 8:5, 25.   **10:6:** Mt 15:24; 10:23.   **10:7–8:** Lk 9:2; 10:9–11; Mt 4:17.   **10:9–14:** Mk 6:8–11; Lk 9:3–5; 10:4–12; 22:35–36.   **10:10:** 1 Cor 9:14; 1 Tim 5:18.   **10:14:** Acts 13:51.   **10:15:** Mt 11:24; Lk 10:12; J::de 7; 2 Pet 2:6.   **10:16:** Lk 10:3; Gen 3:1; Rom l6:19.   **10:17–22:** Mk 13:9–13; Lk 12:11–12; 21:12–19; Jn 16:2.   **10:18:** Acts 25:24–26.   **10:20:** Jn 16:7–11.   **10:21:** Mt 10:35–36; Lk 12:52–53.   **10:22:** Jn 15:18; Mt 24:9.   **10:23:** Mt 16:27; 1 Thess 4:17.   **10:24:** Lk 6:40; Jn 13:16; 15:20.   **10:25:** Mt 9:34; 12:24; Mk 3:22; Lk 11:15; 2 Kings 1:2.   **10:26–33:** Lk 12:2–9.   **10:26:** Mk 4:22; Lk 8:17; Eph 5:13.   **10:28:** Heb 10:31.   **10:31:** Mt 12:12.   **10:32:** Mk 8:38; Lk 9:26; Rev 3:5; 2 Tim 2:12.

10:5 nowhere among the Gentiles: Jesus sends the apostles only to the Israelites of Galilee (10:6). This reflects the order and direction of salvation history. Since God adopted them as his "own possession" (Ex 19:5) and lavished them with privileges (Rom 9:4, 5), it was appropriate that they first hear the New Covenant gospel (cf. Acts 1:8; Rom 1:16). After Jesus' Resurrection, the apostles are sent also to the Gentiles (28:18–20; Mk 16:16; CCC 543). See note on 4:12.

10:14 shake off the dust: Palestinian Jews shook dust from their sandals when leaving Gentile territory and reentering the Holy Land. It was a derogatory statement against the uncleanness of Gentiles as pagans. Jesus commands a similar gesture to signify judgment on those who reject the gospel (Lk 10:10–12; Acts 13:51).

10:23 before the Son of man: Jesus promised to come again within the generation of the living apostles (16:28; 24:34). As a prelude to his Second Coming, this initial "coming" refers to his visitation of destruction upon unfaithful Jerusalem in A.D.

70, an event that destroyed his enemies and vindicated his words of judgment (24:2). See note on 24:1—25:46 and topical essay: *Jesus the Son of Man* at Lk 17.

10:25 Beelzebul: A Philistine god worshiped at Ekron (2 Kings 1:2–16). It translates something like "Prince Baal", a well-known god of the Canaanites. Jews mockingly changed its meaning to "lord of flies" or "lord of dung". In the Gospels, it refers to Satan, "the prince of demons" (9:34; 12:24–27; Mk 3:22; Lk 11:15).

10:28 do not fear: Human agents of persecution are not to be feared. Men can impose suffering and death on the body but cannot force spiritual death on the soul. Jesus uses this distinction between body and soul to contrast the relative value of earthly life with the absolute good of eternal life in heaven (CCC 363). **rather fear him:** Since Satan deceives and tempts souls into sin, he should be feared and resisted as our worst enemy (Eph 6:11; Jas 4:7; 1 Pet 5:8–10). In view of the similar expression in Is 8:12–13, God should also be feared. He alone administers perfect justice and can send the faithless to eternal punishment (3:12; 25:41). A holy fear of God is thus necessary to avoid sin and its consequences (Ex 20:20; Phil 2:12).

ʸ Or *slave*.   ᶻ Greek *Gehenna*.

34

Not Peace, but a Sword

34 "Do not think that I have come to bring peace on earth; I have not come to bring peace, but a sword. ³⁵For I have come to set a man against his father, and a daughter against her mother, and a daughter-in-law against her mother-in-law; ³⁶and a man's foes will be those of his own household. ³⁷He who loves father or mother more than me is not worthy of me; and he who loves son or daughter more than me is not worthy of me; ³⁸and he who does not take his cross and follow me is not worthy of me. ³⁹He who finds his life will lose it, and he who loses his life for my sake will find it.

Rewards

40 "He who receives you receives me, and he who receives me receives him who sent me. ⁴¹He who receives a prophet because he is a prophet shall receive a prophet's reward, and he who receives a righteous man because he is a righteous man shall receive a righteous man's reward. ⁴²And whoever gives to one of these little ones even a cup of cold water because he is a disciple, truly, I say to you, he shall not lose his reward."

11 And when Jesus had finished instructing his twelve disciples, he went on from there to teach and preach in their cities.

Messengers from John the Baptist

2 Now when John heard in prison about the deeds of the Christ, he sent word by his disciples ³and said to him, "Are you he who is to come, or shall we look for another?" ⁴And Jesus answered them, "Go and tell John what you hear and see: ⁵the blind receive their sight and the lame walk, lepers are cleansed and the deaf hear, and the dead are raised up, and the poor have good news preached to them. ⁶And blessed is he who takes no offense at me."

Jesus Praises John the Baptist

7 As they went away, Jesus began to speak to the crowds concerning John: "What did you go out into the wilderness to behold? A reed shaken by the wind? ⁸Why then did you go out? To see a man *ᵃ* dressed in soft robes? Behold, those who wear soft robes are in kings' houses. ⁹Why then did you go out? To see a prophet? *ᵇ* Yes, I tell you, and more than a prophet. ¹⁰This is he of whom it is written,

'Behold, I send my messenger before thy face,
who shall prepare thy way before thee.'

¹¹Truly, I say to you, among those born of women there has arisen no one greater than John the Baptist; yet he who is least in the kingdom of heaven is greater than he. ¹²From the days of John the Baptist until now the kingdom of heaven has suffered violence,*ᶜ* and men of violence take it by force. ¹³For all the prophets and the law prophesied until John; ¹⁴and if you are willing to accept it, he is Eli′jah who is to come. ¹⁵He who has ears to hear,*ᵈ* let him hear.

16 "But to what shall I compare this generation? It is like children sitting in the market places and calling to their playmates,

---

10:34–36: Lk 12:51–53; Mt 10:21; Mk 13:12; Mic 7:6.　**10:37–39:** Lk 14:25–27; 17:33; 9:23–24; Mt 16:24–25; Mk 8:34–35; Jn 12:25.　**10:40:** Lk 10:16; Jn 13:20; Gal 4:14; Mk 9:37; Mt 18:5; Lk 9:48.　**10:42:** Mk 9:41; Mt 25:40.　**11:1:** Mt 7:28; 13:53; 19:1; 26:1.　**11:2–19:** Lk 7:18–35.　**11:3:** Mk 1:7–8; Hab 2:3; Jn 11:27.　**11:5:** Is 35:5–6; 61:1; Lk 4:18–19.　**11:9:** Mt 14:5; 21:26; Lk 1:76.　**11:10:** Mal 3:1; Mk 1:2.　**11:12–13:** Lk 16:16.　**11:14:** Mal 4:5; Mt 17:10–13; Jn 1:21; Lk 1:17.　**11:15:** Mt 13:9,43; Mk 4:23; Rev 13:9; 2:7.　**11:16–19:** Lk 7:31–35.

10:38 take his cross: A striking image of the demands and consequences of discipleship. Jews needed no explanation of it, since the Romans utilized crucifixion as a torturous means of execution for many criminals during NT times. Jesus here assures us that faithfulness will entail self-denial, suffering, and possibly death. Before his Passion, the cross symbolized shame and rejection; afterward it symbolizes the glory of Christian martyrdom (CCC 1506). See note on Mk 15:24.

10:42 these little ones: i.e., the apostles. They must rely on the hospitality of others for daily necessities during their mission (11:9–11). Service rendered to them is service to Jesus himself (11:40; 25:34–36). Children are elsewhere used as examples in Jesus' teaching on faith in 18:1–4 and 19:13–15.

11:2 deeds of the Christ: i.e., the works and credentials of the awaited Messiah. Jesus performs messianic signs in Galilee in chaps. 8–9 (11:5). His works stir such great public interest that **John** hears of his ministry even in **prison**.

11:5 the blind . . . the lame . . . lepers: Jesus' miracles recall Isaian prophecy and link him with an agent of God's healing (Is 26:19; 29:18; 35:4–6; 61:1–2; CCC 549). See note on 8:17.

11:7 A reed shaken . . . ?: John is not swayed by earthly comforts or diverted from the path of discipline.

11:10 Behold, I send: John the Baptist's ministry recalls Mal 3:1 (Sir 48:9–10). As in Is 40:3 (Mt 3:3), this **messenger** is also the Lord's forerunner. ● Malachi's prophesies associate the Lord's forerunner with Elijah, the great prophet of the OT (Mal 4:5). Jesus views John as this prophet, who preaches repentance to Israel in the "spirit" of Elijah (Lk 1:17) and offers God's faithful remnant a final opportunity for salvation (11:15). Even John's clothing recalls Elijah's distinctive dress. See note on 3:1.

11:11 no one greater: John is the greatest OT prophet (11:9). In the New Covenant, however, even the least NT saint outshines the most illustrious saints of old. These prophets looked ahead to the New Covenant but did not share fully in its blessings (13:17; 1 Pet 1:10–12). Jesus thus contrasts the Old and New Covenants; he does not undermine the saintly life of John (CCC 523, 719).

11:12 the kingdom . . . has suffered violence: Interpreted along two lines: **(1)** John's personal sacrifice and self-denial are a call for the *violence* of bodily penance. Only those determined to seek God's kingdom through physical discipline take hold of it. **(2)** Satan had attempted to take men from God's kingdom; John himself was imprisoned and executed for announcing it (4:12; 14:10). Jesus likewise suffers a violent death for inaugurating God's kingdom and rebuking those who oppose it (23:13).

ᵃ Or *What then did you go out to see? A man . . . .*
ᵇ Other ancient authorities read *What then did you go out to see? A prophet?*
ᶜ Or *has been coming violently.*
ᵈ Other ancient authorities read *to hear.*

¹⁷ 'We piped to you, and you did not dance;
we wailed, and you did not mourn.'

¹⁸For John came neither eating nor drinking, and they say, 'He has a demon'; ¹⁹the Son of man came eating and drinking, and they say, 'Behold, a glutton and a drunkard, a friend of tax collectors and sinners!' Yet wisdom is justified by her deeds." ^e

Woes to Unrepentant Cities

20 Then he began to upbraid the cities where most of his mighty works had been done, because they did not repent. ²¹"Woe to you, Chora´zin! woe to you, Beth-sa´ida! for if the mighty works done in you had been done in Tyre and Sidon, they would have repented long ago in sackcloth and ashes. ²²But I tell you, it shall be more tolerable on the day of judgment for Tyre and Sidon than for you. ²³And you, Caper´na-um, will you be exalted to heaven? You shall be brought down to Hades. For if the mighty works done in you had been done in Sodom, it would have remained until this day. ²⁴But I tell you that it shall be more tolerable on the day of judgment for the land of Sodom than for you."

Jesus Thanks His Father

25 At that time Jesus declared, "I thank you, Father, Lord of heaven and earth, that thou hast hidden these things from the wise and understanding and revealed them to infants; ²⁶yes, Father, for such was your gracious will.^f ²⁷All things have been delivered to me by my Father; and no one knows the Son except the Father, and no one knows the Father except the Son and any one to whom the Son chooses to reveal him. ²⁸Come to me, all who labor and are heavy laden, and I will give you rest. ²⁹Take my yoke upon you, and learn from me; for I am gentle and lowly in heart, and you will find rest for your souls. ³⁰For my yoke is easy, and my burden is light."

Plucking Grain on the Sabbath

12 At that time Jesus went through the grainfields on the sabbath; his disciples were hungry, and they began to pluck heads of grain and to eat. ²But when the Pharisees saw it, they said to him, "Look, your disciples are doing what is not lawful to do on the sabbath." ³He said to them, "Have you not read what David did, when he was hungry, and those who were with him: ⁴how he

---

11:20–24: Lk 10:13–15.   **11:24:** Mt 10:15; Lk 10:12.   **11:25–27:** Lk 10:21–22; 11:25: 1 Cor 1:26–29.   **11:27:** Jn 3:35; 5:20; 13:3; 7:29; 10:15; 17:25; Mt 28:18.   **11:29:** Jn 13:15; Philemon 2:5; 1 Pet 2:21; Jer 6:16.   **12:1–8:** Mk 2:23–28; Lk 6:1–5. **12:1:** Deut 23:25.   **12:3:** 1 Sam 21:1–6; Lev 24:9.

11:17 Jesus exposes the excuses of his contemporaries. The children's song highlights both the joyousness of a wedding (**we piped**) reflected in Jesus' ministry (11:19; 9:15), and the solemnity of a funeral (**we wailed**) reflected in John's ministry of penance. The unbelievers of Jesus' generation (11:16) refuse invitations to embrace the kingdom.

📖 **11:19 a glutton and a drunkard:** Jesus is accused of dangerous and irreligious behavior. • Many viewed Jesus as a "stubborn and rebellious" son, in accordance with Deut 21:20. Evoking the context of this OT verse, they implied that Jesus should be killed (Deut 21:21). **wisdom . . . her deeds:** Recalls OT traditions that personify wisdom (Prov 8–9; Wis 7:22–8:21; Sir 51:13–30). Jesus transfers these to himself in light of his messianic signs (11:1–5). Paul similarly regards Jesus as "our wisdom" (1 Cor 1:30). See note on 11:28–30.

11:21 Chorazin . . . Bethsaida: Two cities north of the Sea of Galilee. Both are within five miles of Jesus' home in Capernaum, and both are unresponsive to his ministry. Privileged by Jesus' presence and works, they bear greater guilt for rejecting him than the Gentile cities of **Tyre and Sidon**, north of Palestine on the coast of Phoenicia (cf. Lk 12:48).

📖✝ **11:23 Capernaum:** Jesus' home during his Galilean ministry (4:13). Like his childhood home of Nazareth, this city too rejects Jesus and his works (13:53–58; Lk 4:16–30). • Jesus' rebuke upon the city recalls God's judgment on the king of Babylon in Is 14:13–15. • Morally, Capernaum signifies the soul that receives Christ but falls into mortal sin. Because Christ dwelt there, the fallen-away and prideful soul is subject to harsher judgment (2 Pet 2:20–22; CCC 678). **Sodom:** The city destroyed by God in Gen 19:24–25. It was a proverbial OT example of sexual sin and inhospitality that called down God's wrath (Is 1:9; Jer 23:14; Ezek 16:44–46; Amos 4:11).

✝ **11:25–27** Jesus' thanksgiving prayer stands in contrast to the preceding narrative (11:20–24). While several towns reject Christ, there is a remnant (including the disciples) who trust him with the simplicity of **infants** (11:25; cf. 18:1–4;

19:13–15). Jesus' language is similar to several statements in John's Gospel that articulate his unique relationship with the Father (Jn 3:35; 10:14–15; 17:25). • The intimacy between the Father and Son points to their oneness within the Blessed Trinity–i.e., their shared divine knowledge implies a shared divine nature.

📖 **11:28–30** Jesus invites disciples to follow and learn from him as the model of perfect obedience to the Father (11:27; CCC 520). • Jesus evokes "wisdom's" invitation to the humble in the OT. In Sir 51, wisdom calls "Draw near to me" (11:23), "put your neck under the yoke" (11:26), and "see with your eyes that I have labored little and found for myself much rest" (11:27). These parallels reinforce Jesus' self-identification as "wisdom" in 11:19.

11:29 you will find rest: Jesus' invitation cues the following controversies regarding the spiritual significance of the Sabbath (12:1–14). While the Old Covenant celebration of the Sabbath centered on earthly rest from earthly labor (Ex 20:8–11), Jesus offers heavenly rest in the New (Heb 4:1–11).

✝ **12:2 not lawful . . . on the sabbath:** The Pharisees charge the disciples with violating Ex 34:21, which forbids harvesting on the Sabbath. Although Deut 23:25 differentiates between plucking grain and harvesting it, the Pharisees forbade even plucking grain by a rigid extension of the Exodus prohibition. • Allegorically (St. Hilary, Canons), Christ's passing through the field signifies his passing into the world through the Incarnation. The standing grain is the harvest of souls ready to believe in the gospel and be gathered into the Church by the hungry disciples.

📖 **12:3 have you not read:** An insult to the intellectual pride of the Pharisees. Jesus uses the question to humble learned leaders who lack childlike faith (12:5; 19:4; 21:16, 42; 22:31). • Jesus draws on the parallels between 1 Sam 21:1–6 and his own situation. As David's companions were **hungry** (12:1), so were the disciples; as David was heir to the united kingdom of Israel, so Jesus is the son of David. He thus implies that if his disciples are in sin, then David himself would stand guilty–a conclusion nowhere suggested in the OT. This is the first premise of Jesus' response to the Pharisees. See note on 12:7.

---

^e Other ancient authorities read *children* (Luke 7.35).
^f Or *so it was well-pleasing before thee.*

entered the house of God and ate the bread of the Presence, which it was not lawful for him to eat nor for those who were with him, but only for the priests? ⁵Or have you not read in the law how on the sabbath the priests in the temple profane the sabbath, and are guiltless? ⁶I tell you, something greater than the temple is here. ⁷And if you had known what this means, 'I desire mercy, and not sacrifice,' you would not have condemned the guiltless. ⁸For the Son of man is lord of the sabbath."

The Man with a Withered Hand

9 And he went on from there, and entered their synagogue. ¹⁰And behold, there was a man with a withered hand. And they asked him, "Is it lawful to heal on the sabbath?" so that they might accuse him. ¹¹He said to them, "What man of you, if he has one sheep and it falls into a pit on the sabbath, will not lay hold of it and lift it out? ¹²Of how much more value is a man than a sheep! So it is lawful to do good on the sabbath." ¹³Then he said to the man, "Stretch out your hand." And the man stretched it out, and it was restored, whole like the other. ¹⁴But the Pharisees went out and took counsel against him, how to destroy him.

God's Chosen Servant

15 Jesus, aware of this, withdrew from there. And many followed him, and he healed them all, ¹⁶and ordered them not to make him known. ¹⁷This was to fulfil what was spoken by the prophet Isaiah:

¹⁸ "Behold, my servant whom I have chosen,
my beloved with whom my soul is well pleased.
I will put my Spirit upon him,
and he shall proclaim justice to the Gentiles.
¹⁹ He will not wrangle or cry aloud,
nor will any one hear his voice in the streets;
²⁰ he will not break a bruised reed or quench a smoldering wick,
till he brings justice to victory;
²¹ and in his name will the Gentiles hope."

Jesus and Beelzebul

22 Then a blind and mute demoniac was brought to him, and he healed him, so that the mute man spoke and saw. ²³And all the people were amazed, and said, "Can this be the Son of David?" ²⁴But when the Pharisees heard it they said, "It is only by Be-el´zebul, the prince of demons, that this man casts out demons." ²⁵Knowing their thoughts, he said to them, "Every kingdom divided against itself is laid waste, and no city or house divided against itself will stand; ²⁶and if Satan casts out Satan, he is divided against himself; how then will his kingdom stand? ²⁷And if I cast out demons by Be-el´zebul, by whom do your sons cast them out? Therefore they shall be your judges. ²⁸But if it is by the Spirit of God that I cast out demons, then the kingdom of God has come upon you. ²⁹Or how can one enter a strong man's house and plunder his

---

12:5: Nb 28:9–10. **12:6:** Mt 12:41–42; Lk 11:31–32. **12:7:** Hos 6:6; Mt 9:13. **12:8:** Jn 5:1–18; 7:19–24; 9:1–41. **12:9–14:** Mk 3:1–6; Lk 6:6–11. **12:11:** Lk 14:5. **12:12:** Mt 10:31. **12:14:** Mk 14:1; Jn 7:30; 8:59; 10:39; 11:53. **12:15–16:** Mk 3:7–12; Lk 6:17–19. **12:18–21:** Is 42:1–4. **12:22–29:** Mk 3:22–27; Lk 11:14–22. **12:22:** Mt 9:32–33. **12:24:** Mt 9:34; 10:25; Jn 7:20; 8:52; 10:20.

12:5 profane the sabbath: Levitical priests worked every sabbath, replacing the bread of Presence in the Temple (Lev 24:5–9) and offering sacrifice (Num 28:9–10). Nevertheless, they remained **guiltless** (CCC 582, 2173).

12:6 greater than the temple: The Jerusalem Temple was spectacular because it housed the very presence of God among his people. • God's presence in Jesus, as the divine Son, exceeds that in the Temple (1:23). The earthly sanctuary thus prefigured God's more intimate presence in the world through Christ. The NT elsewhere compares the humanity of Jesus Christ to the wilderness Tabernacle (Jn 1:14) and the Temple (Jn 2:19–21) (CCC 590). See chart: *Jesus and the Old Testament*.

12:7 I desire mercy: Quoted from Hos 6:6. Earlier Jesus challenged the Pharisees to study and learn the meaning of this oracle (9:13), and Hosea's words here complete Jesus' apologetic against the Pharisees. His logic proceeds: **(1)** Mercy is more important than Temple regulations (12:3–4); **(2)** the Temple laws themselves take precedence over the Sabbath (12:5); **(3)** therefore, mercy is more important than the Sabbath (CCC 2100).

12:9–14 Jesus asserts his Lordship over the Sabbath (12:8). Since the Sabbath was meant for man's good, doing good works on the Sabbath cannot be construed as unlawful. If the Pharisees are willing to save one of their livestock, they should be more willing to see a crippled man relieved of his burden on the same day. In short, the Sabbath forbids servile works, not works of mercy.

12:14 took counsel: The Pharisees' conspiracy marks their complete rejection of Jesus. See note on 27:1.

12:18–21 A reference to Is 42:1–4. The Father evokes this same passage at Jesus' Baptism (3:17). Note that

servant (Gk. *pais*) can be translated "son". • Matthew cites Isaiah for three reasons. **(1)** It summarizes his portrait of Christ: Jesus is the Father's **beloved** Son (3:17; 4:3; 11:25–27) and the Servant of the Lord (8:17; 11:5), anointed by the **Spirit** (3:16), who brings God's grace to the **Gentiles** (8:5–13). **(2)** The citation is fulfilled when Jesus withdraws from his enemies and ministers to the lowly (12:20)—he has no regard for public acclaim (12:16, 19). **(3)** It points forward to link Jesus' exorcisms with the power of the Spirit (12:28) (CCC 713).

12:23 the Son of David?: The question reflects the Jewish tradition that King Solomon, the son of David, was empowered by God to exorcize demons (cf. Wis 7:20). Similar abilities were expected of the coming Davidic Messiah.

12:24 only by Beelzebul: The Pharisees' spiritual blindness led them to blasphemy—i.e., they thought Jesus was an agent of Satan's kingdom (CCC 574). See note on 10:25.

12:25–26 Jesus uses the images of a **kingdom**, **city**, and **house** as cryptic allusions to the city and Temple of Jerusalem. By Jesus' day, Jerusalem had reached a point of spiritual crisis. Long known as the Holy City, it was now the center of diabolical resistance to Jesus, with its leadership squarely opposed to the kingdom of heaven. Even the Temple was by then "forsaken and desolate" (23:38). The Pharisees' conspiracy (12:14) thus exposes them as unwitting collaborators and representatives of Satan's kingdom. With Jesus' Crucifixion, the power of Satan is finally destroyed—a fact later evidenced by the plundering of his city (Jerusalem) and house (Temple) in A.D. 70 (12:29) (CCC 550). See notes on 23:38 and 24:1–25:46.

JESUS AND THE OLD TESTAMENT

Matthew frequently quotes OT passages to establish Jesus' credentials as the Messiah. However, Jesus and Matthew often allude to the OT in more subtle ways by drawing comparisons between ancient persons, places, and events and Jesus himself. This form of OT interpretation is called *typology*. A typological reading of the OT is attuned to distinctive "rhymes" in salvation history where God acts in similar (or typical) ways each time he reveals himself and delivers his people. Thus the Father teaches us about himself through the use of things and events long familiar in the minds of his people; in short, he uses old truths to instruct us about new ones. Jesus and Matthew look back on several OT figures and institutions to bring the surpassing glory of Christ and the New Covenant into focus. The great heroes and memories of old bring clarity to the greater person of Christ. The coming of Jesus marks the dramatic climax to the OT story as he fulfills all of the *types* that God prepared throughout the history of salvation.

NEW MOSES

As the supreme lawgiver of the Old Covenant, Moses prefigures Christ, who gives the New Law in the Sermon on the Mount (chaps. 5-7). Jesus also reenacts experiences from Moses' infancy and the prophet's 40 days of fasting in solitude (4:2; Ex 34:28). Finally, Moses bears witness to Jesus' greater glory at the Transfiguration (17:1-5), where Jesus is showcased as the prophet-like-Moses (17:5; Deut 18:15).

NEW DAVID

As Israel's ideal king, David foreshadows the role of Jesus, who assumes his royal throne forever (1:1; 2:2; Lk 1:32–33). Jesus is greater than David (22:41-45); his hungry disciples, like David's companions, are permitted to breech the Sabbath (12:3). As David gave Israel rest from its enemies (2 Sam 7:1), Jesus saves Israel from its sins (1:21).

NEW TEMPLE

The Jerusalem Temple housed the presence of God in the midst of Israel. Similarly, Jesus comes bearing within himself God's glory in a more profound way; he embodies divine holiness (1:23; 12:6; Jn 1:14; 2:19-21). It is thus the Temple—God's dwelling among his people—that prepared Israel to accept Christ's Incarnation. His presence is likewise embodied in a new spiritual Temple, the Church (16:18; 18:20).

NEW ISRAEL

As Israel's Messiah, Jesus reenacts the experience of the Israelites and their Exodus from Egypt (2:15). He endures a 40-day period of testing in the wilderness, corresponding to Israel's 40 years of testing. Unlike wayward Israel, Jesus prevails over the devil through his obedience and trust in God (4:1-11). Jesus' disciples are now assigned Israel's vocation to be a light to the world (5:14; Is 42:6).

NEW SOLOMON

Solomon the "son of David", prefigures Jesus as the royal Son of God (16:16; 2 Sam 7:14). Like Solomon, he receives gifts from the nations (2:11; 1 Kings 10:23-25). As the wise Solomon (1 Kings 3:12) built Israel's Temple (2 Sam 7:12-14), Jesus is wisdom-in-the-flesh (11:19; 12:42) and God's designated builder of the new Temple, the Church (16:18).

NEW JONAH

Jonah was a Hebrew prophet. His experience sleeping on a ship and calming a storm (Jon 1:1-16) anticipates that of Jesus with his disciples (8:23-27). Jonah's three days in the belly of the great fish foreshadows the death and third-day Resurrection of Jesus (12:39-41). In addition, the ministry of Jonah to the Ninevites beyond the borders of Israel anticipates the spread of Christ's gospel to all nations (28:18-20).

goods, unless he first binds the strong man? Then indeed he may plunder his house. ³⁰He who is not with me is against me, and he who does not gather with me scatters. ³¹Therefore I tell you, every sin and blasphemy will be forgiven men, but the blasphemy against the Spirit will not be forgiven. ³²And whoever says a word against the Son of man will be forgiven; but whoever speaks against the Holy Spirit will not be forgiven, either in this age or in the age to come.

A Tree and Its Fruit

33 "Either make the tree good, and its fruit good; or make the tree bad, and its fruit bad; for the tree is known by its fruit. ³⁴You brood of vipers! how can you speak good things, when you are evil? For out of the abundance of the heart the mouth speaks. ³⁵The good man out of his good treasure brings forth good, and the evil man out of his evil treasure brings forth evil. ³⁶I tell you, on the day of judgment men will render account for every careless word they utter; ³⁷for by your words you will be justified, and by your words you will be condemned."

The Sign of Jonah

38 Then some of the scribes and Pharisees said to him, "Teacher, we wish to see a sign from you." ³⁹But he answered them, "An evil and adulterous generation seeks for a sign; but no sign shall be given to it except the sign of the prophet Jonah. ⁴⁰For as Jonah was three days and three nights in the belly of the whale, so will the Son of man be three days and three nights in the heart of the earth. ⁴¹The men of Nin´eveh will arise at the judgment with this generation and condemn it; for they repented at the preaching of Jonah, and behold, something greater than Jonah is here. ⁴²The queen of the South will arise at the judgment with this generation and condemn it; for she came from the ends of the earth to hear the wisdom of Solomon, and behold, something greater than Solomon is here.

The Return of the Unclean Spirit

43 "When the unclean spirit has gone out of a man, he passes through waterless places seeking rest, but he finds none. ⁴⁴Then he says, 'I will return to my house from which I came.' And when he comes he finds it empty, swept, and put in order. ⁴⁵Then he goes and brings with him seven other spirits more evil than himself, and they enter and dwell there; and the last state of that man becomes worse than the first. So shall it be also with this evil generation."

The True Kindred of Jesus

46 While he was still speaking to the people, behold, his mother and his brethren stood outside, asking to speak to him.ᵍ ⁴⁸But he replied to the

---

12:30: Lk 11:23; Mk 9:40.　12:31–32: Mk 3:28–30; Lk 12:10.　12:33–35: Lk 6:43–45; Mt 7:16–20; Jas 3:11–12; Mt 15:18. 12:38–42: Lk 11:16, 29–32; Mk 8:11–12; Mt 16:1–4; Jn 2:18; 6:30; 1 Cor 1:22.　12:40: Jon 1:17.　12:41: Jon 3:5. 12:42: 1 Kings 10:1–10; 2 Chron 9:1–12.　12:43–45: Lk 11:24–26; 2 Pet 2:20.　12:46–50: Mk 3:31–35; Lk 8:19–21. 12:46: Jn 2:1–12; 19:25–27; 7:1–10; Mk 6:3; 1 Cor 9:5.

12:31 blasphemy against the Spirit: i.e., the sin of attributing to Satan the work of God. It is a mature spiritual hardness that directs sinners away from God's mercy and ends in final impenitence. One who blasphemes the Spirit cannot receive forgiveness when he refuses to repent and seek forgiveness. It is this sin that the Pharisees commit in 12:24 (CCC 1864). See note on Mk 3:29.

12:36 every careless word: Spoken insults call down God's judgment (5:21–26). The NT frequently notes that gossip, slandering, and lies are serious sins, inconsistent with holiness and purity of speech (2 Cor 12:20; Eph 4:25–32; Jas 3:1–12).

12:41 greater than Jonah: Jesus' teaching (16:4) and experiences (8:23–27) recall the ministry of the prophet Jonah. ● Jonah prefigures Jesus in two ways: (1) His three days in the whale foreshadow Jesus' Resurrection on the third day (12:40; 16:21); (2) he prefigures Jesus as a prophet to the Gentiles. As Jonah preached to Nineveh in Assyria (Jon 3:2), so Jesus ministers to Gentiles (8:5–13; 15:21–28) and commissions the international spread of the gospel (28:19; Lk 24:45–47). See chart: *Jesus and the Old Testament.*

12:42 greater than Solomon: The connections between Jesus and King Solomon are elsewhere more implicit (2:11; 12:23; 16:18). ● Solomon was the quintessential wise man and Temple builder of the OT (1 Kings 4:29-34; 5-8). As the son of David and heir to his kingdom, Solomon reigned over all Israel and extended his dominion over other nations (1 Kings 4:20-21). He thus prefigured Christ as the son of David (1:1), the embodiment of wisdom (11:19), the new Temple builder (16:18), and the divine ruler of both the 12 tribes of Israel (19:28) and the nations of the world (28:19). See chart: *Jesus and the Old Testament.*

12:44-46 A parable about Jesus' generation. It may be understood in two ways. (1) It is a warning to those who benefit from Jesus' *ministry* without embracing his *message* and its demands. Since one must be not only emptied of evil but filled with divine goodness, the messianic works of Jesus should lead people to accept his messianic kingdom; otherwise they land themselves in a worse state than before (2 Pet 2:20–22). (2) The controversy over exorcisms in the preceding context (12:22–29) sets the stage for Jesus to establish the superiority of his New Covenant ministry over the Old as administered by the Pharisees. Although the Pharisees expel evil spirits ("your sons", 12:27), they leave a vacuum that exposes individuals to more severe counterattacks from Satan. Jesus also drives out demons, but, unlike the Pharisees, he fills believers with the greater power of his kingdom through the Spirit (12:28). Jesus' contemporaries must prefer these blessings of his kingdom ministry to the real but limited benefits of the Pharisees' ministry; otherwise they are left vulnerable to spiritual catastrophes worse than before.

12:45 this evil generation: Many in Jesus' day refused their inheritance, i.e., God's heavenly kingdom. ● The expression recalls Deut 1:35 and description of Israel in the wilderness. They saw many signs during the Exodus but refused to trust God. God thus swore their "evil generation" would perish in the desert (Num 14:21–23). Jesus sees a parallel situation before him: granting the Pharisees a "sign" (12:38) is useless; they have no intention of trusting him but want only to "destroy him" (12:14).

12:46 his brethren: The NT often mentions Jesus' brethren (13:55; Mk 3:31; 6:3; Lk 8:19; Jn 2:12; 7:3; Acts 1:14; Gal 1:19). The Church maintains, however, that Jesus' Mother, Mary, remained a virgin throughout her life. These so-called brethren of Jesus are thus his relatives but not children of Mary. Four observations support the Church's tradition: (1) These

---

ᵍ Other ancient authorities insert verse 47, *Some one told him, "Your mother and your brethren* are standing outside, asking to speak to you".*

man who told him, "Who is my mother, and who are my brethren?" [49]And stretching out his hand toward his disciples, he said, "Here are my mother and my brethren! [50]For whoever does the will of my Father in heaven is my brother, and sister, and mother."

The Parable of the Sower

13 That same day Jesus went out of the house and sat beside the sea. [2]And great crowds gathered about him, so that he got into a boat and sat there; and the whole crowd stood on the beach. [3]And he told them many things in parables, saying: "A sower went out to sow. [4]And as he sowed, some seeds fell along the path, and the birds came and devoured them. [5]Other seeds fell on rocky ground, where they had not much soil, and immediately they sprang up, since they had no depth of soil, [6]but when the sun rose they were scorched; and since they had no root they withered away. [7]Other seeds fell upon thorns, and the thorns grew up and choked them. [8]Other seeds fell on good soil and brought forth grain, some a hundredfold, some sixty, some thirty. [9]He who has ears,[h] let him hear."

The Purpose of the Parables

10 Then the disciples came and said to him, "Why do you speak to them in parables?" [11]And he answered them, "To you it has been given to know the secrets of the kingdom of heaven, but to them it has not been given. [12]For to him who has will more be given, and he will have abundance; but

from him who has not, even what he has will be taken away. [13]This is why I speak to them in parables, because seeing they do not see, and hearing they do not hear, nor do they understand. [14]With them indeed is fulfilled the prophecy of Isaiah which says:

'You shall indeed hear but never understand,
　　and you shall indeed see but never perceive.
[15] For this people's heart has grown dull,
　　and their ears are heavy of hearing,
　　and their eyes they have closed,
lest they should perceive with their eyes,
　　and hear with their ears,
and understand with their heart,
　　and turn for me to heal them.'

[16]But blessed are your eyes, for they see, and your ears, for they hear. [17]Truly, I say to you, many prophets and righteous men longed to see what you see, and did not see it, and to hear what you hear, and did not hear it.

The Parable of the Sower Explained

18 "Hear then the parable of the sower. [19]When any one hears the word of the kingdom and does not understand it, the evil one comes and snatches away what is sown in his heart; this is what was sown along the path. [20]As for what was sown on rocky ground, this is he who hears the word and immediately receives it with joy; [21]yet he has no root in himself, but endures for a while, and when tribulation or persecution arises on account of the

---

12:50: Jn 15:14.　**13:1–9:** Mk 4:1–9; Lk 8:4–8; 5:1–3.　**13:10–13:** Mk 4:10–12; Lk 8:9–10.
13:12: Mk 4:25; Lk 8:18; Mt 25:29; Lk 19:26　**3:14–15:** Is 6:9–10; Mk 8:18; Jn 12:39–41; Acts 28:26–27
13:16–17: Lk 10:23–24; Jn 8:56; Heb 11:13; 1 Pet 1:10–12　**13:18–23:** Mk 4:13–20; Lk 8:11–15.

---

brethren are never called the children of Mary, although Jesus himself is (Jn 2:1; 19:25; Acts 1:14). **(2)** Two names mentioned, **James** and **Joseph**, are sons of a different "Mary" in 27:56 (Mk 15:40). **(3)** It is unlikely that Jesus would entrust his Mother to the Apostle John at his Crucifixion if she had other natural sons to care for her (Jn 19:26–27). **(4)** The word "brethren" (Gk. *adelphoi*) has a broader meaning than blood brothers. Since ancient Hebrew had no word for "cousin", it was customary to use "brethren" in the Bible for relationships other than blood brothers. In the Greek OT, a "brother" can be a nearly related cousin (1 Chron 23:21–22), a more remote kinsman (Deut 23:7; 2 Kings 10:13–14), an uncle or a nephew (Gen 13:8), or the relation between men bound by covenant (2 Sam 1:26; cf. 1 Sam 18:3). Continuing this OT tradition, the NT often uses "brother" or "brethren" in this wider sense. Paul uses it as a synonym for his Israelite kinsmen in Rom 9:3. It also denotes biologically unrelated Christians in the New Covenant family of God (Rom 8:29; 12:1; Col 1:2; Heb 2:11; Jas 1:2; CCC 500).

12:50 will of my Father: Obedience to God the Father creates relationships greater than natural family bonds. Although Jesus had no biological siblings, his spiritual brothers and sisters are the adopted children of God (Rom 8:29; 1 Jn 3:1). They are empowered to obey the Father as he did (cf. Jn 8:29; 1 Jn 3:7–10). See note on 12:46. **mother:** Far from undermining the role of Mary, Jesus reveals the true greatness of her divine maternity. After all, she was not merely his *natural* mother through generation, but she became the Mother of God precisely by embracing the Father's will (Lk 1:38, 43). Her relation-

ship to Jesus—physical and spiritual—is thus magnified by Jesus' statement (CCC 495).

13:1–51 The parables of the kingdom. Jesus speaks of the hidden mysteries of God's kingdom present in the Church. Of the seven, the parables of the Wheat and the Weeds (13:24–30), the Hidden Treasure (13:44), the Pearl of Great Value (13:45–46), and the Dragnet (13:47–50) are found only in Matthew.

⚒ **13:11 to you:** Jesus speaks parables to the "great crowds" (13:2) but explains them only to his disciples. While the illustrations are clear enough—drawn from everyday life—the underlying truths remain obscure to the faithless (13:9, 13). **secrets of the kingdom:** The inner circle of disciples accept Jesus with faith and are privileged to know God's mysteries (13:36–43). ● Jesus' private instruction of his disciples reflects his intention to arrange the Church hierarchically. He invests his authority in the apostles (and their successors) to administer the sacraments (28:19; Jn 20:23; 1 Cor 11:25) and transmit God's truth through their teaching (28:20; Jn 17:17–20; 1 Cor 4:1; CCC 888–90).

📖 **13:14–15** A reference to Is 6:9–10. ● In context, God commissioned Isaiah to preach judgment to the Israelites for their covenant infidelity. Similarly, Jesus uses parables to proclaim God's judgment on the faithless of his generation (cf. Mk 4:12; Lk 8:10).

13:18–23 The parable of the Sower illustrates how indifferent responses to the **word of the kingdom** (13:19) prove unfruitful (CCC 29). Distractions come from the world (13:22; 19:24), the flesh (13:21; 10:22; 26:41), and the devil (13:19; 10:28). On the other hand, **fruit** brought forth from the responsive heart abounds (13:23). Fruit is a common biblical image for

---

[h] Other ancient authorities add here and in verse 43 *to hear.*

word, immediately he falls away.[i] [22]As for what was sown among thorns, this is he who hears the word, but the cares of the world and the delight in riches choke the word, and it proves unfruitful. [23]As for what was sown on good soil, this is he who hears the word and understands it; he indeed bears fruit, and yields, in one case a hundredfold, in another sixty, and in another thirty."

The Parable of Weeds among the Wheat

24 Another parable he put before them, saying, "The kingdom of heaven may be compared to a man who sowed good seed in his field; [25]but while men were sleeping, his enemy came and sowed weeds among the wheat, and went away. [26]So when the plants came up and bore grain, then the weeds appeared also. [27]And the servants[j] of the householder came and said to him, 'Sir, did you not sow good seed in your field? How then has it weeds?' [28]He said to them, 'An enemy has done this.' The servants[j] said to him, 'Then do you want us to go and gather them?' [29]But he said, 'No; lest in gathering the weeds you root up the wheat along with them. [30]Let both grow together until the harvest; and at harvest time I will tell the reapers, 'Gather the weeds first and bind them in bundles to be burned, but gather the wheat into my barn.'"

The Parable of the Mustard Seed

31 Another parable he put before them, saying, "The kingdom of heaven is like a grain of mustard seed which a man took and sowed in his field; [32]it is the smallest of all seeds, but when it has grown it is the greatest of shrubs and becomes a tree, so that the birds of the air come and make nests in its branches."

The Parable of the Yeast

33 He told them another parable. "The kingdom of heaven is like leaven which a woman took and hid in three measures of meal, till it was all leavened."

The Use of Parables

34 All this Jesus said to the crowds in parables; indeed he said nothing to them without a parable. [35]This was to fulfil what was spoken by the prophet:[k]

"I will open my mouth in parables,
I will utter what has been hidden since the foundation of the world."

Jesus Explains the Parable of the Weeds

36 Then he left the crowds and went into the house. And his disciples came to him, saying, "Explain to us the parable of the weeds of the field."

13:22: Mt 19:23; 1 Tim 6:9–10, 17.   **13:24–30:** Mk 4:26–29.   **13:31–32:** Mk 4:30–32; Lk 13:18–19; Mt 17:20.
13:33: Lk 13:20–21; Gal 5:9; Gen 18:6.   **13:34:** Mk 4:33–34; Jn 10:6; 16:25.   **13:35:** Ps 78:2.

---

the good works and faithfulness that flow from God's grace (7:17; 12:33; cf. Ps 1:1–3; Jer 17:10; Jn 15:5; Gal 5:22–23).

13:25 sowed weeds: Probably "darnel", a slightly poisonous plant resembling wheat in the early stages of growth. Only when it fully matures can it be distinguished and separated from wheat (13:30).

📖 **13:32 becomes a tree:** The parable of the Mustard Seed illustrates the contrast in size between the seed and the mature shrub, reaching nearly ten feet in height. Jesus likewise sows the kingdom in a small band of disciples, expecting it to grow into a worldwide Church. • Similar metaphors used in the OT represent great empires as great trees (Ezek 31:1–13; Dan 4:12), including the kingdom of Israel (Ezek 17:22–24). In these instances, **birds** represent Gentile nations. Jesus' parable thus points to the spread of the gospel and acceptance of Gentiles into the Church (28:19).

13:33 like leaven: Sometimes symbolic of evil in the world (16:5–12; 1 Cor 5:6–8). It has positive symbolism here. At one level, leaven represents the grace of the kingdom that sanctifies the world through the Church. At the personal level, leaven is the individual Christian called to bring the gospel to those around him. **three measures:** i.e., about 50 pounds of **meal**, which here symbolizes the world. The parable thus highlights a great disproportion: the little leaven is hidden yet actively raising a significant amount of meal.

13:35 by the prophet: A reference to Ps 78:2, attributed to Asaph. In 2 Chron 29:30 of the Greek OT, Asaph is called a "prophet". In any case, all OT writers were inspired by the Spirit and thus prophets (cf. 22:43; 2 Pet 1:20–21). **what has been hidden:** Psalm 78:2 accents the positive function of parables: they enlighten the humble by revealing God's mysteries. See word study: *Parables*.

13:36–43 The final separation of good and evil. Accordingly, God's forbearance toward sin and evil in the world will last only until the Last Judgment; in the meantime, saints and

sinners will continue side by side in the Church. See note on 25:31–46.

13:36 went into the house: Jesus shifts attention from the

WORD STUDY

Parables (13:3)

Parabolē (Gk.): A spoken or literary "comparison" between two things for illustration. The word is found 48 times in the Synoptic Gospels for short stories that use familiar images and word pictures to illustrate a truth or challenge a common outlook on life and religion. The term is found also in the Greek OT, where it frequently translates the Hebrew word *mashal*, a term for literary forms such as proverbs (1 Sam 10:12; 1 Kings 4:32), riddles (Ps 49:4; Sir 47:15), and allegories (Ezek 17:2; 24:3). Jesus uses parables in the NT for two purposes: to reveal and to conceal divine mysteries. **(1)** Parables invite the humble to reach behind the images and lay hold of God's truth (11:25; Mk 4:33). Parables sketch out earthly scenarios that reveal heavenly mysteries. **(2)** Conversely, they obstruct the proud and conceal divine mysteries from the unworthy. Parables thus have a second, albeit negative, function and are spoken as judgments on the faithless (cf. Is 6:9–10). In Matthew, Jesus shifts from straightforward teaching (chaps. 5–7) to parables (chap. 13) immediately following his rejection by the Pharisees (12:14). Like the OT prophets Jotham (Judg 9:7–15) and Nathan (2 Sam 12:1–6), Jesus speaks parables for the benefit of the faithful and the judgment of unbelievers.

---

[i] Or *stumbles*.   [j] Or *slaves*.
[k] Other ancient authorities read *the prophet Isaiah*.

[37]He answered, "He who sows the good seed is the Son of man; [38]the field is the world, and the good seed means the sons of the kingdom; the weeds are the sons of the evil one, [39]and the enemy who sowed them is the devil; the harvest is the close of the age, and the reapers are angels. [40]Just as the weeds are gathered and burned with fire, so will it be at the close of the age. [41]The Son of man will send his angels, and they will gather out of his kingdom all causes of sin and all evildoers, [42]and throw them into the furnace of fire; there men will weep and gnash their teeth. [43]Then the righteous will shine like the sun in the kingdom of their Father. He who has ears, let him hear.

Three Parables

44 "The kingdom of heaven is like treasure hidden in a field, which a man found and covered up; then in his joy he goes and sells all that he has and buys that field.

45 "Again, the kingdom of heaven is like a merchant in search of fine pearls, [46]who, on finding one pearl of great value, went and sold all that he had and bought it.

47 "Again, the kingdom of heaven is like a net which was thrown into the sea and gathered fish of every kind; [48]when it was full, men drew it ashore and sat down and sorted the good into vessels but threw away the bad. [49]So it will be at the close of the age. The angels will come out and separate the evil from the righteous, [50]and throw

them into the furnace of fire; there men will weep and gnash their teeth.

Treasures New and Old

51 "Have you understood all this?" They said to him, "Yes." [52]And he said to them, "Therefore every scribe who has been trained for the kingdom of heaven is like a householder who brings out of his treasure what is new and what is old."

The Rejection of Jesus at Nazareth

53 And when Jesus had finished these parables, he went away from there, [54]and coming to his own country he taught them in their synagogue, so that they were astonished, and said, "Where did this man get this wisdom and these mighty works? [55]Is not this the carpenter's son? Is not his mother called Mary? And are not his brethren James and Joseph and Simon and Judas? [56]And are not all his sisters with us? Where then did this man get all this?" [57]And they took offense at him. But Jesus said to them, "A prophet is not without honor except in his own country and in his own house." [58]And he did not do many mighty works there, because of their unbelief.

The Death of John the Baptist

14 At that time Herod the tetrarch heard about the fame of Jesus; [2]and he said to his servants, "This is John the Baptist, he has been raised from the dead; that is why these powers are at work in him." [3]For Herod had seized John and bound him and put him in prison, for the sake of

---

13:38: Jn 8:44; 1 Jn 3:10.   **13:41:** Mt 24:31.   **13:42:** Mt 13:50; 8:12; 22:13; 24:51; 25:30; Lk 13:28.   **13:47–50:** Mt 13:40–42.
13:53: Mt 7:28; 11:1; 19:1; 26:1.   **13:54–58:** Mk 6:1–6; Lk 4:16–30.
14:1–2: Mk 6:14–16; Lk 9:7–9; Mk 8:28.   **14:3–4:** Mk 6:17–18; Lk 3:19–20; Lev 18:16; 20:21.

"great crowds" (13:2) to his private instruction of the disciples. See note on 13:11.

13:39 the harvest: A biblical image for the Day of the Lord—i.e., the time when God will judge all nations (3:12; cf. Jer 51:33; Hos 6:11; Joel 3:13; Rev 14:14–16).

13:42 gnash their teeth: The wicked will experience punishment (CCC 1034). See note on 8:12.

13:43 shine like the sun: Those resurrected to eternal life share in Jesus' glory. • The expression evokes Dan 12:3. In context, Daniel foresees the general resurrection, when the "wise" will be delivered from God's judgment and "shine" for ever (Dan 12:1–4).

13:44–46 Two parables, the Hidden Treasure (13:44) and the Pearl of Great Value (13:45–46), that underscore the same point. Both stress that the kingdom's value is inestimable, and surrendering earthly attachments is required to obtain it (19:21, 29; Phil 3:8). This may entail literal poverty (religious) or spiritual poverty (5:3) for those whose state in life involves ownership of property (laity) (CCC 546). • *Allegorically* (St. Irenaeus, *AH* 4, 26, 1), Christ himself is the great treasure hidden within the field of the OT Scriptures. Only in light of his Cross and Resurrection can the mysteries of the Old be fully understood to announce the advent of God's Son.

13:47–50 The parable of the Dragnet mirrors the parable of the Wheat and the Weeds (13:24–30, 36–43); both foresee the same destiny for the wicked (13:42, 50). The Greek expression behind **fish of every kind** (13:47) is literally "every kind of thing". Thus, the separation between good and evil may envision a sorting of fish from other useless things in the dragnet

(e.g., seaweed, trash, algae, etc.). Like the "field" in 13:38, the **sea** (13:47) represents the world.

13:52 every scribe: Legal experts in first-century Judaism. Here it denotes the apostles instructed for the **kingdom**. Jesus equips them to evangelize and catechize (28:18–20) the world about the treasures hidden in the **old** Covenant and manifest in the **new**. Matthew's own ministry follows this pattern: he continually cites the OT to explain its fulfillment in Jesus Christ.

13:55 his brethren: See note on 12:46.

14:1–12 John the Baptist's martyrdom is a narrative "flashback" on events of the past. Matthew's account has a double purpose: **(1)** It marks a clear distinction between John and Jesus in light of popular rumors about their identity (14:2; 16:14). **(2)** It underscores the high cost of Christian discipleship (5:10–11; 10:39). The execution of John by governing authorities anticipates the fate of Jesus (17:12) and the early Christian martyrs (Rev 20:4).

14:1 Herod the tetrarch: Herod Antipas, son of Herod the Great, who governed Galilee and Perea from 4 B.C. until A.D. 39. See note on 2:22.

14:4 It is not lawful: John publicly denounced the union of Herod Antipas and his mistress, Herodias. While the NT gives little background, extrabiblical history details how Antipas desired Herodias while she was married to his half-brother Herod Philip. Antipas and Herodias then abandoned their respective spouses in order to be united. The Mosaic Law, however, forbids the union of a man with his brother's wife while the brother is still living (Lev 18:16; 20:21). Since Philip was yet living, John the Baptist spoke out against the union of

Hero´di-as, his brother Philip's wife;[l] [4]because John said to him, "It is not lawful for you to have her." [5]And though he wanted to put him to death, he feared the people, because they held him to be a prophet. [6]But when Herod's birthday came, the daughter of Hero´di-as danced before the company, and pleased Herod, [7]so that he promised with an oath to give her whatever she might ask. [8]Prompted by her mother, she said, "Give me the head of John the Baptist here on a platter." [9]And the king was sorry; but because of his oaths and his guests he commanded it to be given; [10]he sent and had John beheaded in the prison, [11]and his head was brought on a platter and given to the girl, and she brought it to her mother. [12]And his disciples came and took the body and buried it; and they went and told Jesus.

Feeding the Five Thousand
13 Now when Jesus heard this, he withdrew from there in a boat to a lonely place apart. But when the crowds heard it, they followed him on foot from the towns. [14]As he went ashore he saw a great throng; and he had compassion on them, and healed their sick. [15]When it was evening, the disciples came to him and said, "This is a lonely place, and the day is now over; send the crowds away to go into the villages and buy food for themselves." [16]Jesus said, "They need not go away; you give them something to eat." [17]They said to him, "We have only five loaves here and two fish." [18]And he said, "Bring them here to me." [19]Then he ordered the crowds to sit down on the grass; and taking the five loaves and the two fish he looked up to heaven, and blessed, and broke and gave the loaves to the disciples, and the disciples gave them to the crowds. [20]And they all ate and were satisfied. And they took up twelve baskets full of

the broken pieces left over. [21]And those who ate were about five thousand men, besides women and children.

Jesus Walks on the Water
22 Then he made the disciples get into the boat and go before him to the other side, while he dismissed the crowds. [23]And after he had dismissed the crowds, he went up into the hills by himself to pray. When evening came, he was there alone, [24]but the boat by this time was many furlongs distant from the land,[m] beaten by the waves; for the wind was against them. [25]And in the fourth watch of the night he came to them, walking on the sea. [26]But when the disciples saw him walking on the sea, they were terrified, saying, "It is a ghost!" And they cried out for fear. [27]But immediately he spoke to them, saying, "Take heart, it is I; have no fear."

28 And Peter answered him, "Lord, if it is you, bid me come to you on the water." [29]He said, "Come." So Peter got out of the boat and walked on the water and came to Jesus; [30]but when he saw the wind,[n] he was afraid, and beginning to sink he cried out, "Lord, save me." [31]Jesus immediately reached out his hand and caught him, saying to him, "O man of little faith, why did you doubt?" [32]And when they got into the boat, the wind ceased. [33]And those in the boat worshiped him, saying, "Truly you are the Son of God."

Jesus Heals the Sick in Gennesaret
34 And when they had crossed over, they came to land at Gennesaret. [35]And when the men of that place recognized him, they sent round to all that region and brought to him all that were sick, [36]and begged him that they might only touch the fringe of his garment; and as many as touched it were made well.

14:5–12: Mk 6:19–29. **14:13–21:** Mk 6:32–44; Lk 9:10–17; Jn 6:1–13; Mt 15:32–38. **14:19:** Mk 14:22; Lk 24:30. **14:22–23:** Mk 6:45–46; Jn 6:15–17. **14:24–33:** Mk 6:47–52; Jn 6:16–21 **14:26:** Lk 24:37. **14:29:** Jn 21:7. **14:31:** Mt 6:30; 8:26; 16:8. **14:33:** Mt 28:9, 17. **14:34–36:** Mk 6:53–56; Jn 6:22–26. **14:36:** Mk 3:10; Nb 15:38; Mt 9:20.

Herod Antipas and Herodias and publicly disgraced them (Mk 6:19).

14:9 he commanded it: Herod succumbed to peer pressure by swearing an illicit oath (14:7) before his distinguished guests (14:9). Condemning an innocent man without trial, he stands in a stream of immorality historically linked with the Herodian dynasty. See notes on 2:16 and 2:22.

14:13–21 Jesus' multiplication of loaves appears in every Gospel. The event anticipates the Eucharist, a point that Matthew reinforces by using the same series of verbs (**taking . . . blessed . . . broke . . . gave**) here (14:19) and at the Last Supper (26:26; Mk 14:22). • The miracle also recalls the similar OT episode in 2 Kings 4:42–44, where the prophet Elisha multiplied 20 barley loaves (Jn 6:9) to feed 100 men, with some left over (CCC 1335). • *Morally* (St. John, Patriarch of Alexandria; Theophylact), the five loaves signify alms given to the poor (cf. 6:2–4). As here, the size of the donation is less significant than the generosity of one's heart (cf. Lk 21:1–4; 2

Cor 9:6–8). Gifts given to the poor are, in return, multiplied by God back to the giver as treasure in heaven (6:19–21; CCC 1434).

14:19 the disciples gave them: Jesus feeds the crowd through the hands of the apostles. • The disciples' intermediary role points forward to their priesthood (cf. 15:36). They distribute the bread provided by Jesus in anticipation of the eucharistic liturgy, where the priests of the New Covenant give the Bread of Life as Holy Communion to the Church (1 Cor 10:16; CCC 1329).

14:25 the fourth watch: The 12 hours of the night between 6 P.M. and 6 A.M. were divided into four "watches" (cf. Mk 13:35). This event took place between 3 and 6 A.M. and suggests the disciples were battling the storm most of the night. **walking on the sea**: See note on 8:27.

14:27 it is I: Literally, "I am." • In light of his power over nature, Jesus' statement may allude to God's self-revelation at the burning bush (Ex 3:14; cf. Jn 8:58; 18:5, 6). Jesus thus goes beyond reassuring the disciples and claims for himself a divine identity and authority (14:33).

14:33 you are the Son of God: Anticipates the confessions of Jesus' divinity by Peter (16:16) and the centurion (27:54).

---

[l] Other ancient authorities read *his brother's wife*.
[m] Other ancient authorities read *was out on the sea*.
[n] Other ancient authorities read *strong wind*.

The Tradition of the Elders

15 Then Pharisees and scribes came to Jesus from Jerusalem and said, [2]"Why do your disciples transgress the tradition of the elders? For they do not wash their hands when they eat." [3]He answered them, "And why do you transgress the commandment of God for the sake of your tradition? [4]For God commanded, 'Honor your father and your mother,' and, 'He who speaks evil of father or mother, let him surely die.' [5]But you say, 'If any one tells his father or his mother, What you would have gained from me is given to God,*°* he need not honor his father.' [6]So, for the sake of your tradition, you have made void the word*ᵖ* of God. [7]You hypocrites! Well did Isaiah prophesy of you, when he said:

[8] 'This people honors me with their lips,
   but their heart is far from me;
[9] in vain do they worship me,
   teaching as doctrines the precepts of men.' "

Things That Defile

10 And he called the people to him and said to them, "Hear and understand: [11]not what goes into the mouth defiles a man, but what comes out of the mouth, this defiles a man." [12]Then the disciples came and said to him, "Do you know that the Pharisees were offended when they heard this saying?" [13]He answered, "Every plant which my heavenly Father has not planted will be rooted up. [14]Let them alone; they are blind guides. And if a blind man leads a blind man, both will fall into a pit." [15]But Peter said to him, "Explain the parable to us." [16]And he said, "Are you also still without understanding? [17]Do you not see that whatever goes into the mouth passes into the stomach, and so passes on?*q* [18]But what comes out of the mouth proceeds from the heart, and this defiles a man. [19]For out of the heart come evil thoughts, murder, adultery, fornication, theft, false witness, slander. [20]These are what defile a man; but to eat with unwashed hands does not defile a man."

The Canaanite Woman's Faith

21 And Jesus went away from there and withdrew to the district of Tyre and Sidon. [22]And behold, a Canaanite woman from that region came out and cried, "Have mercy on me, O Lord, Son of David; my daughter is severely possessed by a demon." [23]But he did not answer her a word. And his disciples came and begged him, saying, "Send her away, for she is crying after us." [24]He answered, "I was sent only to the lost sheep of the house of Israel." [25]But she came and knelt before him, saying, "Lord, help me." [26]And he answered, "It is not

---

15:1-20: Mk 7:1–23.   **15:4:** Ex 20:12; Deut 5:16; Ex 21:17; Lev 20:9.   **15:8–9:** Is 29:13.
15:11: Acts 10:14–15; 1 Tim 4:3.   **15:13:** Is 60:21; Jn 15:2.   **15:14:** Lk 6:39; Mt 23:16, 24; Rom 2:19.
15:19: Gal 5:19–21; 1 Cor 6:9–10; Rom 14:14.   **15:21-28:** Mk 7:24–30.   **15:24:** Mt 10:6, 23.   **15:25:** Mt 8:2; 18:26; 20:20; Jn 9:38.

15:1–20 Jesus' clash with religious leaders centers on oral traditions added to the Mosaic Law. Addressing the Pharisees, Jesus designates ceremonial washing (15:2, 20) and the custom of dedication (15:5) as **your tradition** (15:6). He denies that these Pharisaic customs hold the same weight and authority as the Law of God (cf. Col 2:8). The Pharisees were violating the **word of God** (15:6) by overemphasizing the importance of their own traditions at the expense of the Law. Only traditions that stem from Christ and the apostles have divine authority, since they are not human in their origin (1 Cor 11:2; 2 Thess 2:15; 3:6). See note on Mk 7:3 and topical essay: *Who Are the Pharisees?* at Mk 2 (CCC 83–84).

15:5 is given to God: The Pharisees sometimes withheld financial support from parents in order to donate money to the Temple. This tradition of dedication was probably enforced by a vow, and money offered to the Temple could not be repossessed. While the practice of Temple donations appeared pious, its practical effect marginalized God's commandment to **honor** one's parents (15:4; Ex 20:12).

15:19 out of the heart: Real defilement is spiritual and moral, not ceremonial. The scribes and Pharisees unduly emphasized external ceremonies and compromised the true spirit of Israel's religion. Real defilement stems from evil intentions within and is manifest through sinful deeds (5:28). Jesus stresses the need for inner purity of heart, not ritual purity of the body (CCC 2517). See note on 5:8.

15:21 Tyre and Sidon: Gentile cities in Phoenicia, north of Palestine. According to the table of nations in Gen 10, Sidon was the first-born son of Canaan (Gen 10:15), and thus the woman is a "Canaanite" (15:22). Mark refers to her more proximate geographical background as "Syrophoenician" (Mk 7:26).

15:26 the children's bread: i.e., Israel and its inherited right to God's blessings. As in 8:5–13, Jesus heals a faith-

MAP — Jesus' Ministry beyond Galilee. In the region of Tyre and Sidon, Jesus cast out a demon from the daughter of a Syrophoenician woman (Mk 7:24–30). In the region of Caesarea Philippi, Peter made his great declaration of faith in Jesus as God's Messiah (Mt 16:13–19). Jesus returned to Galilee via the Decapolis region, crossing the Jordan River south of the Sea of Galilee.

° Or *an offering.*   *ᵖ* Other ancient authorities read *law.*   *q* Or *is evacuated.*

fair to take the children's bread and throw it to the dogs." [27]She said, "Yes, Lord, yet even the dogs eat the crumbs that fall from their masters' table." [28]Then Jesus answered her, "O woman, great is your faith! Let it be done for you as you desire." And her daughter was healed instantly.

Jesus Cures Many People

29 And Jesus went on from there and passed along the Sea of Galilee. And he went up into the hills, and sat down there. [30]And great crowds came to him, bringing with them the lame, the maimed, the blind, the mute, and many others, and they put them at his feet, and he healed them, [31]so that the throng wondered, when they saw the mute speaking, the maimed whole, the lame walking, and the blind seeing; and they glorified the God of Israel.

Feeding the Four Thousand

32 Then Jesus called his disciples to him and said, "I have compassion on the crowd, because they have been with me now three days, and have nothing to eat; and I am unwilling to send them away hungry, lest they faint on the way." [33]And the disciples said to him, "Where are we to get bread enough in the desert to feed so great a crowd?" [34]And Jesus said to them, "How many loaves have you?" They said, "Seven, and a few small fish." [35]And commanding the crowd to sit down on the ground, [36]he took the seven loaves and the fish, and having given thanks he broke them and gave them to the disciples, and the disciples gave them to the crowds. [37]And they all ate and were satisfied; and they took up seven baskets full of the broken pieces left over. [38]Those who ate were four thousand men, besides women and children. [39]And sending away the crowds, he got into the boat and went to the region of Mag'adan.

The Demand for a Sign

16 And the Pharisees and Sad'ducees came, and to test him they asked him to show them a sign from heaven. [2]He answered them,[r] "When it is evening, you say, 'It will be fair weather; for the sky is red.' [3]And in the morning, 'It will be stormy today, for the sky is red and threatening.' You know how to interpret the appearance of the sky, but you cannot interpret the signs of the times. [4]An evil and adulterous generation seeks for a sign, but no sign shall be given to it except the sign of Jonah." So he left them and departed.

The Yeast of the Pharisees and Sadducees

5 When the disciples reached the other side, they had forgotten to bring any bread. [6]Jesus said to them, "Take heed and beware of the leaven of the Pharisees and Sad'ducees." [7]And they discussed it among themselves, saying, "We brought no bread." [8]But Jesus, aware of this, said, "O men of little faith, why do you discuss among yourselves the fact that you have no bread? [9]Do you not yet perceive? Do you not remember the five loaves of the five thousand, and how many baskets you gathered? [10]Or the seven loaves of the four thousand, and how many baskets you gathered? [11]How is it that you fail to perceive that I did not speak about bread? Beware of the leaven of the Pharisees and Sad'ducees." [12]Then they understood that he did not tell them to beware of the leaven of bread, but of the teaching of the Pharisees and Sad'ducees.

Peter's Declaration That Jesus Is the Christ

13 Now when Jesus came into the district of Caesare'a Philip'pi, he asked his disciples, "Who do men say that the Son of man is?" [14]And they said, "Some say John the Baptist, others say Eli'jah, and others Jeremiah or one of the proph-

---

15:28: Mt 9:22, 28; Mk 10:52; Lk 7:50; 17:19.   **15:29–31:** Mk 7:31–37.
15:32–39: Mk 8:1–10; Mt 14:13–21.   **15:32:** Mt 9:36.   **16:1–4:** Mk 8:11–12; Lk 11:16, 29; 12:54–56; Mt 12:38–39; Jn 2:18; 6:30
16:4: Jon 3:4–5.   **16:5–12:** Mk 8:13–21.   **16:6:** Lk 12:1.   **16:8:** Mt 6:30; 8:26; 14:31.   **16:9:** Mt 14:17–21.
16:10: Mt 15:34–38.   **16:13–16:** Mk 8:27–30; Lk 9:18–21.   **16:14:** Mt 14:2; Mk 6:15; Lk 9:7–8; Jn 1:21.

---

filled Gentile despite his intention to minister to Israel first (15:24; 10:6; cf. Rom 1:16). **the dogs:** Literally, "little dogs" or "puppies". See note on 7:6. • *Morally* (St. John Chrysostom, *Hom. in Matt.* 52), the Canaanite woman signifies repentant souls. Incapable of boasting, contrite sinners lean wholly on God's mercy; they recognize their weakness before God and can only beg for blessings, unable to demand from God gifts that he freely bestows. Only the humble and faith-filled are rewarded with spiritual healing.

15:32–39 The feeding of the 4,000 is similar to the episode in 14:13–21. Differences lie in the number of people (15:38; 14:21), the number of loaves (15:34; 14:17), and the number of leftover baskets involved (15:37; 14:20). Both narratives emphasize the miraculousness of Jesus' sign and the abundance of bread provided (cf. 16:9–10). See note on Mk 8:19.

16:1 a sign from heaven: These leaders interpret signs in heaven to predict the weather, yet they are blind in spiritual matters (15:14; 23:16). Jesus refuses to perform miracles for those unconvinced of his authority—it is something already manifest through his healings (11:2–5; 1 Cor 1:22).

16:4 the sign of Jonah: A reference to Jesus' Resurrection. See note on 12:41.

16:11 the leaven: Symbolic of an effective and hidden influence (13:33). It is here a negative symbol of the dangerous teaching of the **Pharisees** and **Sadducees,** who prevent others from entering the kingdom (cf. 12:24; 22:23; 23:13). Jesus' warning prepares for the following episode, where he ensures the transmission of true Christian doctrine through Peter.

16:13–20 The Gospels generally highlight Peter's preeminence among the disciples (10:2; Lk 22:31–32; Jn 1:42; 21:15–18). This episode defines his role explicitly. • Jesus' blessing on Peter draws from OT traditions about the Davidic covenant. The key concepts and images (**Christ / Son of God / rock / build / gates of Hades / keys / kingdom**) are all connected with Israel's kingdom established under David and confirmed by Solomon and his construction of the Temple (cf. 2 Sam 7:4–17; Ps 2:7; 89; 132). Although David's empire crumbled in 586 B.C., Jesus announces its restoration in the New Covenant (cf. Mk 11:10; Lk 1:32–33; Acts 15:15–18). Christ is the long-awaited "son of David", who rebuilds and transforms the ancient kingdom in the Church. See introduction: *Themes.* • Vatican I (1870) cited this episode as biblical support for the primacy of Peter and successive popes. The

---

[r] Other ancient authorities omit the following words to the end of verse 3.

ets." [15]He said to them, "But who do you say that I am?" [16]Simon Peter replied, "You are the Christ, the Son of the living God." [17]And Jesus answered him, "Blessed are you, Simon Bar-Jona! For flesh and blood has not revealed this to you, but my Father who is in heaven. [18]And I tell you, you are Peter,[s] and on this rock[t] I will build my church, and the powers of death[u] shall not prevail against it. [19]I will give you the keys of the kingdom of heaven, and whatever you bind on earth shall be bound in heaven, and whatever you loose on earth shall be loosed in heaven." [20]Then he strictly charged the disciples to tell no one that he was the Christ.

Jesus Foretells His Death and Resurrection

21 From that time Jesus began to show his disciples that he must go to Jerusalem and suffer many things from the elders and chief priests and scribes, and be killed, and on the third day be raised. [22]And Peter took him and began to rebuke him, saying, "God forbid, Lord! This shall never happen to you." [23]But he turned and said to Peter, "Get behind me, Satan! You are a hindrance[v] to me; for you are not on the side of God, but of men."

16:16: Mt 1:16; Jn 11:27; 1:49. **16:17:** 1 Cor 15:50; Gal 1:16; Eph 6:12; Heb 2:14
16:18: Jn 1:40–42; 21:15–17; 1 Cor 15:5. **16:19:** Is 22:22; Rev 1:18; Mt 18:18; Jn 20:23. **16:20:** Mt 8:4; Mk 3:12; 5:43; 7:36; 9:9
16:21-28: Mk 8:31–9:1; Lk 9:22–27. **16:21:** Mt 17:22–23; 20:17–19;; Lk 17:25; Mt 17:12; 26:2. **16:23:** Mt 4:10.

Council's interpretation touches five points of doctrine: **(1)** The Magisterium built upon Peter is instituted by Jesus Christ; **(2)** Peter is given a unique role as chief teacher and ruler (primacy of jurisdiction) over the Church; **(3)** Peter is the visible head of the Church; **(4)** Peter's authority is passed on through successors; **(5)** through Peter, Christ himself assures the infallible preservation of the gospel in the Church.

16:13 Caesarea Philippi: A predominantly Gentile city north of Palestine. It was originally known as Panion (or Paneas) because of a shrine built there to the Greco-Roman god Pan. When Herod the Great's son Philip became tetrarch of that region (4 B.C.–A.D. 33), he rebuilt the city and renamed it in honor of Tiberius Caesar, adding his own name to distinguish it from the Judean coastal city of Caesarea.

16:16 Son of the living God: The confession is double-sided: **(1)** Peter proclaims the mystery of Christ's divinity as the head and spokesman of the Church (cf. 11:25–27; 14:33). **(2)** Peter sees Jesus as the awaited Messiah-king of Israel (26:63; Jn 1:49). The close relationship between the titles **Christ** and *Son* reflects OT traditions, where Israel's kings enjoyed unique relationships with God as his sons (2 Sam 7:14; Ps 2:7; 89:27; CCC 436, 439, 442). See word study: *Christ* at Mk 14.

16:17 Blessed are you: Jesus blesses Peter and elevates him to be the chief patriarch of the New Covenant. • Parallels between Genesis and Jesus' words (16:17-19) suggest that Peter assumes a role in salvation history similar to Abraham's. **(1)** Both are blessed by God (Gen 14:19); **(2)** both respond with heroic faith (Heb 11:8); **(3)** both receive a divine mission (Gen 12:1-3); **(4)** both have their names changed (Gen 17:5); **(5)** both are called a "rock" (Is 51:1-2); and **(6)** both are assured a victory over the "gate" of their enemies (Gen 22:17). **Simon Bar-Jona:** Literally means "Simon son of Jonah". Since Peter's father is actually named "John" (Jn 1:42), the title may be symbolic. **(1)** Jesus' role as a new Jonah (12:39-41) may suggest he views Peter as his spiritual son. **(2)** Since the Hebrew name "Jonah" means "dove", Jesus may point to the relationship between Peter and the Holy Spirit. Indeed, the same Spirit who confirmed Jesus' Sonship in the form of a dove (3:16) now inspires Peter's confession. **flesh and blood:** A Semitic idiom for human beings, emphasizing their natural limitations and weaknesses (Sir 14:18; Gal 1:16).

16:18 I will build: Jesus portrays the Church as a spiritual Temple (cf. 1 Cor 3:16–17; 2 Cor 6:16; Eph 2:19–22; 1 Pet 2:4–8). • As Solomon was the son of David and the anointed Temple builder in the OT, so Jesus is the Davidic "Son" of God (16:16) and the anointed Messiah who builds the Church in the New. Jesus elsewhere sees himself as both similar and superior to King Solomon (12:42). See note on 7:24. **my church:** Among the Gospels, Matthew alone uses the word *church* (18:17). The word is used often in the Greek OT for the "congregation" or "assembly" of Israel united to God. Jesus uses it in a similar way for the New Covenant community. **the**

powers of death: Literally, "the gates of Hades". • In the OT, Hades—also called "Sheol" or "the Pit"—is the place of the dead where souls descend through its gates (Ps 9:13, 17; Wis 16:13; Is 38:10; Jon 2:2). It is not hell, but a temporary realm where souls are detained until the Last Judgment (Rev 20:13–15). By extension, Hades is also the habitation of evil forces that bring about death and deception (Rev 6:8; 20:1-3). According to Jewish tradition, the foundation stone (Heb. *'eben shetiyyah*) of the Jerusalem Temple capped off and sealed a long shaft leading down to the netherworld (Rev 9:1–2; 20:1–3). The Temple, resting securely on a rock, was thus the center of the cosmos, the junction between heaven and Hades. Drawing from this background, Jesus guarantees that the powers of death and deception will not overcome the Church—i.e., the new Temple built on Peter. He enables Peter (and his successors) to hold error at bay and faithfully proclaim the gospel (CCC 552).

16:19 the keys: A symbol of teaching authority (Lk 11:52). Jesus consecrates Peter as the Church's chief teacher, whose office will continue on through successors. The plural use of *keys* may imply a connection with the "gates" in 16:18 and mean that Peter's position includes, among other things, the authority to release the righteous souls who are detained in Hades but destined for heaven. • In the OT Davidic empire, the king appointed a cabinet of ministers for specific tasks in the kingdom (1 Kings 4:1–6; 2 Kings 18:37). Of these, a prime minister was elevated to unique status of authority, ranking second only to the king. This government structure was common among kingdoms in the ancient Near East (cf. Gen 41:39–43; Esther 3:1–2). Jesus here evokes Is 22:15–25, where the prime minister's office is handed on to a successor by the symbolic act of handing on the "key of the house [i.e., kingdom] of David" (Is 22:22). In Matthew, Jesus is the new Davidic king, who appoints Peter the prime minister over the **kingdom of heaven** in the Church. As in Is 22, Peter's position is designed for him and his successors; the office is meant to endure as long as the kingdom itself. Entrusted with the keys, Peter wields Christ's own royal authority (cf. Rev 1:18; 3:7). **whatever you bind . . . loose:** Familiar language in early Jewish literature. The metaphor carries several connotations: **(1)** It signifies teaching authority and the ability to render binding decisions. Rabbis were said to make "binding" interpretations of the Law. **(2)** It denotes authority to include or exclude members of a religious community. **(3)** It signals the forgiveness of sins (*Tg Neof* in Gen 4:7). The verb *loose* is used this way in Rev 1:5 (translated "freed") and by the early Church Fathers (cf. Jn 20:23). Peter is thus invested with Christ's authority as the kingdom's chief teacher and administrator; through him **heaven** governs the Church on **earth** (cf. Jn 21:15–17; 1 Tim 3:15; CCC 553, 1445).

16:23 Satan: In contrast to the blessing of Peter in 16:17, Jesus here rebukes him. Peter's confession (16:16) was inspired by the Father; here his natural instincts object to a suffering Messiah. On his own, he cannot see the spiritual necessity of Jesus' Passion for sinners.

---

[s] Greek *Petros*. [t] Greek *Petra*. [u] Greek *the gates of Hades*.

The Cross and Self-Denial

24 Then Jesus told his disciples, "If any man would come after me, let him deny himself and take up his cross and follow me. ²⁵For whoever would save his life will lose it, and whoever loses his life for my sake will find it. ²⁶For what will it profit a man, if he gains the whole world and forfeits his life? Or what shall a man give in return for his life? ²⁷For the Son of man is to come with his angels in the glory of his Father, and then he will repay every man for what he has done. ²⁸Truly, I say to you, there are some standing here who will not taste death before they see the Son of man coming in his kingdom."

The Transfiguration

17 And after six days Jesus took with him Peter and James and John his brother, and led them up a high mountain apart. ²And he was transfigured before them, and his face shone like the sun, and his garments became white as light. ³And behold, there appeared to them Moses and Eli′jah, talking with him. ⁴And Peter said to Jesus, "Lord, it is well that we are here; if you wish, I will make three booths here, one for you and one for Moses and one for Eli′jah." ⁵He was still speaking, when behold, a bright cloud overshadowed them, and a voice from the cloud said, "This is my beloved Son,ʷ with whom I am well pleased; listen to him." ⁶When the disciples heard this, they fell on their faces, and were filled with awe. ⁷But Jesus came and touched them, saying, "Rise, and have no fear." ⁸And when they lifted up their eyes, they saw no one but Jesus only.

9 And as they were coming down the mountain, Jesus commanded them, "Tell no one the vision, until the Son of man is raised from the dead." ¹⁰And the disciples asked him, "Then why do the scribes say that first Eli′jah must come?" ¹¹He replied, "Eli′jah does come, and he is to restore all things; ¹²but I tell you that Eli′jah has already come, and they did not know him, but did to him whatever they pleased. So also the Son of man will

16:24–26: Mt 10:38–39; Lk 14:27; 17:33; Jn 12:25.   **16:27:** Mt 10:33; Lk 12:9; 1 Jn 2:28; Rom 2:6; Rev 22:12.
16:28: Mt 10:23; 1 Cor 16:22; 1 Thess 4:15–18; Rev 1:7; Jas 5:7.   **17:1–9:** Mk 9:2–10; Lk 9:28–36; 2 Pet 1:17–18.
17:1: Mt 26:37; Mk 5:37; 13:3.   **17:5:** Mt 3:17; Is 42:1; Ps 2:7; Jn 12:28.   **17:9:** Mt 8:4; 16:20; Mk 3:12; 5:43; 7:36.
17:10–13: Mk 9:11–13; Mt 11:14; Mal 4:5.   **17:12:** Mt 16:21; 17:22; 20:17; 26:2; Lk 17:25.

16:24 take up his cross: Jesus' challenge follows his first Passion prediction (16:21). He indicates that suffering and self-denial are central to the Christian life (cf. Rom 8:17; Col 1:24; CCC 618). See note on 10:38.

17:1–8 Jesus' Transfiguration confirms his divine Sonship (3:17; 16:16). It also strengthens three early Church leaders (**Peter, James,** and **John**) after Jesus' first Passion prediction (16:21). Being **transfigured before them** (17:2), Jesus unveils his glory, later manifest in his Resurrection and shared by his angels (28:2–3) and Virgin Mother in heaven (Rev 12:1) (CCC 555–56). • The OT background for this event is God's self-revelation to Moses on Mt. Sinai. (1) Both take place on the seventh day (17:1; Ex 24:16); (2) both occur on a mountain (17:1; Ex 24:13, 15); (3) both Jesus and Moses take three companions with them (17:1; Ex 24:1); (4) the faces of both Jesus and Moses shine with God's glory (17:2; Ex 34:29); (5) both involve the glory-cloud of God's Presence; (6) and both events involve God speaking through a heavenly voice (17:5; Ex 24:16). • *Anagogically* (Dionysius, *The Divine Names* 1.4), the glory that shone around the disciples on the Mount of Transfiguration prefigures the contemplation of God in eternity, when the minds of the saints will be for ever lifted up from lower concerns and engulfed in the blazing light of the Trinity.

17:3 Moses and Elijah: The two OT representatives of the Law and prophets (cf. 5:17; 7:12). They are the only OT figures to hear God's voice atop Mt. Sinai, also called Horeb (Ex 24:18; 1 Kings 19:8–18). They here witness to the surpassing glory of Jesus as the lawgiver and prophet of the New Covenant (cf. Jn 5:39; Rev 11:3–6).

17:4 I will make three booths: Peter desires to prolong the heavenly experience. The booths are small, tentlike shelters erected yearly at the Jewish Feast of Booths (Lev 23:39–43). This liturgical feast became an early Church symbol of the ongoing joys of heaven (cf. Rev 7:9–10).

17:5 beloved Son . . . listen to him: A similar proclamation was made at Jesus' baptism (3:17; cf. Is 42:1). • The final statement, "listen to him," evokes Deut 18:15. In context, God promised that a prophet like Moses (Messiah) would come to Israel to be heeded by his people (cf. Acts 3:20–22). See note on 2:16.

17:6 fell on their faces: The posture of those overwhelmed by God's glory (Gen 17:3; Ezek 1:28; Rev 1:17).

17:11 to restore all things: e.g., family relationships (Mal 4:5-6) and the 12 tribes of Israel (Sir 48:10).

17:12 Elijah has already come: The "scribes" (17:10) were correct in their teaching and expectation (Mal 4:5) but wrong

ᵛ Greek *stumbling block*.   ʷ Or *my Son, my* (or *the*) *Beloved.*

WORD STUDY

Peter (16:18)

Petros (Gk.): A masculine noun meaning "rock" or "stone". Although a common word in Greek, there is no evidence that *Peter* was ever a proper name before Jesus renamed Simon. This accentuates the symbolism of the name: Simon is himself the rock upon which Jesus builds the Church. Further NT evidence suggests that Jesus' words to Peter were originally spoken in Aramaic. In this language, the word *kepha* is the equivalent of *Peter* and denotes a "sizeable rock"—one suitable as a building foundation. This Aramaic name is preserved as "Cephas" 9 times in the NT (Jn 1:42; 1 Cor 1:12; 15:5; Gal 1:18; 2:9, etc.). At another level, Simon's name change recalls the OT episodes where God renamed Abram as Abraham (Gen 17:5) and Jacob as Israel (Gen 32:28). Peter now stands in this biblical tradition where new names signify new God-given roles in salvation history. In Peter's case, Jesus designates him the foundation stone of the New Covenant Church. Just as the Temples of the OT were built upon a great stone (1 Kings 5:17; Ezra 3:10), so Jesus builds his NT Church upon the foundational rock of Peter (cf. Eph 2:20; Rev 21:14).

suffer at their hands." [13]Then the disciples understood that he was speaking to them of John the Baptist.

Jesus Cures a Boy with a Demon

14 And when they came to the crowd, a man came up to him and kneeling before him said, [15]"Lord, have mercy on my son, for he is an epileptic and he suffers terribly; for often he falls into the fire, and often into the water. [16]And I brought him to your disciples, and they could not heal him." [17]And Jesus answered, "O faithless and perverse generation, how long am I to be with you? How long am I to bear with you? Bring him here to me." [18]And Jesus rebuked him, and the demon came out of him, and the boy was cured instantly. [19]Then the disciples came to Jesus privately and said, "Why could we not cast it out?" [20]He said to them, "Because of your little faith. For truly, I say to you, if you have faith as a grain of mustard seed, you will say to this mountain, 'Move from here to there,' and it will move; and nothing will be impossible to you." [x]

Jesus Again Foretells His Death and Resurrection

22 As they were gathering [y] in Galilee, Jesus said to them, "The Son of man is to be delivered into the hands of men, [23]and they will kill him, and he will be raised on the third day." And they were greatly distressed.

Jesus and the Temple Tax

24 When they came to Caper′na-um, the collectors of the half-shekel tax went up to Peter and said, "Does not your teacher pay the tax?" [25]He said, "Yes." And when he came home, Jesus spoke to him first, saying, "What do you think, Simon? From whom do kings of the earth take toll or tribute? From their sons or from others?" [26]And when he said, "From others," Jesus said to him, "Then the sons are free. [27]However, not to give offense to them, go to the sea and cast a hook, and take the first fish that comes up, and when you open its mouth you will find a shekel; take that and give it to them for me and for yourself."

True Greatness

18 At that time the disciples came to Jesus, saying, "Who is the greatest in the kingdom of heaven?" [2]And calling to him a child, he put him in the midst of them, [3]and said, "Truly, I say to you, unless you turn and become like children, you will never enter the kingdom of heaven. [4]Whoever humbles himself like this child, he is the greatest in the kingdom of heaven.

Temptations to Sin

5 "Whoever receives one such child in my name receives me; [6]but whoever causes one of these little ones who believe in me to sin,[z] it would be better for him to have a great millstone fastened round his neck and to be drowned in the depth of the sea.

7 "Woe to the world for temptations to sin! [a] For it is necessary that temptations come, but woe to the man by whom the temptation comes! [8]And if your hand or your foot causes you to sin,[z] cut it off and throw it from you; it is better for you to enter life maimed or lame than with two hands or two feet to be thrown into the eternal fire. [9]And if your eye

---

17:14–18: Mk 9:14–27; Lk 9:37–43. **17:19–21:** Mk 9:28–29. **17:20:** Lk 17:6; Mt 21:21; Mk 11:22–23; 1 Cor 13:2; Mk 9:23
17:22–23: Mk 9:30–32; Lk 9:43–45; Mt 16:21; 20:17–19; 26:2. **17:24:** Ex 30:13; 38:26. **17:25:** Rom 13:7; Mt 22:17–21
17:27: Mt 5:29; 18:6–9; Jn 6:61; 1 Cor 8:13. **18:1–5:** Mk 9:33–37; Lk 9:46–48. **18:3:** Mk 10:15; Lk 18:17; 1 Pet 2:2.
18:5: Mt 10:40; Lk 10:16; Jn 13:20. **18:6–9:** Mk 9:42–48; Lk 17:1–2. **18:8–9:** Mt 5:29–30; 17:27.

---

not to recognize Elijah's arrival in John the Baptist (17:13). See note on 11:10.

17:20 your little faith: Jesus challenges the unbelief of his disciples (8:26; 14:31; 16:8). He suggests their attempts to exorcize demons (17:16) were impeded by presumption, since even a small measure of genuine faith can accomplish great things.

17:24 Capernaum: Jesus' hometown during his Galilean ministry (4:13). **the half-shekel tax:** Literally, the *didrachma*, or "two-drachma tax", required annually of all male Jews over 20 years old. Moses levied a similar tax for the services of the Tabernacle (Ex 30:11–16). This was reimplemented with King Joash for Solomon's Temple (2 Chron 24:6), while a comparable "third part of a shekel" was required for the second Temple (Neh 10:32). **went up to Peter:** Matthew's "fourth book" features the primacy of Peter (14:28–33; 16:13–19; 17:1, 4; see outline). Here the tax collectors recognize and approach him as the apostles' spokesman.

17:26 the sons are free: The divine sonship shared by Jesus (natural) and Peter (adoptive) exempts them from Temple taxes. Nevertheless, they submit their New Covenant liberty to the regulations of the Old. In the early Church, believers maintained certain Old Covenant practices to avoid giving "offense" (17:27) to the Jews and in the hope of winning some

to the gospel (Acts 16:3; 21:17–26; Rom 14:13–21; 1 Cor 9:19–23).

17:27 you will find a shekel: A Greek *stater* worth two *didrachma* (17:24). The full shekel thus pays the half-shekel tax for both Jesus and Peter. ● The single payment for both Christ and Peter underscores the spiritual union between Jesus and his vicar on earth (cf. 16:17–19).

18:1–35 The fourth discourse in Matthew (see outline). Jesus teaches about life in the Church, where the greatness of her leaders is measured by humility, service (18:1–14), and boundless mercy (18:21–35).

18:1 Who is the greatest . . . ?: A question prompted by Jesus' favoritism and honor of Peter in the previous episodes (16:17–19; 17:1, 27).

18:3 like children: Total dependence on God is required to enter the **kingdom**. Childlike simplicity is especially demanded of the apostles, who must lead the Church with a spirit of servanthood and humility. All, however, are called to trust the Father for daily provisions (6:25–33) and the graces necessary for salvation (CCC 2785).

18:6 who believe in me: Religious scandal is a stumbling block for others and may even cause some members of the Church to lose their faith (CCC 2284–85). **a great millstone:** A stone so large that donkeys were required to turn it when milling grain (cf. Rev 18:21). This punishment by drowning was often reserved for the worst criminals.

18:8–9 Jesus' severe language underscores the great dangers of sin. See note on 5:29.

---

[x] Other ancient authorities insert verse 21, *"But this kind never comes out except by prayer and fasting"*.   [y] Other ancient authorities read *abode*.
[z] Greek *causes . . . to stumble*.   [a] Greek *stumbling blocks*.

causes you to sin,*z* pluck it out and throw it from you; it is better for you to enter life with one eye than with two eyes to be thrown into the hell *b* of fire.

The Parable of the Lost Sheep

10 "See that you do not despise one of these little ones; for I tell you that in heaven their angels always behold the face of my Father who is in heaven.*c* 12What do you think? If a man has a hundred sheep, and one of them has gone astray, does he not leave the ninety-nine on the mountains and go in search of the one that went astray? 13And if he finds it, truly, I say to you, he rejoices over it more than over the ninety-nine that never went astray. 14So it is not the will of my*d* Father who is in heaven that one of these little ones should perish.

Binding and Loosing of Sins

15 "If your brother sins against you, go and tell him his fault, between you and him alone. If he listens to you, you have gained your brother. 16But if he does not listen, take one or two others along with you, that every word may be confirmed by the evidence of two or three witnesses. 17If he refuses to listen to them, tell it to the church; and if he refuses to listen even to the church, let him be to you as a Gentile and a tax collector. 18Truly, I say to you, whatever you bind on earth shall be bound in heaven, and whatever you loose on earth shall be loosed in heaven. 19Again I say to you, if two of

you agree on earth about anything they ask, it will be done for them by my Father in heaven. 20For where two or three are gathered in my name, there am I in the midst of them."

Repeated Forgiveness

21 Then Peter came up and said to him, "Lord, how often shall my brother sin against me, and I forgive him? As many as seven times?" 22Jesus said to him, "I do not say to you seven times, but seventy times seven.*e*

The Parable of the Unforgiving Servant

23 "Therefore the kingdom of heaven may be compared to a king who wished to settle accounts with his servants. 24When he began the reckoning, one was brought to him who owed him ten thousand talents;*f* 25and as he could not pay, his lord ordered him to be sold, with his wife and children and all that he had, and payment to be made. 26So the servant fell on his knees, imploring him, 'Lord, have patience with me, and I will pay you everything.' 27And out of pity for him the lord of that servant released him and forgave him the debt. 28But that same servant, as he went out, came upon one of his fellow servants who owed him a hundred denarii;*g* and seizing him by the throat he said, 'Pay what you owe.' 29So his fellow servant fell down and pleaded with him, 'Have patience with me, and I will pay you.' 30He refused and went and put him in

---

18:10: Acts 12:11.   18:11: Lk 19:10.   18:12–14: Lk 15:3–7.
18:15–17: Lk 17:3; 1 Cor 6:1–6; Gal 6:1; Jas 5:19–20; Lev 19:17; Deut 19:15.   18:18: Mt 16:19; Jn 20:23.
18:19–20: Mt 7:7; 21:22; Jas 1:5–7; 1 Jn 5:14; Jn 14:13.   18:21–22: Lk 17:4; Gen 4:24.   18:23: Mt 25:19:18:25: Lk 7:42.
18:26: Mt 8:2.

18:10 their angels: Scripture portrays God's angels as protectors, guides, and helpers of his people (Tob 12:15; Job 33:23–24; Ps 34:7; 91:11; Acts 12:15; Heb 1:14). The elect angels already participate in glory as they **behold the face** of God in heaven (CCC 329, 336). • This verse is traditionally cited as biblical evidence for guardian angels. Several Church Fathers teach that God assigns everyone an angel to watch over him throughout life.

18:12 a hundred sheep: Jesus is often described as a shepherd (25:32; Jn 10:1–18; 1 Pet 2:25). • This parable alludes to the messianic prophecy of Ezek 34:11–31. In context, Ezekiel foretells that God himself would assume the role of a shepherd to seek out and rescue the lost sheep of his fold. • *Allegorically* (St. Hilary, St. Anselm), the lost sheep represent mankind, who went astray in sin. The 99 on the hills are the angels in heaven. In the Incarnation, Christ temporarily descended from the hills to seek the lost souls of men (cf. 15:24; Lk 19:10); through the redemption, Christ restores men to grace and raises them again to the company of the angels (cf. Heb 12:22).

18:15–20 Church discipline is a serious matter for her leaders. Jesus outlines a three-step procedure by (**1**) privately confronting the sinner, (**2**) addressing the sin before a circle of witnesses, and (**3**) bringing the matter before the Church. Emphasis is placed on reconciliation. If the member resists correction, the Church's leaders (apostles and successors) may exercise Christ's authority by disciplining the impenitent. This final decision is backed even by the Father (18:19) (CCC 1463).

18:16 two or three witnesses: Criteria for judicial testimony in Old Covenant Israel (Deut 19:15). Jesus' language reinforces the Church's identity as the restored Israel of the New Covenant (Gal 6:16; cf. 2 Cor 13:1). See note on 5:14.

18:17 the church: Mentioned only here and 16:18 in the Gospels. Whereas 16:18 envisions Peter's authority over the universal Church, this verse pertains to a local congregation of Christians. **Gentile . . . tax collector:** Two groups generally despised by first-century Jews. The choice of these terms suggest that Jesus requires a policy of non-association with those who are disciplined by leaders of the Church (cf. 1 Cor 5:9–13; 2 Cor 6:14–15).

18:18 whatever you bind . . . loose: In 16:19, Peter was invested with Christ's authority as the visible head of the Church. A derivative—but subordinate—authority is given also to the apostles as royal ministers in the kingdom. Jesus' authority in this context is related to Church discipline; by extension, it is also a sacramental authority to forgive sins (cf. Jn 20:23; CCC 553, 1444). See notes on 9:8 and 16:19.

18:22 seventy times seven: Denotes limitless forgiveness and mercy. • Jesus contrasts the behavior expected of the apostles with the boundless vengeance of Lamech in Gen 4:24 (LXX), where the same figures of "seven" and "seventy times seven" are contrasted (CCC 982).

18:24 ten thousand talents: A "talent" (coin) is equivalent to 6,000 denarii, or 20 years' wages for a laborer. The figure is exaggerated for emphasis: the parable accentuates the king's (God's) mercy in forgiving an incalculable debt that was impossible for the servant (man) to repay.

18:28 a hundred denarii: A minor debt, since a "denarius" was equivalent to a single day's wage for a laborer (cf. 20:2). Repayment of 100 days' wages required patience (18:29) but was not impossible.

---

b Greek *Gehenna.*
c Other ancient authorities add verse 11, *For the Son of man came to save the lost.*
d Other ancient authorities omit *your.*
e Or *seventy-seven times.*
f This talent was more than fifteen years' wages of a laborer.
g This denarius was a day's wage for a laborer.

prison till he should pay the debt. [31]When his fellow servants saw what had taken place, they were greatly distressed, and they went and reported to their lord all that had taken place. [32]Then his lord summoned him and said to him, 'You wicked servant! I forgave you all that debt because you pleaded with me; [33]and should not you have had mercy on your fellow servant, as I had mercy on you?' [34]And in anger his lord delivered him to the jailers,[h] till he should pay all his debt. [35]So also my heavenly Father will do to every one of you, if you do not forgive your brother from your heart."

Teaching about Divorce

19 Now when Jesus had finished these sayings, he went away from Galilee and entered the region of Judea beyond the Jordan; [2]and large crowds followed him, and he healed them there.

3 And Pharisees came up to him and tested him by asking, "Is it lawful to divorce one's wife for any cause?" [4]He answered, "Have you not read that he who made them from the beginning made them male and female, [5]and said, 'For this reason a man shall leave his father and mother and be joined to his wife, and the two shall become one'?[i] [6]So they

are no longer two but one.[i] What therefore God has joined together, let no man put asunder." [7]They said to him, "Why then did Moses command one to give a certificate of divorce, and to put her away?" [8]He said to them, "For your hardness of heart Moses allowed you to divorce your wives, but from the beginning it was not so. [9]And I say to you: whoever divorces his wife, except for unchastity,[j] and marries another, commits adultery; and he who marries a divorced woman, commits adultery." [k]

10 The disciples said to him, "If such is the case of a man with his wife, it is not expedient to marry." [11]But he said to them, "Not all men can receive this precept, but only those to whom it is given. [12]For there are eunuchs who have been so from birth, and there are eunuchs who have been made eunuchs by men, and there are eunuchs who have made themselves eunuchs for the sake of the kingdom of heaven. He who is able to receive this, let him receive it."

Jesus Blesses Little Children

13 Then children were brought to him that he might lay his hands on them and pray. The disciples rebuked the people; [14]but Jesus said, "Let the

---

18:35: Mt 6:14.   **19:1:** Mt 7:28; 11:1; 13:53; 26:1.   **19:1–9:** Mk 10:1–12.   **19:5:** Gen 1:27; 2:24; Eph 5:31; 1 Cor 6:16.   **19:7:** Deut 24:1–4.   **19:9:** Mt 5:32; Lk 16:18; 1 Cor 7:10–13.   **19:11:** 1 Cor 7:7–9.   **19:13–15:** Mk 10:13–16; Lk 18:15–17; Mt 18:2–3; 1 Cor 14:20.

18:35 forgive your brother: Jesus demonstrates the folly of mercilessness. One forgiven an eternal debt of sin should readily forgive others of much smaller debts. The lesson is summarized in Jesus' commentary on the Our Father in 6:14–15 (cf. Jas 2:13; CCC 2842–43).

19:1 Judea beyond the Jordan: Marks a geographical shift. Since 4:12, Jesus ministered in Galilee (4:23–25), and his presence here is only brief and transitional—he is advancing toward Jerusalem. This location is linked with the ministry of John the Baptist, who was executed for condemning the divorce and remarriage of Herod Antipas and his mistress, Herodias (3:5; Lk 3:3). This tragedy looms in the background when the Pharisees ask the leading question about divorce (19:3)—a trap in disguise—i.e., they want Jesus to incriminate himself against Herod and reap the same fatal consequences that John did. The fact that this is also the region where Moses promulgated the Deuteronomic laws that once permitted divorce and remarriage (Deut 24:1–4) suggests that Jesus seized the opportunity to nullify these legal concessions near the place beyond the Jordan where Moses first ratified them (Deut 1:5).

19:3–9 Jesus forbids divorce and remarriage (Mk 10:11–12; Lk 16:18) and revokes the lower standard of the Old Law permitting divorce for non-Levitical laymen in Israel (Deut 24:1–4). Jesus thus restores marriage to its original integrity (Gen 2:24) and elevates it to a New Covenant sacrament (Eph 5:22–33; CCC 2382).

19:3 Pharisees . . . tested him: Could also be translated "tempted him" (4:1). Resolved to destroy him (12:14), the Pharisees hope to ensnare Jesus with a question (cf. 22:15; Jn 8:6). They want him to offend Herod Antipas for his divorce and unlawful remarriage to Herodias. They question him "beyond the Jordan" (19:1), fully aware that it lies within the jurisdiction of Antipas (Perea). See note on 14:4. **for any cause:** A trap question. If Jesus answers "Yes", he will discredit himself

for a lax interpretation of the Law (i.e., Deut 24:1–4). If he answers "No", he will insult Herod Antipas and suffer the same fate as John the Baptist (14:9–11). Some suggest the Pharisees wish Jesus to resolve a debate between the rabbinic schools of Hillel and Shammai over the grounds for divorce in Deut 24:1. This is doubtful; taking sides on an intramural dispute among Pharisees would not constitute a trap. Regardless, Jesus advocates lifelong monogamy (19:9) and sides with neither rabbinic school.

19:4 Have you not read?: A counterquestion frequently posed by Jesus to his learned adversaries (i.e., Pharisees and Sadducees). See note on 12:3.

19:6 God has joined together: Citing Gen 2:24 (19:5), Jesus reaffirms that marriage is God's creation, not man's invention. Since God forges the indissoluble bond that unites a married couple, it follows that no civil or religious authority has the power to break it (CCC 1603, 1640). See note on 1 Cor 7:15.

19:9 And I say to you: Jesus invokes his own authority to forbid divorce and remarriage. Matthew's account reflects Jewish cultural conditions, where men alone had the right to divorce (cf. 5:32). Mark more fully records Jesus' statement that both men and women are forbidden to divorce and remarry (Mk 10:11–12; CCC 1614, 2382). See essay: *Jesus on Marriage and Divorce* at Mt 19.

19:10 not expedient to marry: The disciples marvel that Jesus prohibits divorce and remarriage in the New Covenant (19:9), reversing the long-standing permission of the Old (Deut 24:1–4). Their incredulous response makes it certain that Jesus permitted no exceptions for husbands and wives bound together by the sacrament. This new and higher standard leads them to see the comparative superiority of lifelong virginity to married life (CCC 1615).

19:12 eunuchs: i.e., royal servants in charge of a king's wives. To safeguard against sexual temptations, eunuchs in the ancient Near East were either impotent or physically castrated. Jesus speaks metaphorically: those who have **made themselves eunuchs** are those who voluntarily embrace celibacy in imitation of Jesus and for service in his **kingdom**. These men are leaders entrusted with the care of Christ's bride, the

---

[h] Greek *torturers.*   [i] Greek *one flesh.*
[j] Other ancient authorities, after *unchastity*, read *makes her commit adultery.*
[k] Other ancient authorities omit *and he who marries a divorced woman, commits adultery.*

Jesus on Marriage and Divorce

SINCE the dawn of creation, God designed marriage to be permanent, exclusive, and fruitful (Gen 1:28; 2:24; Mt 19:5). However, since man's rebellion against God, the institution of marriage has suffered many distortions that tarnished its God-given beauty. Moses permitted divorce and remarriage as a concession to the sinfulness of Israel under the Old Covenant (Deut 24:1–4). Even so, it was ultimately clear that divorce falls short of God's will and plan for married couples (cf. Mal 2:16).

This leads to an important question: Does Jesus reaffirm the permission of divorce stipulated in Deut 24:1–4, or, rather, does he revoke this concession and announce the indissolubility of marriage for the New Covenant? The Catholic Church has consistently maintained that Jesus forbids divorce and remarriage. The bond that unites a couple in the sacrament of matrimony is created by God (Mt 19:6) and can be dissolved only by the death of one of the spouses (cf. Rom 7:1–3). For men or women to remarry while their spouse is living is to commit adultery (Mt 19:9; Rom 7:3).

Jesus' teaching on marriage, divorce, and remarriage is unfortunately a source of controversy among Christians. Much confusion swirls around his statement in Mt 19:9: "Whoever divorces his wife, *except for unchastity*, and marries another, commits adultery" (cf. Mt 5:32). Does Jesus really make an "exception" to allow for divorce and remarriage? Since the rise of Protestantism in the sixteenth century, many non-Catholic groups have answered "yes". They began to appeal to this "exception clause" to justify divorce and remarriage in extreme circumstances. However, this view fails to interpret Jesus' statement in light of its immediate, biblical context. The disciples' response to Jesus' statement on divorce ("it is not expedient to marry" [19:11]) demonstrates that, in their understanding, Jesus was leaving no room at all for divorce and remarriage. In fact, they viewed celibacy as a preferable alternative to marriage precisely because Jesus' teaching on this matter is so strict—far more so than that of any of his Jewish contemporaries. The disciples' incredulous response to Jesus thus confirms the Catholic Church's constant teaching on the indissolubility of sacramental marriage.

The question, however, still remains: What did Jesus mean when he qualified his teaching on divorce with the phrase "except for unchastity"(19:9)? Three interpretive options have been offered in Catholic tradition to clarify the meaning of this "exception clause". All of them reinforce the harmony between Jesus' revolutionary teaching and the unchanging position of the Catholic Church.

1. Patristic View: Several Church Fathers suggest Jesus allowed for divorce in cases of serious sexual sin like adultery, but he never permitted remarriage. The spouses may separate in these circumstances by a legal arrangement of living apart, but they cannot break the marriage bond, and they are not free to remarry. This view finds support by a consideration of the Greek word *porneia*, translated "unchastity", in Mt 19:9. While the word has a broad range of meaning, it can mean "adultery", as in the Greek OT (also translated "harlotry"; Sir 23:23; Ezek 16:33; Hos 2:2). Thus, an adulterous situation may give cause for separation so long as the spouses do not embark upon a second marriage. This squares with St. Paul's teaching that a separated couple has only two options: be reconciled to one another, or remain single (1 Cor 7:10–11).

2. Levitical Law View: This position interprets "unchastity" in Mt 19:9 as invalid marriages where the spouses are too closely related. Thus, "except for unchastity" (Mt 19:9) means "except where unlawful unions exist". Such unions ought to be severed because of the impediment posed by near blood-relations. A divorce under these conditions does not sunder a true marriage bond because a valid marriage never existed. It is equivalent to an annulment. This view is supported by two NT instances where *porneia* refers to incest. In Acts 15:20, 29, the apostles charge Gentile Christians to abstain from blood and unchastity. The OT background for this decision in Lev 18:6–18 suggests *unchastity* refers to prohibited marriages between closely related kinsfolk. In 1 Cor 5:1–2 (translated "immorality"), *porneia* clearly refers to an illicit union of a man and his father's wife.

3. "No Comment" View: According to this position, Jesus sets aside Jewish debates over the grounds for divorce in the Old Covenant (Deut 24). Because Jesus is revoking the OT concession on divorce, he brackets the whole issue and sets it off to the side as irrelevant. Thus, "except for unchastity" (Mt 19:9) means "regardless of the OT grounds for divorce". Jesus refuses even to comment on Deut 24:1. To do so would blunt the force of his own teaching, since he is not clarifying or reaffirming Moses' permission, he is abolishing it.

Each of these views faithfully upholds Jesus' prohibition against divorce and remarriage (cf. Mk 10:11, 12; Lk 16:18). He restores marriage to its original purity as a lifelong union of love and fidelity. Greater still, Jesus elevates marriage, transforming it into a New Covenant sacrament. Married couples are now called to be an image of Christ and his enduring love for the Church (Eph 5:21–33; cf. Rev 19:6–8). Through the sound principles of biblical interpretation and the guidance of tradition, the revolutionary standard of Jesus' teaching on marriage and divorce is preserved intact in his Church. «

children come to me, and do not hinder them; for to such belongs the kingdom of heaven." ¹⁵And he laid his hands on them and went away.

The Rich Young Man

16 And behold, one came up to him, saying, "Teacher, what good deed must I do, to have eternal life?" ¹⁷And he said to him, "Why do you ask me about what is good? One there is who is good. If you would enter life, keep the commandments." ¹⁸He said to him, "Which?" And Jesus said, "You shall not kill, You shall not commit adultery, You shall not steal, You shall not bear false witness, ¹⁹Honor your father and mother, and, You shall love your neighbor as yourself." ²⁰The young man said to him, "All these I have observed; what do I still lack?" ²¹Jesus said to him, "If you would be perfect, go, sell what you possess and give to the poor, and you will have treasure in heaven; and come, follow me." ²²When the young man heard this he went away sorrowful; for he had great possessions.

23 And Jesus said to his disciples, "Truly, I say to you, it will be hard for a rich man to enter the kingdom of heaven. ²⁴Again I tell you, it is easier for a camel to go through the eye of a needle than for a rich man to enter the kingdom of God." ²⁵When the disciples heard this they were greatly astonished, saying, "Who then can be saved?" ²⁶But Jesus looked at them and said to them, "With men this is impossible, but with God all things are pos-

sible." ²⁷Then Peter said in reply, "Behold, we have left everything and followed you. What then shall we have?" ²⁸Jesus said to them, "Truly, I say to you, in the new world, when the Son of man shall sit on his glorious throne, you who have followed me will also sit on twelve thrones, judging the twelve tribes of Israel. ²⁹And every one who has left houses or brothers or sisters or father or mother or children or lands, for my name's sake, will receive a hundredfold,ᶦ and inherit eternal life. ³⁰But many that are first will be last, and the last first.

The Laborers in the Vineyard

20 "For the kingdom of heaven is like a householder who went out early in the morning to hire laborers for his vineyard. ²After agreeing with the laborers for a denariusᵐ a day, he sent them into his vineyard. ³And going out about the third hour he saw others standing idle in the market place; ⁴and to them he said, 'You go into the vineyard too, and whatever is right I will give you.' So they went. ⁵Going out again about the sixth hour and the ninth hour, he did the same. ⁶And about the eleventh hour he went out and found others standing; and he said to them, 'Why do you stand here idle all day?' ⁷They said to him, 'Because no one has hired us.' He said to them, 'You go into the vineyard too.' ⁸And when evening came, the owner of the vineyard said to his steward, 'Call the laborers and pay them their wages, beginning with the last, up

---

19:16–22: Mk 10:17–22; Lk 18:18–23. **19:16:** Lk 10:25; Lev 18:5. **19:18:** Ex 20:12–16; Deut 5:16–20; Rom 13:9; Jas 2:11. **19:19:** Lev 19:18; Mt 22:39. **19:21:** Lk 12:33; Acts 2:45; 4:34; Mt 6:20. **19:23–26:** Mk 10:23–27; Lk 18:24–27. **19:26:** Gen 18:14; Job 42:2. **19:27–30:** Mk 10:28–31; Lk 18:28–30; Mt 4:18–22. **19:28:** Lk 22:30; Mt 20:21; Rev 3:21. **19:30:** Mt 20:16; Lk 13:30. **20:1:** Mt 21:28, 33. **20:8:** Lev 19:13; Deut 24:15.

Church on earth; embracing consecrated virginity, they live by anticipation the life of heaven (22:30). See note on 9:15. ● The Council of Trent (Sess. 24, can. 10) teaches in accord with Scripture that the objective state of celibacy is higher than the married state, although both vocations are important for the Church's life (1 Cor 7:1–8, 32–35; Rev 14:4; CCC 1618–20).

19:14 the children: Jesus' concern for marriage (19:9) reflects a practical concern for children. God's plan for marriage includes the mutual love of spouses and the responsible upbringing of "Godly offspring" (Mal 2:15; CCC 1646, 1652). In this episode, Jesus blesses children as legitimate members of the **kingdom**, laying a foundation for infant Baptism (cf. Jn 3:5). See note on Lk 18:16.

19:24 easier for a camel: A parable of impossibility. Jesus thus warns that extreme difficulties face the rich and threaten their entrance into the **kingdom**. Only with God's help (19:26) can the wealthy detach themselves from the love of money and material possessions (5:3; 1 Tim 6:9-10; Jas 5:1-6). The young man's refusal (19:22) to embrace poverty proves Jesus' point (CCC 2053).

19:28 the new world: The Greek could be rendered "regeneration" as in Tit 3:5. The historian Josephus uses this expression with reference to Israel's "restoration" after the Exile. This latter connotation is closest to Jesus' meaning here, where the establishment of the universal Church includes the reestablishment of Israel under the leadership of the Twelve. **on twelve thrones:** Jesus portrays the Church as the restored kingdom of Israel (cf. Rev 7:4-8). As the royal son of David (1:1), he recon-

stitutes the Davidic empire that governed the 12 tribes (2 Sam 5:1-5) along with other nations (2 Sam 8:1-15; 1 Kings 4:20-21). He thus appoints the apostles to his royal cabinet and invests them with authority to minister and judge in the new kingdom (Lk 22:28-30). ● Jesus' language recalls Ps 122:3-5. In context, Jerusalem is the city where the thrones of the Davidic kingdom stood and where Israel's tribes went to find justice. In the New Covenant, Christ imparts justice through his apostles in the liturgy of the heavenly Jerusalem (cf. Heb 12:22-24; Rev 21:1-14; CCC 551, 765). See notes on 5:14 and 10:2.

20:1–16 The parable of the Householder highlights God's generosity (20:15). It refers to Israel's labor throughout salvation history and climaxes with the inclusion of the Gentiles in the New Covenant. Despite complaints, there is no violation of justice; God is not unfair to Israel, he is simply generous to late-coming Gentiles, making them equal members of his people (20:12; Eph 2:11–13). ● *Morally* (Origen), the hours of the workday correspond to stages in life when people turn to God. When converted, they are rescued from idle living to serve Christ in his vineyard, where they harvest much fruit for God before the sun sets on their earthly life. Whether converted early in life or later, all are awarded the generous and equal gift of eternal life.

20:1 early in the morning: The day was divided into four nighttime "watches" and several daytime "hours" (6 A.M. to 6 P.M.). The early laborers begin around 6 A.M., and those hired at the "third" (9 A.M.; 20:3), "sixth" (noon; 20:5), and "ninth" (3 P.M.; 20:5) hours each agree to a fair wage. The group hired at the "eleventh hour" (5 P.M.; 20:6) only work about one hour since the Law commanded that workers receive their wages by sundown (Deut 24:14–15).

ᶦ Other ancient authorities read *manifold*.
ᵐ The denarius was a day's wage for a laborer.

to the first.' [9]And when those hired about the eleventh hour came, each of them received a denarius. [10]Now when the first came, they thought they would receive more; but each of them also received a denarius. [11]And on receiving it they grumbled at the householder, [12]saying, 'These last worked only one hour, and you have made them equal to us who have borne the burden of the day and the scorching heat.' [13]But he replied to one of them, 'Friend, I am doing you no wrong; did you not agree with me for a denarius? [14]Take what belongs to you, and go; I choose to give to this last as I give to you. [15]Am I not allowed to do what I choose with what belongs to me? Or do you begrudge my generosity?' [n] [16]So the last will be first, and the first last."

A Third Time Jesus Foretells
His Death and Resurrection

17 And as Jesus was going up to Jerusalem, he took the twelve disciples aside, and on the way he said to them, [18]"Behold, we are going up to Jerusalem; and the Son of man will be delivered to the chief priests and scribes, and they will condemn him to death, [19]and deliver him to the Gentiles to be mocked and scourged and crucified, and he will be raised on the third day."

The Request of the Mother
of James and John

20 Then the mother of the sons of Zeb'edee came up to him, with her sons, and kneeling before him she asked him for something. [21]And he said to her, "What do you want?" She said to him, "Command that these two sons of mine may sit, one at your right hand and one at your left, in your kingdom." [22]But Jesus answered, "You do not know what you are asking. Are you able to drink the cup that I am to drink?" They said to him, "We are able." [23]He said to them, "You will drink my cup, but to sit at my right hand and at my left is not mine to grant, but it is for those for whom it has been prepared by my Father." [24]And when the ten heard it, they were indignant at the two brothers. [25]But Jesus called them to him and said, "You know that the rulers of the Gentiles lord it over them, and their great men exercise authority over them. [26]It shall not be so among you; but whoever would be great among you must be your servant, [27]and whoever would be first among you must be your slave; [28]even as the Son of man came not to be served but to serve, and to give his life as a ransom for many."

Jesus Heals Two Blind Men

29 And as they went out of Jericho, a great crowd followed him. [30]And behold, two blind men sitting by the roadside, when they heard that Jesus was passing by, cried out,[o] "Have mercy on us, Son of David!" [31]The crowd rebuked them, telling them to be silent; but they cried out the more, "Lord, have mercy on us, Son of David!" [32]And Jesus stopped and called them, saying, "What do you want me to do for you?" [33]They said to him, "Lord, let our eyes be opened." [34]And Jesus in pity touched their eyes, and immediately they received their sight and followed him.

Jesus' Triumphal Entry into Jerusalem

21 And when they drew near to Jerusalem and came to Beth'phage, to the Mount of Olives, then Jesus sent two disciples, [2]saying to them, "Go into the village opposite you, and immediately you will find a donkey tied, and a colt with her; untie them and bring them to me. [3]If any one says anything to you, you shall say, 'The Lord has need of

---

20:13: Mt 22:12; 26:50.　**20:15:** Mt 6:23; Mk 7:22; Deut 15:9.　**20:16:** Lk 13:30; Mt 19:30; Mk 10:31.
20:17–19: Mk 10:32–34; Lk 18:31–34; Mt 16:21; 17:12, 22–23; 26:2.　**20:20–24:** Mk 10:35–41.
20:20: Mt 8:2; 9:18; 15:25; 18:26; Jn 9:38.　**20:21:** Mt 19:28.　**20:22:** Mt 26:39; Jn 18:11.　**20:23:** Acts 12:2; Rev 1:9; Mt 13:11
20:25–28: Mk 10:42–45; Lk 22:25–27.　**20:26:** Mt 23:11; Mk 9:35; Lk 9:48.
20:28: Mt 26:28; 1 Tim 2:5–6; Jn 13:15–16; Tit 2:14; 1 Pet 1:18.　**20:29–34:** Mk 10:46–52; Lk 18:35–43; Mt 9:27–31.
21:1–9: Mk 11:1–10; Lk 19:29–38; Jn 12:12–18.

20:2 a denarius: A standard daily wage. See note on 18:28.

20:17–19 Jesus' third Passion prediction is detailed. Unlike in the previous ones (16:21; 17:22–23), he foresees the collaboration of Jewish leaders (20:18) with Roman authorities (20:19) in bringing about his death by means of crucifixion (20:19).

20:20 the sons of Zebedee: James and John (4:21). Along with Peter, they form a privileged inner circle of Jesus' disciples (17:1; 26:37; Mk 5:37).

20:22 drink the cup: An OT metaphor that describes God's wrath poured upon the wicked (Ps 75:8; Is 51:17; Jer 25:15). Here it denotes Jesus' Passion endured for sinners (20:28; 26:39; 1 Pet 2:24). James and John are assured (20:23) a share in this Passion, a prediction partially fulfilled with the martyrdom of James in Acts 12:2.

20:30 two blind men: One of them was Bartimaeus the son of Timaeus (Mk 10:46). **Son of David:** The title may reflect an early belief that the Messiah would possess powers of healing

and exorcism, as did the original son of David, King Solomon. See note on 12:23.

21:1–22 The first actions of Jesus during Passion Week—the triumphal entry (21:1–11), the cleansing of the temple (21:12–17), and the cursing of the fig tree (21:18–22)—are all symbolic gestures. Jesus performs them as prophetic acts to demonstrate that he is the Messiah and that his coming marks the end of the Old Covenant. This provokes Jerusalem's leadership to conspire and have him crucified (26:3–4; 27:1–2; CCC 559–60).

21:1–11 Jesus' triumphal entry recalls Solomon's coronation as king of Israel. ● **(1)** Jesus and Solomon are both the "Son of David" (21:9, 15; Prov 1:1). **(2)** Jesus rides a colt into Jerusalem (21:7) as Solomon rode David's mule into the city (1 Kings 1:32–40). **(3)** Both processions involve a great crowd celebrating the investiture of a new king (21:8–9: 1 Kings 1:39–40). **(4)** In both instances, Jerusalem was in a state of commotion (21:10: 1 Kings 1:45). Similar celebrations are recounted in 1 Mac 13:51 and 2 Mac 10:6–7.

21:1 Bethphage: A small village of an uncertain location but clearly on the **Mount of Olives,** east of Jerusalem. Its Hebrew name means "house of figs".

---

[n] Or *is your eye evil because I am good?*
[o] Other ancient authorities insert *Lord.*

them,' and he will send them immediately." ⁴This took place to fulfil what was spoken by the prophet, saying,

⁵ "Tell the daughter of Zion,
    Behold, your king is coming to you,
    humble, and mounted on a donkey,
    and on a colt, the foal of a donkey."

⁶The disciples went and did as Jesus had directed them; ⁷they brought the donkey and the colt, and put their garments on them, and he sat on them. ⁸Most of the crowd spread their garments on the road, and others cut branches from the trees and spread them on the road. ⁹And the crowds that went before him and that followed him shouted, "Hosanna to the Son of David! Blessed is he who comes in the name of the Lord! Hosanna in the highest!" ¹⁰And when he entered Jerusalem, all the city was stirred, saying, "Who is this?" ¹¹And the crowds said, "This is the prophet Jesus from Nazareth of Galilee."

Jesus Cleanses the Temple

12 And Jesus entered the temple of God ᵖ and drove out all who sold and bought in the temple, and he overturned the tables of the money-changers and the seats of those who sold pigeons. ¹³He said to them, "It is written, 'My house shall be called a house of prayer'; but you make it a den of robbers.'"

14 And the blind and the lame came to him in the temple, and he healed them. ¹⁵But when the chief priests and the scribes saw the wonderful things that he did, and the children crying out in the temple, "Hosanna to the Son of David!" they were indignant; ¹⁶and they said to him, "Do you hear what these are saying?" And Jesus said to them, "Yes; have you never read,

'Out of the mouths of babies and infants
    thou hast brought perfect praise'?"

¹⁷And leaving them, he went out of the city to Bethany and lodged there.

Jesus Curses the Fig Tree

18 In the morning, as he was returning to the city, he was hungry. ¹⁹And seeing a fig tree by the wayside he went to it, and found nothing on it but leaves only. And he said to it, "May no fruit ever come from you again!" And the fig tree withered at once. ²⁰When the disciples saw it they marveled, saying, "How did the fig tree wither at once?" ²¹And Jesus answered them, "Truly, I say to you, if you have faith and never doubt, you will not only do what has been done to the fig tree, but even if you say to this mountain, 'Be taken up and cast into the sea,' it will be done. ²²And whatever you ask in prayer, you will receive, if you have faith."

The Authority of Jesus Questioned

23 And when he entered the temple, the chief priests and the elders of the people came up to him

---

21:5: Is 62:11; Zech 9:9.   **21:8:** 2 Kings 9:13.   **21:9:** Ps 118:26; Lk 2:14; Mt 21:15; 23:39.
21:11: Jn 6:14; 7:40; Acts 3:22; Mk 6:15; Lk 13:33.   **21:12–13:** Mk 11:15–17; Lk 19:45–46; Jn 2:13–17; Ex 30:13; Lev 1:14.
21:13: Is 56:7; Jer 7:11.   **21:15:** Lk 19:39; Mt 21:9.   **21:16:** Ps 8:2.   **21:17–19:** Mk 11:11–14; Lk 13:6–9.
21:20–22: Mk 11:20–24.   **21:21:** Mt 17:20; Lk 17:6; 1 Cor 13:2; Jas 1:6.   **21:22:** Jn 14:13–14; 16:23.
21:23–27: Mk 11:27–33; Lk 20:1–8; Jn 2:18–22

21:5 A combined reference to Is 62:11 and Zech 9:9. • The emphasis of this citation is twofold: (1) Isaiah's prophecy, only partially cited, speaks of a highway to Jerusalem when the Lord declares, "Behold, your salvation comes." The similar wording of Zechariah's prophecy connects this salvation with the coming **king**. (2) The uniqueness of this king is his lowliness and humility; he rides a peaceful **donkey** rather than a "war horse" (Zech 9:10).

21:7 he sat on them: Matthew alone mentions a **donkey** and a **colt** (cf. Mk 11:7; Lk 19:35). That Jesus *sat on them* refers either to the **garments** or indicates that he rode both beasts successively. • *Allegorically* (St. Jerome, *Homily* 81), the two beasts are the nations that Christ brings under his Lordship. The donkey signifies Israel in its long-standing covenant with God; the colt is the younger Gentiles, unfamiliar with God and his Law. Jesus ushers them together into the Church of the heavenly Jerusalem (Gal 4:26; Heb 12:22).

21:8 spread their garments: An expression of homage for a new king. • Similarly in 2 Kings 9:13, garments were laid on the ground for Jehu when he was hailed the king of Israel. See note on Mk 11:8.

21:9 Hosanna: A Hebrew acclamation meaning "Save us" (cf. 2 Sam 14:4; Ps 118:25). **Blessed is he:** Words from Ps 118:26, the last of the Hallel Psalms (113–18), which were sung as hymns at Israel's great feasts of Passover, Weeks, and Booths.

21:13 a house of prayer: Merchants sold sacrificial animals in the Temple as a service to pilgrims celebrating Passover. However, rates of monetary exchange and inflated prices made the selling a profitable enterprise. By citing Is 56:7, Jesus indicts the merchants for profaning the Temple. The Temple is not a common marketplace but a sanctuary for worship. • In context (Is 56:3–8), Isaiah sees God gathering all nations to his Temple. No longer shall Gentiles be excluded from his covenant people; God will join them to himself. The prophecy looks endangered by the present circumstances—animals are being sold in the Temple's outermost court, the court of the Gentiles. This prevents Gentiles from truly worshiping. Drawing from Isaiah, Jesus charges the establishment with obstructing God's intentions. **a den of robbers:** A citation from Jer 7:11. • In context, Jeremiah delivered a sermon of judgment to Israelites in the Temple. They presumed that the Temple guaranteed the Israelites' security and protection, despite their sinful living (Jer 7:4, 8–10). Because Israel disregarded Jeremiah, God destroyed Solomon's Temple in 586 B.C. Jesus here recalls both the circumstances and outcome of Jeremiah's prophecy: If Israel fails to repent, the Temple will again be destroyed (CCC 584).

21:16 Out of the mouths of babies: A citation from Ps 8:2 (LXX). • In context, the psalm describes infants glorifying the Lord—a point that Jesus uses to hint at his divinity (cf. 11:25).

21:19 a fig tree: A symbol of Old Covenant Israel (Jer 8:13; Hos 9:10). Jesus curses it because it is barren and has no figs (Mk 11:21). Symbolically, then, he announces God's curse on the unfaithful of Israel—i.e., those who refuse him as the Messiah and lack the fruits of repentance (3:8–10; 21:41, 43). Israel's faithlessness is a negative example: the Church must learn from the nation's mistakes and pray instead with faith and confidence (21:21; 17:20; Jas 1:6).

ᵖ Other ancient authorities omit *of God*.

as he was teaching, and said, "By what authority are you doing these things, and who gave you this authority?" [24]Jesus answered them, "I also will ask you a question; and if you tell me the answer, then I also will tell you by what authority I do these things. [25]The baptism of John, where was it from? From heaven or from men?" And they argued with one another, "If we say, 'From heaven,' he will say to us, 'Why then did you not believe him?' [26]But if we say, 'From men,' we are afraid of the multitude; for all hold that John was a prophet." [27]So they answered Jesus, "We do not know." And he said to them, "Neither will I tell you by what authority I do these things.

The Parable of the Two Sons

28 "What do you think? A man had two sons; and he went to the first and said, 'son, go and work in the vineyard today.' [29]And he answered, 'I will not'; but afterward he repented and went. [30]And he went to the second and said the same; and he answered, 'I go, sir,' but did not go. [31]Which of the two did the will of his father?" They said, "The first." Jesus said to them, "Truly, I say to you, the tax collectors and the harlots go into the kingdom of God before you. [32]For John came to you in the way of righteousness, and you did not believe him, but the tax collectors and the harlots believed him; and even when you saw it, you did not afterward repent and believe him.

The Parable of the Wicked Tenants

33 "Hear another parable. There was a householder who planted a vineyard, and set a hedge around it, and dug a wine press in it, and built a tower, and leased it to tenants, and went into another country. [34]When the season of fruit drew near, he sent his servants to the tenants, to get his fruit; [35]and the tenants took his servants and beat one, killed another, and stoned another. [36]Again he sent other servants, more than the first; and they did the same to them. [37]Afterward he sent his son to them, saying, 'They will respect my son.' [38]But when the tenants saw the son, they said to themselves, 'This is the heir; come, let us kill him and have his inheritance.' [39]And they took him and cast him out of the vineyard, and killed him. [40]When therefore the owner of the vineyard comes, what will he do to those tenants?" [41]They said to him, "He will put those wretches to a miserable death, and lease the vineyard to other tenants who will give him the fruits in their seasons."

The Stone Which the Builders Rejected

42 Jesus said to them, "Have you never read in the scriptures:

'The very stone which the builders rejected
has become the head of the corner;
this was the Lord's doing,
and it is marvelous in our eyes'?

[43]Therefore I tell you, the kingdom of God will be taken away from you and given to a nation producing the fruits of it. [44]And he who falls on this stone will be broken to pieces; but when it falls on any one, it will crush him." [q]

45 When the chief priests and the Pharisees heard his parables, they perceived that he was speaking about them. [46]But when they tried to arrest him, they feared the multitudes, because they held him to be a prophet.

The Parable of the Wedding Banquet

22 And again Jesus spoke to them in parables, saying, [2]"The kingdom of heaven may be compared to a king who gave a marriage feast for

---

21:26: Mt 11:9; 14:5; Lk 1:76. **21:28:** Mt 20:1; 21:33. **21:32:** Lk 7:29–30.
21:33–46: Mk 12:1–12; Lk 20:9–19; Is 5:1–7. **21:34:** Mt 22:3. **21:41:** Mt 8:11; Acts 13:46; 18:6; 28:28.
21:42: Ps 118:22–23; Acts 4:11; 1 Pet 2:7. **22:1–10:** Lk 14:16–24.

21:28–32 The parable of the Two Sons explains the preceding question about John the Baptist's authority (21:25). The **sons** (21:28) represent two groups of people: the first are sinners who repent at the preaching of **John** (21:32); the second are Israel's leaders, who refuse the Baptist's message, even when **tax collectors** and **harlots** (21:32) respond to him (Lk 7:29–30). By following John's **way of righteousness** (21:32), the former sinners do the **will** of the **father** (21:31).

21:33–41 The parable of the Wicked Tenants is an allegory–i.e., each of its details is important and symbolic (cf. Is 5:1–2). The **householder** is God (21:33) and the **vineyard** is Jerusalem (21:33). The **tenants** are Israel's leaders (21:33, 45) while the **servants** are OT prophets persecuted for warning Israel of its sins (21:34; cf. 23:37). The **son** is Jesus, who will be thrown **out of the vineyard** and crucified outside the city (21:39; cf. Jn 19:17, 20). Because of the wickedness of the tenants, God will put them to **death** (21:41) when he judges Jerusalem in A.D. 70. He will entrust the New Covenant kingdom to the **other tenants** in the Church (16:17–19; 18:17–19). See note on 24:1.

🔲 **21:42 in the Scriptures:** A reference to Ps 118:22. • Jesus states that he (**stone**) is commissioned by God (**the Lord's doing**), despite his rejection by Jerusalem (**the builders**). Scripture thus foresees that the Messiah will paradoxically meet opposition from the leaders of his own people; conversely, the faithful see in the work of Jesus God's **marvelous** deeds. Psalm 118 is elsewhere cited as biblical support for Jesus' vindication and Resurrection (Acts 4:10–11; 1 Pet 2:7; CCC 756).

21:43 given to a nation: God will transfer his **kingdom** from the leaders of the Old Covenant establishment to the shepherds of the New Covenant Church (19:28; Lk 22:28–30).

22:1–14 The parable of the Marriage Feast is an allegory of salvation history culminating in Jesus. The **king** is God (21:2) who prepares a heavenly banquet for his **son** (21:2). The **servants** are OT prophets (21:3) called to summon Israel (21:3). Because some of the **invited** guests ignored the prophets and others **killed** them (21:6; 23:37), God will destroy **their city**, Jerusalem (21:7), and send other **servants** as apostles (21:8) to invite Gentiles, **bad** and **good** (21:10), to the celebration. Those lacking proper attire are cast into the **darkness** of eternal punishment (21:14). The parable highlights God's impartial treatment of all who are called—Jews and Gentiles. He rewards and punishes on the basis of one's acceptance or rejection of his call (cf. Rom 2:6–11) (CCC 546, 796).

🔲 **22:2 marriage feast:** An image of rejoicing and communion with God. • The background is probably Is 25:6–9,

[q] Other ancient authorities omit verse 44.

his son, ³and sent his servants to call those who were invited to the marriage feast; but they would not come. ⁴Again he sent other servants, saying, 'Tell those who are invited, Behold, I have made ready my dinner, my oxen and my fat calves are killed, and everything is ready; come to the marriage feast.' ⁵But they made light of it and went off, one to his farm, another to his business, ⁶while the rest seized his servants, treated them shamefully, and killed them. ⁷The king was angry, and he sent his troops and destroyed those murderers and burned their city. ⁸Then he said to his servants, 'The wedding is ready, but those invited were not worthy. ⁹Go therefore to the streets, and invite to the marriage feast as many as you find.' ¹⁰And those servants went out into the streets and gathered all whom they found, both bad and good; so the wedding hall was filled with guests.

11 "But when the king came in to look at the guests, he saw there a man who had no wedding garment;¹² and he said to him, 'Friend, how did you get in here without a wedding garment?' And he was speechless. ¹³Then the king said to the attendants, 'Bind him hand and foot, and cast him into the outer darkness; there men will weep and gnash their teeth.' ¹⁴For many are called, but few are chosen."

The Question about Paying Taxes

15 Then the Pharisees went and took counsel how to entangle him in his talk. ¹⁶And they sent their disciples to him, along with the Hero´di-ans, saying, "Teacher, we know that you are true, and teach the way of God truthfully, and care for no man; for you do not regard the position of men. ¹⁷Tell us, then, what you think. Is it lawful to pay taxes to Caesar, or not?" ¹⁸But Jesus, aware of their malice, said, "Why put me to the test, you hypocrites? ¹⁹Show me the money for the tax." And they brought him a coin.ʳ ²⁰And Jesus said to them, "Whose likeness and inscription is this?" ²¹They said, "Caesar's." Then he said to them, "Render therefore to Caesar the things that are Caesar's, and to God the things that are God's." ²²When they heard it, they marveled; and they left him and went away.

The Question about the Resurrection

23 The same day Sad´ducees came to him, who say that there is no resurrection; and they asked him a question, ²⁴saying, "Teacher, Moses said, 'If a man dies, having no children, his brother must marry the widow, and raise up children for his brother.' ²⁵Now there were seven brothers among us; the first married, and died, and having no children left his wife to his brother. ²⁶So too the second and third, down to the seventh. ²⁷After them all, the woman died. ²⁸In the resurrection, therefore, to which of the seven will she be wife? For they all had her."

29 But Jesus answered them, "You are wrong,

22:3: Mt 21:34. **22:10:** Mt 13:47. **22:12:** Mt 20:13; 26:50. **22:13:** Mt 8:12; 13:42, 50; 24:51; 25:30; Lk 13:28. **22:15–22:** Mk 12:13–17; Lk 20:20–26. **22:15:** Mk 3:6; 8:15. **22:21:** Rom 13:7. **22:23–33:** Mk 12:18–27; Lk 20:27–38. **22:23:** Acts 4:1–2; 23:6–10. **22:24:** Deut 25:5.

---

where the salvation of God's people is portrayed as a joyful banquet. Its fulfillment takes shape at two levels: (1) *Present Liturgical*. The Holy Eucharist is Christ's banquet of sacramental food and drink (cf. Jn 6:53–58; 1 Cor 10:16; Rev 19:9). (2) *Future Eschatological*. Ultimate communion with Christ takes place in heaven with the unending union of God and his saints.

22:11 no wedding garment: A symbol of righteous deeds that accompany faith (Rev 19:7–8). These deeds are outlined in Matthew as almsgiving (6:2–4), prayer (6:5–15), fasting (6:16–18), and works of mercy (25:34–40).

22:15–22 The collaboration of the Pharisees and Herodians—representing opposite political views—reveals the extreme measures taken to eliminate Jesus (cf. 12:14; 26:4). Their strategy was to trap him: if Jesus opposed the tax, the Herodians could charge him with treason for instigating a tax revolt against Rome. If Jesus approved of it, the Pharisees would charge him as unfaithful to Judaism and its hopes of national independence.

22:16 their disciples: Jewish nationalists opposed to Rome's occupation and rule over Palestine. See topical essay: *Who Are the Pharisees?* at Mk 2. **Herodians:** Supporters of Roman rule, sympathetic to the Herodian dynasty. See notes on 2:1 and 2:22.

22:19 a coin: A "denarius" stamped with a profile portrait of Tiberius Caesar, the Roman Emperor (A.D. 14–37). This tax was especially offensive to the Jews, who knew that God forbade the fashioning of graven images in the likeness of any created thing (Ex 20:4).

22:21 Caesar's . . . God's: Jesus evades the intended trap (22:17) with a subtle and riddle-like response. His words have several implications. (1) At one level, Jesus plays on the word "likeness" (literally, "image"). Caesar's coins could be given back to him in taxes without religious compromise; after all, he minted the coins with his own image and they were his rightful property. (2) More important, everyone has the duty of giving himself—created in the "image" of God (Gen 1:27)—back to God. Jesus implies that this higher duty is incumbent even upon Caesar. (3) Jesus' response turns his adversaries' trap back on themselves. He reminds them that taxation is the result of their own sins—had Israel been giving God his due, they would not have been subjected to the yoke of Roman rule. (4) In the end, Jesus affirms the propriety of fulfilling civil duties while emphasizing our primary duty of serving God (cf. Rom 13:1–7; 1 Pet 2:13–17; CCC 2242).

22:23 Sadducees: Priestly aristocrats centered mostly in Jerusalem. See topical essay: *Who Are the Sadducees?* at Mk 12. **there is no resurrection:** A denial at odds with mainstream Judaism (cf. Acts 23:8). Their apparent acceptance of the doctrine in 22:28 is only a façade; they hope to stump Jesus with an unanswerable question.

22:24 If a man dies: A hypothetical scenario based on the levirate law of Deut 25:5–6. If a married man dies childless, this law requires one of his brothers to marry the widow and so produce offspring for his older brother (cf. Gen 38:6–8). The seven husbands mentioned (22:26) may allude to the situation in Tob 7:11.

22:30 like angels: Against the Sadducees, Jesus affirms the resurrection (cf. Jn 5:28–29). The event will signal the end of earthly marriage and its purposes (1) to beget children and (2) help spouses advance toward holiness. Life in heaven will no longer require populating the Church and sanctifying spouses. Rather, the righteous will live as angels, who beget no offspring and worship God continually (cf. Is 6:2–3; Rev 5:11, 12).

ʳ Greek *a denarius*.

because you know neither the scriptures nor the power of God. [30]For in the resurrection they neither marry nor are given in marriage, but are like angels [s] in heaven. [31]And as for the resurrection of the dead, have you not read what was said to you by God, [32]'I am the God of Abraham, and the God of Isaac, and the God of Jacob'? He is not God of the dead, but of the living." [33]And when the crowd heard it, they were astonished at his teaching.

The Greatest Commandment

34 But when the Pharisees heard that he had silenced the Sad´ducees, they came together. [35]And one of them, a lawyer, asked him a question, to test him. [36]"Teacher, which is the great commandment in the law?" [37]And he said to him, "You shall love the Lord your God with all your heart, and with all your soul, and with all your mind. [38]This is the great and first commandment. [39]And a second is like it, You shall love your neighbor as yourself. [40]On these two commandments depend all the law and the prophets."

A Question about David's Son

41 Now while the Pharisees were gathered together, Jesus asked them a question, [42]saying, "What do you think of the Christ? Whose son is he?" They said to him, "The son of David." [43]He said to them, "How is it then that David, inspired by the Spirit,[t] calls him Lord, saying,

[44] 'The Lord said to my Lord,
Sit at my right hand,
till I put thy enemies under thy feet'?

[45]If David thus calls him Lord, how is he his son?" [46]And no one was able to answer him a word, nor from that day did any one dare to ask him any more questions.

Jesus Denounces Scribes and Pharisees

23 Then said Jesus to the crowds and to his disciples, [2]"The scribes and the Pharisees sit on Moses' seat; [3]so practice and observe whatever they tell you, but not what they do; for they preach, but do not practice. [4]They bind heavy burdens, hard to bear,[u] and lay them on men's shoulders; but they themselves will not move them with their finger. [5]They do all their deeds to be seen by men; for they make their phylacteries broad and their fringes long, [6]and they love the place of honor at feasts and the best seats in the synagogues, [7]and salutations in the market places, and being called rabbi by men. [8]But you are not to be called rabbi, for you have one teacher, and you are all brethren. [9]And call no man your father on earth, for you have one Father, who is in heaven. [10]Neither be called masters, for you have one master, the Christ. [11]He who is greatest among you shall be your servant; [12]whoever exalts himself will be

---

22:32: Ex 3:6.   22:33: Mt 7:28.   22:34–40: Mk 12:28–34; Lk 20:39–40; 10:25–28.   22:35: Lk 7:30; 11:45; 14:3.
22:37: Deut 6:5.   22:39: Lev 19:18; Mt 19:19; Gal 5:14; Rom 13:9; Jas 2:8.
22:41–46: Mk 12:35–37; Lk 20:41–44.   22:44: Ps 110:1; Acts 2:34–35; Heb 1:13; 10:13.   22:46: Mk 12:34, Lk 20:40.
23:4: Lk 11:46; Acts 15:10.   23:5: Mt 6:1, 5, 16; Ex 13:9; Deut 6:8; Mt 9:20.
23:6–7: Mk 12:38–39; Lk 20:46; 14:7–11; 11:43.   23:8: Jas 3:1.   23:11: Mt 20:26; Mk 9:35; 1O:43; Lk 9:48; 22:26.
23:12: Lk 14:11; 18:14; Mt 18:4; 1 Pet 5:6. 23:13: Lk 11:52.

22:32 Abraham . . . Isaac . . . Jacob: The Sadducees lack faith in God's power and thus misinterpret Scripture. At another level, Jesus' controversy with the Sadducees may also involve the canon of the Bible. The Sadducees accepted only the five books of Moses (Gen–Deut) as Sacred Scripture and rejected the full authority of the OT prophets. Jesus appears aware of this, since he could have cited several passages from the prophets that speak clearly of the resurrection (Is 26:19; Ezek 37:1–14; Dan 12:2). Instead, he tailors his response to the Sadducees by strategically citing one of the books of Moses (Ex 3:6). • In context, God revealed himself to Moses in the burning bush as the God of the long-deceased patriarchs (Ex 3:1–6). Jesus draws two conclusions from the text: (1) Abraham, Isaac, and Jacob are still alive with God; (2) their ongoing presence with God is the decisive precondition for their resurrection in the future (CCC 581).

22:40 these two commandments: The 613 commands of the Mosaic Law are distilled into two prescriptions: love God (Deut 6:5) and your neighbor (Lev 19:18). These summarize the spirit of the entire OT (law and the prophets). According also to Paul, love is the greatest theological virtue (1 Cor 13:13) and fulfills God's moral Law (Rom 13:8–10; CCC 1822–24).

22:45 calls him Lord: Jesus' question concerns the meaning of Ps 110:1. The Pharisees (22:42) assume it mentions the Messiah, but their understanding of the verse is partial and inadequate. • Psalm 110 is an enthronement psalm that was probably used at coronation ceremonies for Davidic

kings. In context, David addresses his son as "my Lord" (22:44), a title more appropriate for one's superior. This implies that the expected Messiah would be greater than David himself, a crucial point missed by the Pharisees (cf. Acts 2:34–36). As Messiah, Jesus is the son of David (1:1) and yet greater than David as the Son of God (3:17; 16:16; 17:5) (CCC 439, 447). See note on 1:17.

23:1–36 Jesus warns the crowds and his disciples (23:1) that the scribes and the Pharisees (23:2) are dangerous and their false piety is unworthy of imitation. Jesus takes aim at Pharisaic attitudes (23:2–12) and announces seven "woes" indicting them as murderers (23:34–35).

23:2 Moses' seat: This may be an actual "chair", like those used in later synagogues, or only a symbol of teaching authority. The Pharisees thus preach the Mosaic Law with authority, but their failure to practice its "weightier matters" (23:23) should not be followed by others. See topical essay: *Who Are the Pharisees?* at Mk 2.

23:5 their phylacteries: Small leather boxes containing Scripture verses. These are tied to the forearm and forehead while praying (Deut 6:8; 11:18). Making them broad, the Pharisees sought to parade their piety for public recognition. fringes: See note on 9:20.

23:7 rabbi: A Hebrew word meaning "my great one" and a title for revered Jewish teachers (Jn 1:38).

23:9 call no man your father: Jesus uses hyperbole to post a warning that no one should pridefully desire honorific titles. His words are not meant literally. The NT writers elsewhere use *father* for natural fathers (Heb 12:7–11) and spiritual fathers in the Church (1 Cor 4:15; Philem 10). • The spiritual fatherhood of New Covenant priests is an extension of its application to Old Covenant priests (Judg 17:10; 18:19).

---

[s] Other ancient authorities add *of God.*
[t] Or *David in the Spirit.*
[u] Other ancient authorities omit *hard to bear.*

humbled, and whoever humbles himself will be exalted.

13 "But woe to you, scribes and Pharisees, hypocrites! because you shut the kingdom of heaven against men; for you neither enter yourselves, nor allow those who would enter to go in.*v* [15]Woe to you, scribes and Pharisees, hypocrites! for you traverse sea and land to make a single proselyte, and when he becomes a proselyte, you make him twice as much a child of hell*w* as yourselves.

16 "Woe to you, blind guides, who say, 'If any one swears by the temple, it is nothing; but if any one swears by the gold of the temple, he is bound by his oath.' [17]You blind fools! For which is greater, the gold or the temple that has made the gold sacred? [18]And you say, 'If any one swears by the altar, it is nothing; but if any one swears by the gift that is on the altar, he is bound by his oath.' [19]You blind men! For which is greater, the gift or the altar that makes the gift sacred? [20]So he who swears by the altar, swears by it and by everything on it; [21]and he who swears by the temple, swears by it and by him who dwells in it; [22]and he who swears by heaven, swears by the throne of God and by him who sits upon it.

23 "Woe to you, scribes and Pharisees, hypocrites! for you tithe mint and dill and cummin, and have neglected the weightier matters of the law, justice and mercy and faith; these you ought to have done, without neglecting the others. [24]You blind guides, straining out a gnat and swallowing a camel!

25 "Woe to you, scribes and Pharisees, hypocrites! for you cleanse the outside of the cup and of the plate, but inside they are full of extortion and rapacity. [26]You blind Pharisee! first cleanse the inside of the cup and of the plate, that the outside also may be clean.

27 "Woe to you, scribes and Pharisees, hypocrites! for you are like whitewashed tombs, which outwardly appear beautiful, but within they are full of dead men's bones and all uncleanness. [28]So you also outwardly appear righteous to men, but within you are full of hypocrisy and iniquity.

29 "Woe to you, scribes and Pharisees, hypocrites! for you build the tombs of the prophets and adorn the monuments of the righteous, [30]saying, 'If we had lived in the days of our fathers, we would not have taken part with them in shedding the blood of the prophets.' [31]Thus you witness against yourselves, that you are sons of those who murdered the prophets. [32]Fill up, then, the measure of your fathers. [33]You serpents, you brood of vipers, how are you to escape being sentenced to hell?*w* [34]Therefore I send you prophets and wise men and scribes, some of whom you will kill and crucify, and some you will scourge in your synagogues and persecute from town to town, [35]that upon you may come all the righteous blood shed on

---

23:13: Lk 11:52.   **23:15:** Acts 2:10; 6:5; 13:43.   **23:16–22:** Mt 5:33–37; 15:14.   **23:17:** Ex 30:29.
23:21: 1 Kings 8:13; Ps 26:8.   **23:23–24:** Lk 11:42; Lev 27:30; Mic 6:8.   **23:25–26:** Lk 11:39–41; Mk 7:4.
23:27–28: Lk 11:44; Acts 23:3; Ps 5:9.   **23:29–32:** Lk 11:47–48; Acts 7:51–53.   **23:33:** Mt 3:7; Lk 3:7.
23:34–36: Lk 11:49–51; 2 Chron 36:15–16.   **23:34:** Mt 10:17, 23.   **23:35:** Gen 4:8; Heb 11:4; Zech 1:1; 2 Chron 24:21.

23:13 woe to you: Recalls OT oracles of judgment (Is 5:8–23; Ezek 24:6, 9; Hab 2:6–20). This is the first of seven "woes" in Jesus' denunciation of the Pharisees (23:15–16, 23, 25, 27, 29). He presents a covenant lawsuit against unfaithful Israel and pronounces "woes" as covenant curses upon the impenitent (cf. Deut 27:15–26). In Matthew, these seven "woes" stand opposite the New Covenant "blessings" in the Beatitudes (5:3–12; cf. Lk 6:24–26). • The OT background is likely Lev 26 and God's promise to exact "sevenfold" vengeance upon the Israelites if they violate his covenant (Lev 26:18, 21, 24, 28).

23:15 a single proselyte: i.e, a convert to Pharisaic Judaism.

23:16–22 The Pharisees made false and hair-splitting distinctions between oaths, supposing the object invoked (Temple, gold, altar) determined the binding force of sworn statements. Their distinctions, which made some oaths less binding than others, abused and devalued the sacredness of the practice (CCC 2153). See note on 5:33.

23:23 mint and dill and cummin: Small seasoning herbs. According to the Law, a tenth part (**tithe**) of all produce must be offered to God (Lev 27:30; Deut 14:22–23). The Pharisees scrupulously adhered to this small command but neglected greater and more important principles; for **justice, mercy,** and **faith** are the foundations of the Mosaic Law and should inspire all obedience to God (cf. 9:13).

23:24 a gnat: One of the smaller unclean animals, which Jews were forbidden to eat (Lev 11:41–43). The Pharisees dutifully poured beverages through a cloth to strain them out before drinking. **a camel:** One of the larger unclean animals (Lev 11:4). Jesus' contrast exposes the Pharisees for observing the minute laws of God at the expense of greater principles of the spiritual life.

23:27 whitewashed tombs: Since contact with the dead makes Jews temporarily unclean, it was customary to whitewash grave sites to make them visible and help prevent inadvertent contact (Num 19:11–20). According to Jesus, the practice illustrates how the visible piety of many Pharisees only disguises their interior corruption and hypocrisy.

23:35 Abel to . . . Zechariah: Some see this as a reference to the first (Gen 4:8) and last (2 Chron 24:20–22) murders in the OT. This is based on the Palestinian arrangement of the OT, where Genesis is the first book and 2 Chronicles is the last. This is difficult to maintain, because the Zechariah in 2 Chron 24:20 is the "son of Jehoiada", not the **son of Barachiah**. Zechariah the "son of Barachiah" is rather the OT prophet (Zech 1:1) whose death is nowhere recorded in the Bible. Jesus may instead be drawing from ancient tradition, just as Isaiah's martyrdom is never mentioned in the OT but alluded to in Heb 11:37 as the prophet "sawn in two". In fact, later rabbinic tradition maintains that Zechariah the son of Barachiah was killed in the Temple. In any case, the cup of iniquity filled throughout history begins to overflow with the Pharisees' intent to murder Jesus (12:14). By rejecting God's Messiah, Jesus' generation calls down divine judgment stored up from the ages.

---

v Other ancient authorities add here (or after verse 12) verse 14, *Woe to you, scribes and Pharisees, hypocrites! for you devour widows' houses and for a pretense you make long prayers; therefore you will receive the greater condemnation.*
w Greek *Gehenna.*

earth, from the blood of innocent Abel to the blood of Zechari′ah the son of Barachi′ah, whom you murdered between the sanctuary and the altar. ³⁶Truly, I say to you, all this will come upon this generation.

The Lament over Jerusalem

37 "O Jerusalem, Jerusalem, killing the prophets and stoning those who are sent to you! How often would I have gathered your children together as a hen gathers her brood under her wings, and you would not! ³⁸Behold, your house is forsaken and desolate.ˣ ³⁹For I tell you, you will not see me again, until you say, 'Blessed is he who comes in the name of the Lord.' "

The Destruction of the Temple Foretold

24 Jesus left the temple and was going away, when his disciples came to point out to him the buildings of the temple. ²But he answered them, "You see all these, do you not? Truly, I say to you, there will not be left here one stone upon another, that will not be thrown down."

Signs of the End of the Age

3 As he sat on the Mount of Olives, the disciples came to him privately, saying, "Tell us,

when will this be, and what will be the sign of your coming and of the close of the age?" ⁴And Jesus answered them, "Take heed that no one leads you astray. ⁵For many will come in my name, saying, 'I am the Christ,' and they will lead many astray. ⁶And you will hear of wars and rumors of wars; see that you are not alarmed; for this must take place, but the end is not yet. ⁷For nation will rise against nation, and kingdom against kingdom, and there will be famines and earthquakes in various places: ⁸all this is but the beginning of the sufferings.

Persecutions Foretold

9 "Then they will deliver you up to tribulation, and put you to death; and you will be hated by all nations for my name's sake. ¹⁰And then many will fall away,ʸ and betray one another, and hate one another. ¹¹And many false prophets will arise and lead many astray. ¹²And because wickedness is multiplied, most men's love will grow cold. ¹³But he who endures to the end will be saved. ¹⁴And this gospel of the kingdom will be preached throughout the whole world, as a testimony to all nations; and then the end will come.

23:36: Mt 10:23; 16:28; 24:34.   **23:37–39:** Lk 13:34–35.   **23:38:** 1 Kings 9:7; Jer 22:5.   **23:39:** Mt 21:9; Ps 118:26.
24:1–35: Mk 13:1–31; Lk 21:1–33.   **24:2:** Mt 26:61; 27:39–40; Lk 19:44; Jn 2:19.   **24:3:** Lk 17:20; Mt 13:39, 40, 49; 28:20; 16:27.
24:5: Mt 24:11, 23–24; 1 Jn 2:18.   **24:6–7:** Rev 6:3–8, 12–17; Is 19:2.   **24:9:** Mt 10:17–18, 22; Jn 15:18; 16:2.
24:13: Mt 10:22; Rev 2:7.   **24:14:** Mt 28:19; Rom 10:18.

23:37 as a hen: The Holy City persistently rejected God's messengers. Jesus too stands rejected, though he desired to protect and gather its faithful (CCC 558). • Jesus' language evokes Is 31:5 and the Lord's protection of Jerusalem. Other OT texts similarly portray God as a winged bird protecting Israel (Deut 32:10–12; Ps 91:4). • Allegorically (Auctor Imperfecti), the hen signifies the Church's Magisterium; the brood are the citizens of the New Jerusalem, the Church. It is the Magisterium who continually calls her children, born through Baptism, to a life of faith in Christ. As a mother, the Church protects the faithful from error and danger while nourishing them with truth.

23:38 your house is forsaken: The Jerusalem Temple is devoid of God's presence (cf. Jer 12:7; Dan 9:17). Jesus, God-in-flesh, symbolically enacts this by exiting the Temple (24:1) and walking to the Mount of Olives (24:3). • Jesus' Temple exit recalls Ezekiel's vision in the OT. He witnessed God's glory leaving Solomon's Temple and resting on the Mount of Olives, east of the city (Ezek 10:18; 11:23). God's departure was soon followed by the Temple's first destruction in 586 B.C.

24:1–25:46 The Olivet Discourse is Jesus' final sermon in Matthew (see outline). His words have two shades of meaning: **(1)** At the literal-historical level, Jesus forewarns the disciples that Jerusalem and the Temple will be destroyed. The Holy City is about to reject Jesus as the Messiah and erect itself as a barrier to God's New Covenant. The Temple, an architectural symbol of the Old Covenant, must be eliminated to make way for the Church, the new Temple of God (cf. 16:18; Eph 2:19–22; 1 Pet 2:4–8). Jesus uses dramatic imagery—called "apocalyptic" language—and draws heavily on the OT to forecast this coming military catastrophe. Forty years later, in A.D. 70, the prophecy was fulfilled when Roman troops marched on Jerusalem, destroying the city and Temple. **(2)** On a spiritual level, the Temple's devastation foreshadows the destruction of the world itself to make way for the eternal dwelling of heaven. This will coincide with Jesus' Second

Coming and the General Judgment of all nations (CCC 585–86). See topical essay: End of the World? at Mt 24. • The earliest summaries of the Church's faith—the Apostles' Creed and the Nicene Creed—affirm Jesus' Second Coming in glory. The Church has always maintained that Christ will come again from heaven as mankind's Judge and Lord (Acts 1:11; CCC 671, 681).

24:3 Mount of Olives: See note on 21:1. **Tell us:** The disciples respond to Jesus' Temple prophecy with a two-part question (**when?** / **what?**). Different views attempt to explain this. **(1)** Two-Question View: The disciples ask Jesus two separate questions: When will the Temple fall, and what signs will precede his Second Coming at the end of history? Jesus thus answers the first in 24:4–35 and handles the second question in 24:36–25:46. This view is weakened by Jesus' teaching elsewhere. In Lk 17:22–37, the same images that span Mt 24 (lightning, 24:27; Noah, 24:37; housetop, 24:17; women grinding, 24:41; body, 24:28; eagles, 24:28) are shuffled in a different sequence, and all refer to a single event—i.e., the Temple's downfall. Luke's arrangement thus undermines an artificial division of Jesus' discourse in Mt 24–25 into two parts dealing with two different subjects. **(2)** Single-Question View: Matthew 24–25 is Jesus' single response to a single, two-sided question about the Temple. In 24:4–35, Jesus reveals proximate signs that will precede the Temple's doom; in 24:36–25:46, he conceals the precise day and hour of God's judgment. Accordingly, 24:36 marks a shift of emphasis, not a change of subject. This view more aptly squares Jesus' predictions with the Temple's destruction in A.D. 70, within one generation of His prophecy (16:28; 24:34; 26:64). See note on 24:34. **close of the age:** The Old Covenant age will terminate with Jerusalem's destruction. This "closing" is linked with God's rescue of the righteous and his judgment of the wicked (13:39–43, 48–50).

24:8 the sufferings: Literally, "the birth pangs." • An OT prophetic image for grief, which overcomes sinners when God comes as Judge (Is 26:17–18; Jer 6:24; Hos 13:13).

24:14 throughout the whole world: This language is elsewhere used to denote the scope of Christianity's presence in

---

ʷ Greek Gehenna.
ˣ Other ancient authorities omit and desolate.   ʸ Or stumble.

End of the World?

ESUS' Olivet Discourse in Mt 24–25 is difficult to interpret (cf. Mk 13; Lk 21). He speaks extensively about cosmic catastrophes, heavenly signs, and the future judgment of God. This has led some to think that Jesus was predicting his Second Coming and the end of the visible world. This interpretation appears to take Jesus' words seriously and at their face value. Nevertheless, it leads to a troublesome scenario: Jesus expected these world-shaking events to occur soon after his Ascension. After all, he told the disciples, "Truly, I say to you, this generation will not pass away till all these things take place" (Mt 24:34). Was Jesus mistaken? Should we feel uncomfortable because the world is still with us almost two thousand years after he prophesied its frightful end?

A closer look at Jesus' words in the context of ancient Judaism reveals a better interpretation. Namely, Jesus was predicting the demise of the Jerusalem Temple—the architectural symbol of the Old Covenant. At the literal-historical level, Jesus' entire discourse is an extension of his cryptic comment about the Temple: "There will not be left here one stone upon another, that will not be thrown down" (Mt 24:2). Hearing this, the disciples were probably reminded of a similar event in the OT when God allowed the Temple to be destroyed in 586 B.C. as punishment for Israel's sins (2 Kings 25:8–10). Interpreting Jesus' words in this way does more adequate justice to the symbolism of his language and the testimony of history. Ancient sources confirm his prophecy: the Romans destroyed Jerusalem and the Temple in A.D. 70, a tragedy that claimed the lives of more than 1 million Jews. From this perspective Jesus stands vindicated, since his words did come to pass within the lifetime of his contemporaries.

But how are the details of Jesus' strange language to be understood? Could he expect us to associate cosmic upheavals like national warfare (Mt 24:6–7), earthly catastrophes (Mt 24:7–8), the darkening of the sun and the moon (Mt 24:29), and stars falling out of the sky (Mt 24:29) with the collapse of a sacred building? The answer lies in biblical and traditional views of the Temple. Like many religions in the Near East, the Israelites regarded their Temple as a miniature replica or microcosm of the world; it was an architectural model of the universe fashioned by God. Conversely, the universe itself was a macrotemple, where God also dwells with his people. This is best summarized by the Psalmist, "He built his sanctuary like the high heavens, like the earth, which he has founded for ever" (Ps 78:69). Other indications of this Temple theology are found in OT parallels and Jewish traditions that link the Temple and the world closely together:

(1) The Place of God's Rest

After the week-long construction of the world, "God rested from all his work which he had done in creation" (Gen 2:3). Likewise, when God established order and gave the Israelites "rest" from their enemies (2 Sam 7:1), He commissioned the building of the Temple by Solomon as his "resting place for ever" (Ps 132:14; cf. 2 Chron 6:41; Sir 24:11; Is 66:1).

(2) Symbolism of Seven

God's creation of the world is described as the construction of a Temple (Job 38:4–6; Amos 9:6) that is completed and blessed on the seventh day (Gen 2:2–3). Similarly, Solomon built the Jerusalem Temple in seven years (1 Kings 6:38) and dedicated it in the seventh month (1 Kings 8:2) during the seven-day Feast of Booths (1 Kings 8:65).

(3) A House of Glory

Isaiah's vision of the Lord (Is 6:1–7) makes an implicit comparison: the Temple and the cosmos are mutually and interchangeably filled with divine glory. As the train of God's robe "filled the temple" (Is 6:1) and God's house is "filled with smoke" (Is 6:4), so the angels cry out "the whole earth is full of his glory" (Is 6:3).

(4) Jewish Tradition

Jewish writers of Jesus' day describe in great detail the Temple as a model of the universe. Josephus, Philo, and later rabbinic writings interpret the Temple's divisions, furniture, colors, and architecture as symbols of the cosmos. One tradition links the three divisions of the Temple with three realms of the world: heaven is the most holy place, the land is the holy place, and the sea is the outer courtyard and the bronze laver of water.

These considerations help make sense of Jesus' words in their historical context. With the dawning of the New Covenant, God had to clear away the central symbol of the Old Covenant, the Temple. The Church is God's new and spiritual Temple, built with the living stones of Christian believers (Mt 16:18; Eph 2:20–22; 1 Pet 2:4–5). In this light, the devastation of the Temple and the judgment of Israel in A.D. 70 can be seen as an overture to greater things. That is, the termination of the Old Covenant world prefigures the destruction of the universe, God's macrotemple, and the judgment of all nations by Christ (cf. 2 Pet 3:5–7). Thus Jesus' Olivet Discourse (Mt 24–25) is initially fulfilled in the first century as he said (Mt 24:34). But imbedded in Christ's words are spiritual truths that point forward to his Second Coming in glory and the end of the visible world. «

The Desolating Sacrilege

15 "So when you see the desolating sacrilege spoken of by the prophet Daniel, standing in the holy place (let the reader understand), 16then let those who are in Judea flee to the mountains; 17let him who is on the housetop not go down to take what is in his house; 18and let him who is in the field not turn back to get a coat. 19And alas for those who are with child and for those who are nursing in those days! 20Pray that your flight may not be in winter or on a sabbath. 21For then there will be great tribulation, such as has not been from the beginning of the world until now, no, and never will be. 22And if those days had not been shortened, no human being would be saved; but for the sake of the elect those days will be shortened. 23Then if any one says to you, 'Behold, here is the Christ!' or 'There he is!' do not believe it. 24For false Christs and false prophets will arise and show great signs and wonders, so as to lead astray, if possible, even the elect. 25Behold, I have told you beforehand. 26So, if they say to you, 'Behold, he is in the wilderness,' do not go out; if they say, 'Behold, he is in the inner rooms,' do not believe it. 27For as the lightning comes from the east and shines as far as the west, so will be the coming of the Son of man. 28Wherever the body is, there the eagles z will be gathered together.

The Coming of the Son of Man

29 "Immediately after the tribulation of those days the sun will be darkened, and the moon will not give its light, and the stars will fall from heaven, and the powers of the heavens will be shaken; 30then will appear the sign of the Son of man in heaven, and then all the tribes of the earth will mourn, and they will see the Son of man coming on the clouds of heaven with power and great glory; 31and he will send out his angels with a loud trumpet call, and they will gather his elect from the four winds, from one end of heaven to the other.

24:15: Dan 9:27; 11:31; 12:11.   **24:17–18:** Lk 17:31.   **24:19:** Lk 23:29.   **24:21:** Dan 12:1; Joel 2:2.
24:26–27: Lk 17:22–24; Rev 1:7.   **24:28:** Lk 17:37; Job 39:30.
24:29: Rev 8:12; Is 13:10; Ezek 32:7; Joel 2:10–11; Zeph 1:15.   **24:30:** Mt 16:27; Dan 7:13; Rev 1:7.
24:31: 1 Cor 15:52; 1 Thess 4:16; Is 27:13; Zech 9:14.

---

the Roman Empire (Rom 1:8; Col 1:6, 23). The gospel was substantially spread throughout the Roman world by the middle of the first century A.D. (cf. 1 Thess 1:8).

24:15 the desolating sacrilege: Recalls Dan 9:27, 11:31, and 12:11. • In context, Daniel foresees the desecration of the Jerusalem Temple by the Gentile ruler Antiochus Epiphanes IV (167 B.C.). Antiochus burned Jerusalem, plundered the Temple of its sacred articles, and erected an idol to the Greek god Zeus within its precincts (1 Mac 1:31, 37, 54). Jesus draws from this episode and projects it forward to announce the Temple's ultimate destruction and desecration by the Roman army in A.D. 70 (cf. Lk 21:20).

24:16 flee to the mountains: A warning for early Christians to escape Jerusalem before its judgment and to resist temptations to defend the city. According to the Church Father Eusebius (A.D. 340), Christians living in the city fled to Pella, east of the Jordan River. • Jesus' command evokes Zech 14. In context, Zechariah envisions a day of judgment for Jerusalem, when the faithful are beckoned to "flee" the city (Zech 14:5; cf. Joel 2:32; Obad 17). Similarly, in 1 Mac 1:37–39 and 2:27–28, the righteous had to evacuate the sinful cities of Jerusalem and Modein in times of crisis.

24:27 lightning: Points to the swiftness of God's judgment on the city. • The OT similarly depicts God's presence and frightful punishment as a raging storm (Ps 97:4; Is 29:5–6; Zech 9:14). **the coming:** See word study: *Coming* at Mt 24:3.

24:28 the eagles: Scavengers (Romans) who eat the remains of a carcass (Jerusalem). It is noteworthy that Roman military standards featured eagles as symbols of the empire. • In the OT, the eagle (also translated "vulture") symbolized pagan nations who brought suffering upon Israel (Deut 28:49; Hab 1:8; cf. Hos 8:1).

24:29 sun . . . moon . . . stars: Images of cosmic catastrophe underscore the magnitude of Jerusalem's coming doom. • Depictions of heavenly chaos are used by the OT prophets to predict the downfall of pagan kingdoms (Is 13:9–10; 34:4; Ezek 32:7–8; Joel 2:10, 31; Amos 8:9). Jesus redirects this language toward Jerusalem: the kingdom of Old Covenant Israel will be devastated for corrupting itself like the pagans and rejecting Jesus.

24:30 the Son of man: An allusion to Dan 7:13. • In context, Daniel beholds "a son of man" coming to God with the **clouds of heaven**; he is given a royal "kingdom" (Dan 7:14) and "everlasting dominion" over all nations (cf. 28:18). Daniel's vision takes historical shape (initially) with Jesus' Resurrection and Ascension to the Father (Mk 16:19; Acts 1:9). Jesus' victory over his enemies will be visibly manifest with Jerusalem's judgment and the termination of the Old Covenant. See topical essay: *Jesus the Son of Man* at Lk 17.

24:31 his angels: The Greek word *angelos* can refer to an angel (pure spirit) or a human messenger such as John the Baptist in 11:10. Initially, it may denote the apostles sent to evangelize all nations (28:18–20). **trumpet call:** An allusion to Is 27:13 (cf. Zech 9:14). • Isaiah's prophecy depicts the restoration of Israel as the Israelites are saved from their exile among pagan nations. Gathering his faithful into the Church, God

WORD STUDY

Coming (24:3)

Parousia (Gk.): literally means "presence" but can denote "appearing" or "visitation". The word is used four times in Mt 24 and 20 times in the rest of the NT. It is sometimes used in Greek literature to describe the visitation of a king or high official to a city he has previously conquered. In this sense, it presumes a period of absence before the king's return. The Bible uses it in a similar way for the arrival of important people (Jud 10:18; 2 Mac 8:12; 2 Cor 7:6; Phil 1:26). More important, it denotes the coming of Jesus Christ, who brings judgment upon his enemies (Mt 24:37, 39; 2 Thess 2:8) and rescues his faithful disciples (1 Cor 15:23; 1 Thess 3:13; 1 Jn 2:28). The word can refer both to Christ's "visitation" of destruction upon Jerusalem in A.D. 70 as well as to his Second Advent at the end of time as Judge of the living and the dead (cf. Acts 1:11; 2 Tim 4:1).

---

z Or *vultures*.

The Lesson of the Fig Tree

32 "From the fig tree learn its lesson: as soon as its branch becomes tender and puts forth its leaves, you know that summer is near. ³³So also, when you see all these things, you know that he is near, at the very gates. ³⁴Truly, I say to you, this generation will not pass away till all these things take place. ³⁵Heaven and earth will pass away, but my words will not pass away.

The Necessity for Watchfulness

36 "But of that day and hour no one knows, not even the angels of heaven, nor the Son,ᵃ but the Father only. ³⁷As were the days of Noah, so will be the coming of the Son of man. ³⁸For as in those days before the flood they were eating and drinking, marrying and giving in marriage, until the day when Noah entered the ark, ³⁹and they did not know until the flood came and swept them all away, so will be the coming of the Son of man. ⁴⁰Then two men will be in the field; one is taken and one is left. ⁴¹Two women will be grinding at the mill; one is taken and one is left. ⁴²Watch therefore, for you do not know on what day your Lord is coming. ⁴³But know this, that if the householder had known in what part of the night the thief was coming, he would have watched and would not have let his house be broken into. ⁴⁴Therefore you also must be ready; for the Son of man is coming at an hour you do not expect.

The Faithful or the Unfaithful Servant

45 "Who then is the faithful and wise servant, whom his master has set over his household, to give them their food at the proper time? ⁴⁶Blessed is that servant whom his master when he comes will find so doing. ⁴⁷Truly, I say to you, he will set him over all his possessions. ⁴⁸But if that wicked servant says to himself, 'My master is delayed,' ⁴⁹and begins to beat his fellow servants, and eats and drinks with the drunken, ⁵⁰the master of that servant will come on a day when he does not expect him and at an hour he does not know, ⁵¹and will punish ᵇ him, and put him with the hypocrites; there men will weep and gnash their teeth.

The Parable of the Ten Bridesmaids

25 "Then the kingdom of heaven shall be compared to ten maidens who took their lamps and went to meet the bridegroom.ᶜ ²Five of them were foolish, and five were wise. ³For when the foolish took their lamps, they took no oil with them; ⁴but the wise took flasks of oil with their lamps. ⁵As the bridegroom was delayed, they all slumbered and slept. ⁶But at midnight there was a

---

24:34: Mt 16:28.   **24:35:** Mt 5:18; Lk 16:17.   **24:36:** Acts 1:6–7.   **24:37–39:** Lk 17:26–27; Gen 6:5–8; 7:6–24   **24:40–41:** Lk 17:34–35.   **24:42:** Mk 13:35; Lk 12:40; Mt 25:13.   **24:43–51:** Lk 12:39–46.   **24:43:** 1 Thess 5:2; Rev 3:3; 16:15; 2 Pet 3:10.   **24:45:** Mt 25:21, 23.   **24:49:** Lk 21:34.   **24:51:** Mt 8:12; 13:42, 50; 22:13; 25:30; Lk 13:28.   **25:1:** Lk 12:35–38; Mk 13:34.   **25:2:** Mt 7:24–27.

---

rescues the righteous from the collapsing Old Covenant and the Gentiles from paganism (cf. Eph 2:11–16). **the four winds:** The four cardinal directions of the earth (cf. 8:11; Lk 13:29). • The OT similarly depicts God gathering his people from their exile among the nations (Deut 30:4; Is 11:12; Zech 2:6).

24:34 this generation: The Greek denotes about a forty-year time span. Jesus' words would thus be accomplished within the lifetime of some of his hearers (cf. 10:23; 16:28; 23:36). **will not pass away:** The identical expression is used in the following verse, implying a close connection between the termination of Old Covenant era and the end of the visible world. Just as signs of chaos and catastrophe precede the collapse of the Old age and the coming of Christ's kingdom (24:3-30), so similar signs are expected before the final days of the New age and Christ's Second Coming in glory.

📖 **24:35 Heaven and earth will pass away:** A solemn prediction, not a hypothetical contrast. Jesus thus prophesies the termination of the Old Covenant order, i.e., the old creation awaiting renewal in Christ (cf. 2 Cor 5:17; Rev 21:1). As the OT era gave way to the NT age established by Christ's powerful **words,** so even the NT age will give way to eternal life at the end of history. • Jesus' statement recalls OT oracles that describe God's word (Is 40:8) and salvation (Is 51:6) outlasting the frail elements of the cosmos.

24:36–25:46 Jesus turns from revealing general prophesies to concealing specific details. Jerusalem's doom will be preceded by proximate signs (24:5-8, 30, 33), but the precise time of the city's judgment will remain unknown (24:42, 44; 25:13).

✳ **24:36 nor the Son, but the Father:** This saying is comparable to 20:23, where Jesus says that the Father, not the Son, makes royal appointments of rank. Here also **only** the Father appoints the time of the Son's royal return in glory.

Christ's professed ignorance of this **day** and **hour** may be understood as hyperbole (overstatement), a teaching device used by Jewish rabbis and Jesus himself (5:34; 23:9; Lk 14:26). • Tradition maintains that Jesus' apparent ignorance is not a literal statement, but a figurative expression; for the Father and the Son share everything in common, including their divine knowledge: 11:27; Jn 3:35; 10:15; 17:25). Here Jesus does not display any human knowledge of the time when the Father will send the Son to judge all nations, because this mystery lies beyond the scope of what the Father intends the Son to reveal (CCC 472-74).

24:38 The lesson from **the flood** is based on unexpected catastrophe (cf. Dan 9:26). Except for **Noah** and his family, the rest of his generation showed no concern for God. They were distracted by the concerns of the world and were destroyed in God's judgment.

24:40 one is taken . . . one is left: This scenario follows Jesus' example of Noah and the flood (24:37). The righteous will be left, just as Noah and his family were spared (Sir 44:17); the wicked will be taken, as Noah's generation was swept away by the flood (24:39; 2 Pet 2:4-10).

24:42 Watch therefore: A prominent theme in Jesus' teaching (24:43; 25:13; 26:38-41). It addresses the glorious **coming** of Christ at three levels. **(1)** *Past historical.* The disciples were to look vigilantly for Christ's judgment on Jerusalem A.D. 70, lest they fail to heed his words and evacuate the city before its demise (24:16). **(2)** *Present liturgical.* Disciples must look with faith to see the coming of Christ in the Eucharist. Here too Jesus' presence must be discerned to avoid divine judgment when he comes in the sacrament (1 Cor 11:27-29). **(3)** *Future eschatological.* Disciples must watch for Christ's Second Coming in glory at the end of history. Being vigilant in faith and good works is necessary to inherit eternal life with Christ (25:34-36). See word study *Coming* at Mt 24.

✠ **25:1-13** The parable of the Ten Maidens emphasizes the need for watchfulness (25:13). Its story line centers on a

---

ᵃ Other ancient authorities omit *nor the Son.*
ᵇ Or *cut him in pieces.*
ᶜ Other ancient authorities add *and the bride.*

cry, 'Behold, the bridegroom! Come out to meet him.' [7]Then all those maidens rose and trimmed their lamps. [8]And the foolish said to the wise, 'Give us some of your oil, for our lamps are going out.' [9]But the wise replied, 'Perhaps there will not be enough for us and for you; go rather to the dealers and buy for yourselves.' [10]And while they went to buy, the bridegroom came, and those who were ready went in with him to the marriage feast; and the door was shut. [11]Afterward the other maidens came also, saying, 'Lord, lord, open to us.' [12]But he replied, 'Truly, I say to you, I do not know you.' [13]Watch therefore, for you know neither the day nor the hour.

The Parable of the Talents

14 "For it will be as when a man going on a journey called his servants and entrusted to them his property; [15]to one he gave five talents,[d] to another two, to another one, to each according to his ability. Then he went away. [16]He who had received the five talents went at once and traded with them; and he made five talents more. [17]So also, he who had the two talents made two talents more. [18]But he who had received the one talent went and dug in the ground and hid his master's money. [19]Now after a long time the master of those servants came and settled accounts with them. [20]And he who had received the five talents came forward, bringing five talents more, saying, 'Master, you delivered to me five talents; here I have made five talents more.' [21]His master said to him, 'Well done, good and faithful servant; you have been faithful over a little, I will set you over much; enter into the joy of your master.' [22]And he also who had the two talents came forward, saying, 'Master, you delivered to me two talents; here I have made two talents more.' [23]His master said to him, 'Well done, good and faithful servant; you have been faithful over a little, I will set you over much; enter into the joy of your master.' [24]He also who had received the one talent came forward, saying, 'Master, I knew you to be a hard man, reaping where you did not sow, and gathering where you did not winnow; [25]so I was afraid, and I went and hid your talent in the ground. Here you have what is yours.' [26]But his master answered him, 'You wicked and slothful servant! You knew that I reap where I have not sowed, and gather where I have not winnowed? [27]Then you ought to have invested my money with the bankers, and at my coming I should have received what was my own with interest. [28]So take the talent from him, and give it to him who has the ten talents. [29]For to every one who has will more be given, and he will have abundance; but from him who has not, even what he has will be taken away. [30]And cast the worthless servant into the outer darkness; there men will weep and gnash their teeth.'

The Judgment of the Nations

31 "When the Son of man comes in his glory, and all the angels with him, then he will sit on his glorious throne. [32]Before him will be gathered all the nations, and he will separate them one from

---

25:10: Rev 19:9.   **25:11–12:** Lk 13:25; Mt 7:21–23.   **25:13:** Mt 24:42; Mk 13:35; Lk 12:40.   **25:14–30:** Lk 19:12–28.
25:19: Mt 18:23.   **25:21:** Lk 16:10; Mt 24:45.   **25:29:** Mt 13:12; Mk 4:25; Lk 8:18.   **25:30:** Mt 8:12; 13:42, 50; 22:13; Lk 13:28
25:31: Mt 16:27; 19:28.   **25:32:** Ezek 34:17.

Jewish marital custom: following the period of betrothal, the groom would lead a procession to bring his new wife to their home, and they would celebrate a week-long banquet with family and friends. Here the **bridegroom** (25:6; 9:15) arrives to begin the joyous procession and take his wife to the **marriage feast**. Unprepared and without **oil** (25:3), the **foolish** maidens are excluded from the celebration (22:1–14) while the **wise** participate fully. Likewise, Christians are called to be spiritually prepared: the moment Jesus brings judgment on Jerusalem is unknown, as is the time of his Second Coming as Judge (CCC 672, 796). See note on 1:18. • *Morally* (Origen, St. Hilary), awaiting the bridegroom signifies one's uncertain life-span—no one knows the hour of his death and judgment. The lamp is Christian faith, while the oil represents good works; thus faith without works is useless (Jas 2:17). Souls must prepare for their personal encounter with Christ (bridegroom) by loving God and neighbor (25:35–40; 1 Jn 3:7), since those lacking good works will be shut out of heaven's banquet.

25:14–30 The parable of the Talents is about stewardship. It warns against the dangers of sloth, whereby God-given blessings and abilities are squandered because of fear (25:25) and laziness (25:26–28). Personal diligence, however, is greatly rewarded with superior gifts and responsibilities (25:21, 23). Accountability to Christ entails risk and challenges; God's endowments must be invested in and for the good of others to increase heavenly earnings.

25:14 on a journey: A sufficient time for servants to multiply their master's wealth. In the context of Jesus' sermon, the journey represents the delay between his Ascension and God's judgment on Jerusalem in A.D. 70 (Lk 19:11–27). At the personal level, it indicates one's lifetime, during which God expects his gifts to be cultivated (1 Pet 4:10).

25:15 talents: Coins representing sizable sums of money. The modern notion of God-given "talents" (i.e., abilities) is derived from this parable (CCC 1936–37). See note on 18:24.

25:26 slothful servant!: The master rebuked his servant for more than laziness—he was **wicked**. The servant was presumably insulted when the master entrusted him with only a single talent (25:15), while others received more. Despising his master, then, he refused to trade with—or even invest—the talent, lest his master should benefit from his stewardship. The parable thus warns against sloth that is fueled by envy (cf. Lk 19:14).

25:28 Failure to use and cultivate one's talents results in their loss.

25:31-46 Jesus' prophesy of the Last Judgment unfolds at two historical levels. **(1)** He initially foretells the judgment of Old Covenant Israel. This involves his "coming" to Jerusalem (A.D. 70) as the Shepherd who separates the faithful sheep of Israel from the wicked goats (10:23; 16:27-28; cf. Ezek 34:17-22). **(2)** He ultimately foretells the General Judgment at the end of history. This will involve Christ's Second Coming and the general resurrection of all people before his throne to be **blessed** (25:34) or **cursed** (25:41) according to their deeds (Jn 5:25-29; Rev 20:11-12; CCC 1038-39).

---

[d] This talent was more than fifteen years' wages of a laborer.

Matthew 25, 26

another as a shepherd separates the sheep from the goats, [33]and he will place the sheep at his right hand, but the goats at the left. [34]Then the King will say to those at his right hand, 'Come, O blessed of my Father, inherit the kingdom prepared for you from the foundation of the world; [35]for I was hungry and you gave me food, I was thirsty and you gave me drink, I was a stranger and you welcomed me, [36]I was naked and you clothed me, I was sick and you visited me, I was in prison and you came to me.' [37]Then the righteous will answer him, 'Lord, when did we see thee hungry and feed thee, or thirsty and give thee drink? [38]And when did we see thee a stranger and welcome thee, or naked and clothe thee? [39]And when did we see thee sick or in prison and visit thee?' [40]And the King will answer them, 'Truly, I say to you, as you did it to one of the least of these my brethren, you did it to me.' [41]Then he will say to those at his left hand, 'Depart from me, you cursed, into the eternal fire prepared for the devil and his angels; [42]for I was hungry and you gave me no food, I was thirsty and you gave me no drink, [43]I was a stranger and you did not welcome me, naked and you did not clothe me, sick and in prison and you did not visit me.' [44]Then they also will answer, 'Lord, when did we see thee hungry or thirsty or a stranger or naked or sick or in prison, and did not minister to thee?' [45]Then he will answer them, 'Truly, I say to you, as you did it not to one of the least of these, you did it not to me.' [46]And they will go away into eternal punishment, but the righteous into eternal life."

The Plot to Kill Jesus

26 When Jesus had finished all these sayings, he said to his disciples, [2]"You know that after two days the Passover is coming, and the Son of man will be delivered up to be crucified."

[3]Then the chief priests and the elders of the people gathered in the palace of the high priest, who was called Ca´iaphas, [4]and took counsel together in order to arrest Jesus by stealth and kill him. [5]But they said, "Not during the feast, lest there be a tumult among the people."

The Anointing at Bethany

[6]Now when Jesus was at Bethany in the house of Simon the leper, [7]a woman came up to him with an alabaster jar of very expensive ointment, and she poured it on his head, as he sat at table. [8]But when the disciples saw it, they were indignant, saying, "Why this waste? [9]For this ointment might have been sold for a large sum, and given to the poor." [10]But Jesus, aware of this, said to them, "Why do you trouble the woman? For she has done a beautiful thing to me. [11]For you always have the poor with you, but you will not always have me. [12]In pouring this ointment on my body she has done it to prepare me for burial. [13]Truly, I say to you, wherever this gospel is preached in the whole world, what she has done will be told in memory of her."

Judas Agrees to Betray Jesus

[14]Then one of the twelve, who was called Judas Iscariot, went to the chief priests [15]and said, "What will you give me if I deliver him to you?" And they paid him thirty pieces of silver. [16]And from that moment he sought an opportunity to betray him.

The Passover with the Disciples

[17]Now on the first day of Unleavened Bread the disciples came to Jesus, saying, "Where will you have us prepare for you to eat the passover?" [18]He said, "Go into the city to such a one, and say to him, 'The Teacher says, My time is at hand; I will keep the passover at your house with my disciples.'" [19]And the disciples did as Jesus had directed them, and they prepared the passover.

25:34: Lk 12:32; Mt 5:3; Rev 13:8; 17:8.   **25:35–36:** Is 58:7; Jas 1:27; 2:15–16; Heb 13:2; 2 Tim 1:16.   **25:40:** Mt 10:42; Mk 9:41; Heb 6:10; Prov 19:17.   **25:41:** Mk 9:48; Lk 16:23; Rev 20:10.   **25:46:** Dan 12:2; Jn 5:29.
26:1: Mt 7:28; 11:1; l3:53; 19.l.   **26:2–5:** Mk 14:1–2; Lk 22:1–2; Jn 11:47–53.   **26:6–13:** Mk 14:3–9; Jn 12:1–8; Lk 7:36–38
26:11: Deut 15:11.   **26:12:** Jn 19:40.   **26:14–16:** Mk 14:10–11; Lk 22:3–6.   **26:15:** Ex 21:32; Zech 11:12.
26:17–19: Mk 14:12–16; Lk 22:7–13.   **26:18:** Mt 26:45; Jn 7:6; 12:23; 13:1; 17:1.   **26:19:** Mt 21:6; Deut 16:5–8.

25:40 you did it to me: Jesus identifies himself with all men, especially the poor and afflicted. Thus by serving others we serve Christ; by performing works of mercy we hope to find mercy (Jas 2:1-13). Indeed, Jesus' own ministry was marked by concern for the disadvantaged (4:23-24; 8:1-17; 11:4-6).

25:41 the eternal fire: A description of hell. Here the wicked are consigned to everlasting punishment with the **devil** and his fallen **angels** (cf. Mk 9:48; 2 Pet 2:4; Rev 20:10; CCC 1033–35).

26:1–27:66 All four Gospels give more attention to Jesus' final days than to the rest of his ministry. In Matthew, Passion Week (chaps. 21-28) comprises nearly one-third of his Gospel. This unparalleled emphasis reflects the centrality of Jesus' Passion and Resurrection in the gospel message.

26:2 the Passover: One of the great feasts of the Jewish calendar. It commemorates God's deliverance of Israel from Egypt (Ex 12) and is celebrated on the 15th of Nisan (or Abib), the first month of the OT liturgical year (March/April). With Weeks (Pentecost) and Booths (Tabernacles), it is one of three feasts that required Israelites to travel to Jerusalem (Ex 23:14; Lev 23:4-8; Deut 16:16). By NT times, the Passover was cel-

ebrated in conjunction with the feast of Unleavened Bread (26:17).

26:3 Caiaphas: The Jerusalem high priest from A.D. 18 to 36.

26:6 Bethany: A small village about two miles from Jerusalem (Jn 11:18). It is on the eastern hillside of the Mount of Olives and was the hometown of Jesus' friends Mary, Martha, and Lazarus (Jn 11:1).

26:7 expensive ointment: A costly extract from pure nard that was poured **on his head** and his feet (Mk 14:3; Jn 12:3).

26:12 for burial: Jesus' anointing is a twofold sign: **(1)** It points to the immeasurable value of Jesus' presence. The costly ointment is not wasted but used in a generous act of reverence and worship. **(2)** It points forward to Jesus' Passion and death as his own priceless gift for man's salvation.

26:15 thirty pieces of silver: The price of a slave (Ex 21:32). Judas' betrayal for "blood money" (27:6) stands in contrast to the lavish gesture of the woman (26:6-13). He places little value on Jesus and prefers instead personal gain.

26:17 first day of Unleavened Bread: Begins with the day of Passover. During this feast, the Jews ate only unleavened bread for seven days (Ex 12:14-20).

20 When it was evening, he sat at table with the twelve disciples;*e* ²¹and as they were eating, he said, "Truly, I say to you, one of you will betray me." ²²And they were very sorrowful, and began to say to him one after another, "Is it I, Lord?" ²³He answered, "He who has dipped his hand in the dish with me, will betray me. ²⁴The Son of man goes as it is written of him, but woe to that man by whom the Son of man is betrayed! It would have been better for that man if he had not been born." ²⁵Judas, who betrayed him, said, "Is it I, Master?"*f* He said to him, "You have said so."

The Institution of the Lord's Supper

26 Now as they were eating, Jesus took bread, and blessed, and broke it, and gave it to the disciples and said, "Take, eat; this is my body." ²⁷And he took a cup, and when he had given thanks he gave it to them, saying, "Drink of it, all of you; ²⁸for this is my blood of the *g* covenant, which is poured out for many for the forgiveness of sins. ²⁹I tell you I shall not drink again of this fruit of the vine until that day when I drink it new with you in my Father's kingdom."

Peter's Denial Foretold

30 And when they had sung a hymn, they went out to the Mount of Olives. ³¹Then Jesus said to them, "You will all fall away because of me this night; for it is written, 'I will strike the shepherd, and the sheep of the flock will be scattered.' ³²But after I am raised up, I will go before you to Galilee." ³³Peter declared to him, "Though they all fall away because of you, I will never fall away." ³⁴Jesus said to him, "Truly, I say to you, this very night, before the cock crows, you will deny me three times." ³⁵Peter said to him, "Even if I must die with you, I will not deny you." And so said all the disciples.

Jesus Prays in Gethsemane

36 Then Jesus went with them to a place called Gethsem'ane, and he said to his disciples, "Sit here, while I go over there and pray." ³⁷And taking with him Peter and the two sons of Zeb'edee, he began to be sorrowful and troubled. ³⁸Then he said to them, "My soul is very sorrowful, even to death; remain here, and watch*h* with me." ³⁹And going a little farther he fell on his face and prayed, "My Father, if it be possible, let this cup pass from me; nevertheless, not as I will, but as thou wilt." ⁴⁰And he came to the disciples and found them sleeping; and he said to Peter, "So, could you not watch*h* with me one hour? ⁴¹Watch*h* and pray that you may not enter into temptation; the spirit indeed is willing, but the flesh is weak." ⁴²Again, for the second time, he went away and prayed, "My Father, if this cannot pass unless I drink it, thy will be done." ⁴³And again he came and found them sleeping, for their eyes were heavy. ⁴⁴So, leaving them again, he went

26:20–24: Mk 14:17–21; Lk 22.14, 21–23; Jn 13:21–30.   26:24: Ps 41:9; Lk 24:25; 1 Cor 15:3; Acts 17:2–3; Mt 18:7.
26:26–29: Mk 14:22–25; Lk 22:17–19; 1 Cor 10:16; 11:23-26; Mt 14:19; 15:36.   26:28: Heb 9:20; Mt 20:28; Mk 1:4; Ex 24:6–8.
26:30–35: Mk 14:26–31; Lk 22:33–34, 39; Jn 14:31; 18:1; 13:36–38[?].   26:31: Zech 13:7; Jn 16:32.   26:32: Mt 28:7, 10, 16
26:36–46: Mk 14:32–42; Lk 22:40–46.   26:38: Jn 12:27; Heb 5:7–8.   26:39: Jn 18:11; Mt 20:22.   26:41: Mt 6:13; Lk 11:4.
26:42: Jn 4:34; 5:30; 6:38.

26:26–29 Matthew's Last Supper account highlights three aspects of the Eucharist (CCC 1339-40). **(1)** Jesus identifies the unleavened **bread** and the **cup** with his **body** and **blood** (26:26-28). Through his spoken words the mystery of "transubstantiation" takes place: his body and blood replace the entire substance of the bread and wine. Although his presence remains undetected by the senses, the force of the verb "is" (Gk. *estin*) should not be reduced to "represents" or "symbolizes". The Church's faith rests entirely on Jesus' solemn words (cf. Jn 6:68; 2 Cor 5:7). **(2)** Jesus links the Eucharist with his forthcoming sacrifice on the Cross (27:35; Jn 19:34). The expression **poured out** (26:28) recalls how Old Covenant priests poured the blood of sacrificial offerings at the base of the Temple's altar to make atonement for sin (Lev 4:16–20; cf. Deut 12:26, 27; Is 53:12). Shedding his own blood, Jesus is both the high priest and the sacrificial victim of the New Covenant; his priestly offering is present in an unbloody manner in the sacrament and secures for us the **forgiveness of sins**. **(3)** Christ's presence in the Eucharist makes the sacrament a true communion with Jesus (1 Cor 10:16). The phrase **blood of the covenant** is drawn from Ex 24:8, where God entered a covenant of love and communion with Israel through sacrifice. The consumption of blood—always forbidden under the Old Covenant (Lev 17:11–12)—is now enjoined in the New, since it communicates Christ's divine life to the believer (Jn 6:53; CCC 1329, 1374, 1381).

26:26 The Eucharist is prefigured when Jesus multiplies bread for the crowds. See note on 14:13–21. ● *Anagogi-*

cally (St. Thomas Aquinas, *Office of the Adorable Sacrament*), the Eucharist is a pledge and sign of heavenly glory. While the sacrament is a true communion with Christ in the present, it points also to our perfect communion with him in eternity. In heaven, the sacraments will give way to the saints' direct and unmediated union with the Trinity (CCC 1402).

26:30 sung a hymn: The Passover liturgy included the singing of various Hallel Psalms. Normally Psalms 113-14 were sung before the main meal, while Psalms 115-18 were sung afterward.

26:31 I will strike the shepherd: A citation from Zech 13:7. Its fulfillment unfolds when the disciples flee from Gethsemane (26:56). Jesus' assurance of a later appearance in "Galilee" (26:32) implies that the apostles will abandon him only temporarily—they will be regathered (28:16; cf. Lk 22:31-32).

26:34 before the cock crows: Possibly the bugle call that signaled the end of the third watch of the night. The Romans referred to this watch (midnight to 3 A.M.) as the "cockcrow" (Mk 13:35). See note on 14:25.

26:36 Gethsemane: A Hebrew word meaning "oil press". It is a garden traditionally located near the foot of the Mount of Olives, facing Jerusalem (cf. Jn 18:1).

26:37 The third episode when Peter, James, and John alone are privileged to accompany Jesus. They also witnessed the raising of Jairus' daughter (Mk 5:37) and the Transfiguration (17:1).

26:39 let this cup pass: Jesus fears his Passion and Crucifixion. As a man, he has a natural aversion to suffering that is both physical (crucifixion) and spiritual (bearing the sins of the world). As God's Son, he could have suppressed these human passions by divine effort, but he chose to embrace the Father's plan even in agony. This ordeal in the garden is traditionally

e Other ancient authorities omit *disciples*.
f Or *Rabbi*.   *g* Other ancient authorities insert *new*.   *h* Or *keep awake*.

away and prayed for the third time, saying the same words. ⁴⁵Then he came to the disciples and said to them, "Are you still sleeping and taking your rest? Behold, the hour is at hand, and the Son of man is betrayed into the hands of sinners. ⁴⁶Rise, let us be going; see, my betrayer is at hand."

The Betrayal and Arrest of Jesus

47 While he was still speaking, Judas came, one of the twelve, and with him a great crowd with swords and clubs, from the chief priests and the elders of the people. ⁴⁸Now the betrayer had given them a sign, saying, "The one I shall kiss is the man; seize him." ⁴⁹And he came up to Jesus at once and said, "Hail, Master!" ⁱ And he kissed him. ⁵⁰Jesus said to him, "Friend, why are you here?" ʲ Then they came up and laid hands on Jesus and seized him. ⁵¹And behold, one of those who were with Jesus stretched out his hand and drew his sword, and struck the slave of the high priest, and cut off his ear. ⁵²Then Jesus said to him, "Put your sword back into its place; for all who take the sword will perish by the sword. ⁵³Do you think that I cannot appeal to my Father, and he will at once send me more than twelve legions of angels? ⁵⁴But how then should the scriptures be fulfilled, that it must be so?" ⁵⁵At that hour Jesus said to the crowds, "Have you come out as against a robber, with swords and clubs to capture me? Day after day I sat in the temple teaching, and you did not seize me. ⁵⁶But all this has taken place, that the scriptures of the prophets might be fulfilled." Then all the disciples deserted him and fled.

Jesus before the High Priest

57 Then those who had seized Jesus led him to Ca´iaphas the high priest, where the scribes and the elders had gathered. ⁵⁸But Peter followed him at a distance, as far as the courtyard of the high priest, and going inside he sat with the guards to see the end. ⁵⁹Now the chief priests and the whole council sought false testimony against Jesus that they might put him to death, ⁶⁰but they found none, though many false witnesses came forward. At last two came forward ⁶¹and said, "This fellow said, 'I am able to destroy the temple of God, and to build it in three days.'" ⁶²And the high priest stood up and said, "Have you no answer to make? What is it that these men testify against you?" ⁶³But Jesus was silent. And the high priest said to him, "I adjure you by the living God, tell us if you are the Christ, the Son of God." ⁶⁴Jesus said to him, "You have said so. But I tell you, hereafter you will see the Son of man seated at the right hand of Power, and coming on the clouds of heaven." ⁶⁵Then the high priest tore his robes, and said, "He has uttered

---

26:45: Mt 26:18; Jn 12:23; 13:1; 17:1. **26:47–56:** Mk 14:43–50; Lk 22:47–53; Jn 18:2–11. **26:50:** Mt 20:13; 22:12. **26:52:** Gen 9:6; Rev 13:10. **26:55:** Lk 19:47; Jn 18:19–21. **26:57–75:** Mk 14:53–72; Lk 22:54–71; Jn 18:12–27. **26:61:** Mt 24:2; 27:40; Acts 6:14; Jn 2:19. **26:63:** Mt 27:11; jn 18:33. **26:64:** Mt 16:28; Dan 7:13; Ps 110:1. **26:65:** Nb 14:6; Acts 14:14; Lev 24:16.

---

viewed as Satan's most aggressive assault on Jesus (Lk 22:53) (CCC 612). See note on 20:22. **not as I will:** Jesus entrusts himself to the Father despite his fear of death (cf. Phil 2:8; Heb 5:7). Note that his human will is in perfect harmony with the divine will (cf. Jn 6:38; CCC 475).

26:45 sleeping: The slumber of the disciples is clear evidence that "the flesh is weak" (26:41). The privilege of their presence with Jesus at his time of distress was wasted by their lack of attention and prayer. See note on Mk 14:38.

26:52 Put your sword back: Jesus rebukes Peter for responding with violence, recoiling from any attempt at frustrating the Father's plan. His obedience and life-giving love fulfills the Scriptures (26:54; cf. Is 53:4–12; CCC 2262).

26:53 twelve legions: In the Roman army, a "legion" consisted of nearly 6,000 soldiers. Here it is not the Father's will to dispatch angelic armies to deliver Jesus from sinners; his betrayal and Crucifixion are essential to God's plan of redemption.

26:56 the scriptures: A fulfillment of Zech 13:7, quoted earlier in 26:31. • Jesus' betrayal recalls the conspiracy against King David in 2 Sam 17. Judas Iscariot's role in particular parallels the treachery of Ahithophel, who planned to seek out David at night (2 Sam 17:1; Mt 26:31) when he was "weary and discouraged", so that David's companions would flee (2 Sam 17:2; Mt 26:38, 56). He then prepared to "strike down the king only" (2 Sam 17:2; Mt 26:31). When Ahithophel's plans fell apart, he "hanged himself" (2 Sam 17:23; Mt 27:5).

26:57 Caiaphas: The Jerusalem high priest (A.D. 18–36) and representative head of Israel. He presided over the Sanhedrin, the supreme court of the Jews, during Jesus' trial (cf. Jn 11:49; 18:14).

26:59 the whole council: The entire membership (71) of the Sanhedrin. Their primary function was to regulate and judge the internal affairs of Judaism. Their attempts to procure "false witnesses" (26:60) underscores the extreme measures taken by Jerusalem's leaders to condemn Jesus. See note on Mk 14:55.

26:61 the temple . . . in three days: A distortion of Jesus' words in Jn 2:19. Jesus was predicting his bodily Resurrection, not announcing a plan to reconstruct a fallen building (Jn 2:21).

26:64 You have said so: Jesus breaks silence under oath. According to Mk 14:62, Jesus' response to Caiaphas is unambiguous: he accepts fully the charge to be Israel's divine Messiah and king. **But I tell you:** Jesus appears to be the victim, but he claims to be the victor. Drawing from two OT texts (Ps 110:1 and Dan 7:13), Jesus anticipates his vindication by God. • In context, Ps 110 and Dan 7 share common images. Both envision a heavenly throne room in God's presence (Ps 110:1; Dan 7:9); both depict a royal Messiah who reigns with God (Ps 110:1; Dan 7:14); and both present this figure triumphing over his enemies (Ps 110:2, 5–6; Dan 7:23–27). Jesus here weaves these texts into a self-portrait: he is the royal **Son of man** soon to be vindicated over his enemies and enthroned at God's **right hand**. By contrast, the high priest and the council are cast as the Messiah's adversaries seeking his death. Caiaphas in particular is toppled from his high position. As Israel's head representative, he is the only person permitted to enter the Temple's innermost chamber. Jesus claims something still greater for himself: as Messiah, he is now the true head of faithful Israel in the Church and will assume his throne in the inner shrine of God's heavenly presence at his Ascension (Mk 16:19; CCC 663–64).

26:65 tore his robes: A gesture of extreme distress and wrongdoing—the Mosaic Law forbade the **high priest** to tear his sacred vestments (Lev 10:6; 21:10). **blasphemy:** The coun-

---

ⁱ Or *Rabbi.*
ʲ Or *do that for which you have come.*

blasphemy. Why do we still need witnesses? You have now heard his blasphemy. ⁶⁶What is your judgment?" They answered, "He deserves death." ⁶⁷Then they spat in his face, and struck him; and some slapped him, ⁶⁸saying, "Prophesy to us, you Christ! Who is it that struck you?"

Peter's Denial of Jesus
69 Now Peter was sitting outside in the courtyard. And a maid came up to him, and said, "You also were with Jesus the Galilean." ⁷⁰But he denied it before them all, saying, "I do not know what you mean." ⁷¹And when he went out to the porch, another maid saw him, and she said to the bystanders, "This man was with Jesus of Nazareth." ⁷²And again he denied it with an oath, "I do not know the man." ⁷³After a little while the bystanders came up and said to Peter, "Certainly you are also one of them, for your accent betrays you." ⁷⁴Then he began to invoke a curse on himself and to swear, "I do not know the man." And immediately the cock crowed. ⁷⁵And Peter remembered the saying of Jesus, "Before the cock crows, you will deny me three times." And he went out and wept bitterly.

Jesus Brought before Pilate
27 When morning came, all the chief priests and the elders of the people took counsel against Jesus to put him to death; ²and they bound him and led him away and delivered him to Pilate the governor.

The Suicide of Judas
3 When Judas, his betrayer, saw that he was condemned, he repented and brought back the thirty pieces of silver to the chief priests and the elders, ⁴saying, "I have sinned in betraying innocent blood." They said, "What is that to us? See to it yourself." ⁵And throwing down the pieces of silver in the temple, he departed; and he went and hanged himself. ⁶But the chief priests, taking the pieces of silver, said, "It is not lawful to put them into the treasury, since they are blood money." ⁷So they took counsel, and bought with them the potter's field, to bury strangers in. ⁸Therefore that field has been called the Field of Blood to this day. ⁹Then was fulfilled what had been spoken by the prophet Jeremiah, saying, "And they took the thirty pieces of silver, the price of him on whom a price had been set by some of the sons of Israel, ¹⁰and they gave them for the potter's field, as the Lord directed me."

Pilate Questions Jesus
11 Now Jesus stood before the governor; and the governor asked him, "Are you the King of the Jews?" Jesus said to him, "You have said so." ¹²But when he was accused by the chief priests and elders, he made no answer. ¹³Then Pilate said to him, "Do you not hear how many things they testify against you?" ¹⁴But he gave him no answer, not even to a single charge; so that the governor wondered greatly.

26:75: Mt 26:34. **27:1–2:** Mk 15:1; Lk 23:1; Jn 18:28. **27:3–10:** Acts 1:16–20. **27:3:** Mt 26:15; Ex 21:32.
27:6: Deut 23:18. **27:9:** Zech 11:12–13; Jer 32:6–15; 18:2–3. **27:11–26:** Mk 15:2–15; Lk 23:3, 18–25; Jn 18:29–19:16.
27:14: Lk 23:9; Mt 26:62; Mk 14:60; 1 Tim 6:13.

---

cil charges Jesus with blaspheming the name of God and issues a death sentence (Lev 24:16). The Romans, however, reserved for themselves the sole authority to administer capital punishment in NT Palestine (Jn 18:31). For this reason, the council delivers Jesus to the Roman governor, Pilate (27:2), in hopes of enforcing their judgment (CCC 591, 596).
26:73 your accent: Peter's Galilean *accent* was foreign to natives of Jerusalem (Mk 14:70).
26:74 the cock crowed: Peter is unwilling to identify with Jesus and denies even knowing him. Hearing the cock, he recalls Jesus' prophecy (26:34) and probably his foolish overconfidence (26:35). See note on 26:34. • *Morally* (St. Laurence Giustiniani, *de Christi agone*, chap. 9), Peter typifies man's proneness to sin. The cock is the informed conscience that accuses us of sins, reminding us of God's commandments and stirring the soul to contrition. As with Peter, the informed conscience directs sinners away from despair and toward genuine repentance.
27:1 took council: Depicts the conspiracy of Jesus' adversaries (12:14; 22:15; 26:4). • Matthew's description of the plot alludes to Ps 2:2 (Acts 4:25–27). In context, David describes rulers who "take council together against the LORD and his anointed" (i.e., the Messiah).
27:2 Pilate the governor: Pontius Pilate, the Roman procurator of Judea, Idumea, and Samaria from A.D. 26 to 36. He is known from first-century sources as a harsh tyrant. Although he considers Jesus innocent of a capital crime (27:23), he lacks the integrity to release him by his own authority. He is now immortalized in the Apostles' Creed as responsible for the suffering and Crucifixion of Christ.
27:5 hanged himself: The suicide of Judas is difficult to in-

terpret. Matthew describes a hanging, but Acts 1:18 suggests his death involved a headlong fall whereby his "bowels gushed out". Since both the hanging (Mt) and the fall (Acts) seem to involve some height or elevation related to the incident, the two accounts should be considered complementary, although the precise course of events is unknown. See note on 26:56.
27:6 blood money: The priests deem it inappropriate to use Judas' betrayal money as a religious donation to the Temple.
27:8-10 An allusion to OT passages from both **Jeremiah** and Zechariah. • The central scenario of buying a **potter's field** links these prophets. **(1)** Jeremiah made a famous visit to a potter (Jer 18:1-11) and was commissioned by God to purchase a field (Jer 32:6-9), **(2)** while Zechariah narrates how the wicked shepherds of Israel valued the Lord at a mere "thirty shekels of silver" (Zech 11:12), a price so worthless it was thrown away to a "potter" (see text note *q* at Zech 11:13). The wider context of Jeremiah gives these oracles a geographical focus: the prophet also smashed a potter's vessel in the valley of Hinnom (i.e., Gehenna / Topheth) as a sign that Jerusalem and Judea would be destroyed for shedding innocent blood (Jer 19:1-15). Ancient tradition locates Judas' burial site (**Field of Blood**) in this same valley of Hinnom, precisely where Jeremiah smashed the pot and foretold its destiny as a future graveyard (Jer 19:11). Matthew may think of the smashed vessel, originally a sign of Judea's demise, as also a prophetic sign of Judas' destruction.
27:11 King of the Jews?: The Jerusalem leaders give Jesus a title with obvious political overtones. This would appear to threaten Rome and give legal cause for the **governor** to execute Jesus for treason.

Barabbas or Jesus?

15 Now at the feast the governor was accustomed to release for the crowd any one prisoner whom they wanted. [16]And they had then a notorious prisoner, called Barab′bas.[k] [17]So when they had gathered, Pilate said to them, "Whom do you want me to release for you, Barab′bas[k] or Jesus who is called Christ?" [18]For he knew that it was out of envy that they had delivered him up. [19]Besides, while he was sitting on the judgment seat, his wife sent word to him, "Have nothing to do with that righteous man, for I have suffered much over him today in a dream." [20]Now the chief priests and the elders persuaded the people to ask for Barab′bas and destroy Jesus. [21]The governor again said to them, "Which of the two do you want me to release for you?" And they said, "Barab′bas." [22]Pilate said to them, "Then what shall I do with Jesus who is called Christ?" They all said, "Let him be crucified." [23]And he said, "Why, what evil has he done?" But they shouted all the more, "Let him be crucified."

Pilate Hands Jesus Over to Be Crucified

24 So when Pilate saw that he was gaining nothing, but rather that a riot was beginning, he took water and washed his hands before the crowd, saying, "I am innocent of this righteous man's blood;[l] see to it yourselves." [25]And all the people answered, "His blood be on us and on our children!" [26]Then he released for them Barab′bas, and having scourged Jesus, delivered him to be crucified.

The Soldiers Mock Jesus

27 Then the soldiers of the governor took Jesus into the praetorium, and they gathered the whole battalion before him. [28]And they stripped him and put a scarlet robe upon him, [29]and plaiting a crown of thorns they put it on his head, and put a reed in his right hand. And kneeling before him they mocked him, saying, "Hail, King of the Jews!" [30]And they spat upon him, and took the reed and struck him on the head. [31]And when they had mocked him, they stripped him of the robe, and put his own clothes on him, and led him away to crucify him.

The Crucifixion of Jesus

32 As they were marching out, they came upon a man of Cyre′ne, Simon by name; this man they compelled to carry his cross. [33]And when they came to a place called Gol′gotha (which means the place of a skull), [34]they offered him wine to drink, mingled with gall; but when he tasted it, he would not drink it. [35]And when they had crucified him, they divided his garments among them by casting lots; [36]then they sat down and kept watch over him there. [37]And over his head they put the charge against him, which read, "This is Jesus the King of the Jews." [38]Then two robbers were crucified with him, one on the right and one on the left. [39]And those who passed by derided him, wagging their heads [40]and saying, "You who would destroy the temple and build it in three days, save yourself! If you are the Son of God, come down from the cross." [41]So also the chief priests, with the scribes and elders, mocked him, saying, [42]"He saved others; he cannot save himself. He is the King of Israel; let him come down now from the cross, and we will believe in him. [43]He trusts in God; let God deliver him now, if he desires him; for he said, 'I am the Son of God.'" [44]And the robbers who were crucified with him also reviled him in the same way.

27:19: Lk 23:4. 27:21: Acts 3:13–14. 27:24: Deut 21:6–9; Ps 26:6. 27:25: Acts 5:28; Josh 2:19.
27:27–31: Mk 15:16–20; Lk 23:11; Jn 19:2–3. 27:32: Mk 15:21; Lk 23:26; Jn 19:17; Heb 13:12.
27:33–44: Mk 15:22–32; Lk 23:33–39; Jn 19:17–24. 27:35: Ps 22:18. 27:39: Ps 22:7–8; 109:25.
27:40: Mt 26:61; Acts 6:14; Jn 2:19.

27:19 a dream: Matthew alone records this episode with Pilate's **wife**. As in the Infancy Narratives, dreams are channels for divine warning and instruction (1:20; 2:12–13, 22).

27:24 a riot: The same word is translated "tumult" (Gk. *thorybos*) in 26:5. The Jerusalem leaders originally hoped to avoid a public upheaval but now instigate one to their own advantage. **washed his hands:** Pilate's vain gesture to excuse himself from the responsibility of Jesus' death. See note on 27:2.

27:25 His blood be on us: An oath formula (cf. Josh 2:17–19). The Jerusalem mob invokes a curse upon itself, staking their lives on their decision. Sadly, their oath was rash and inappropriate; they did not take seriously the responsibilities attached to crucifying Jesus. Their guilt eventually brought judgment on the Holy City (cf. Jer 26:15; Acts 5:28; CCC 597–598). See note on 5:33.

27:27 praetorium: The residence of a Roman official (Pilate) in Jerusalem.

27:28 a scarlet robe: The military cloak of a Roman soldier.

✝ **27:29 King of the Jews!:** A title suggested by the Sanhedrin and used mockingly by the soldiers (Lk 23:2).

It is also the transcription on Jesus' Cross (27:37). The wise men are the only figures in Matthew to use the title in a positive and honorable way (2:2). ● *Allegorically*, the title and articles used to slander Jesus signify his kingship and triumph over sin. The scarlet robe (27:28) represents Jesus' defeat of Satan through his shed blood; the crown of thorns (27:29) points to the crown of glory that adorns Jesus at his Ascension; the reed (27:29) signifies the scepter of his heavenly kingdom. Through these images, Christ's victory is paradoxically announced in the midst of his apparent defeat.

27:33 Golgotha: An Aramaic term meaning "skull". The Vulgate translation of this word (Lat. *Calvariae*) is the source of the modern term "Calvary". Golgotha lies outside Jerusalem's walls (Jn 19:20) and probably acquired its name as a site commonly used for executing criminals.

27:34 gall: A mixture of herbs and myrrh used as a narcotic (cf. Mk 15:23). Jesus' refusal of painkillers signifies his total acceptance of the Father's will and the extent of his sacrificial love (cf. Jn 10:17–18; Rom 5:8).

27:35 crucified him: Crucifixion was designed to facilitate a slow and torturous death. Victims died from a combination of blood loss and asphyxiation. See note on Mk 15:24. **divided his garments:** An allusion to Ps 22:18. This psalm is quoted by Jesus before his death (27:46; cf. Jn 19:24).

---

[k] Other ancient authorities read *Jesus Barabbas*.
[l] Other ancient authorities omit *righteous* or *man's*.

The Death of Jesus

45 Now from the sixth hour there was darkness over all the land *m* until the ninth hour. [46]And about the ninth hour Jesus cried with a loud voice, "Eli, Eli, la´ma sabach-tha´ni?" that is, "My God, my God, why hast thou forsaken me?" [47]And some of the bystanders hearing it said, "This man is calling Eli´jah." [48]And one of them at once ran and took a sponge, filled it with vinegar, and put it on a reed, and gave it to him to drink. [49]But the others said, "Wait, let us see whether Eli´jah will come to save him." *n* [50]And Jesus cried again with a loud voice and yielded up his spirit.

51 And behold, the curtain of the temple was torn in two, from top to bottom; and the earth shook, and the rocks were split; [52]the tombs also were opened, and many bodies of the saints who had fallen asleep were raised, [53]and coming out of the tombs after his resurrection they went into the holy city and appeared to many. [54]When the centurion and those who were with him, keeping watch over Jesus, saw the earthquake and what took place, they were filled with awe, and said, "Truly this was the Son *x* of God!"

55 There were also many women there, looking on from afar, who had followed Jesus from Galilee, ministering to him; [56]among whom were Mary Mag´dalene, and Mary the mother of James and Joseph, and the mother of the sons of Zeb´edee.

The Burial of Jesus

57 When it was evening, there came a rich man from Arimathe´a, named Joseph, who also was a disciple of Jesus. [58]He went to Pilate and asked for the body of Jesus. Then Pilate ordered it to be given to him. [59]And Joseph took the body, and wrapped it in a clean linen shroud, [60]and laid it in his own new tomb, which he had hewn in the rock; and he rolled a great stone to the door of the tomb, and departed. [61]Mary Mag´dalene and the other Mary were there, sitting opposite the tomb.

The Guard at the Tomb

62 Next day, that is, after the day of Preparation, the chief priests and the Pharisees gathered before Pilate [63]and said, "Sir, we remember how that impostor said, while he was still alive, 'After three days I will rise again.' [64]Therefore order the tomb to be made secure until the third day, lest his disciples go and steal him away, and tell the people, 'He has risen from the dead,' and the last fraud will be worse than the first." [65]Pilate said to them, "You have a guard *o* of soldiers; go, make it as secure as you can." *p* [66]So they went and made the tomb secure by sealing the stone and setting a guard.

The Resurrection of Jesus

28 Now after the sabbath, toward the dawn of the first day of the week, Mary Mag´dalene and the other Mary went to see the tomb. [2]And behold, there was a great earthquake; for an angel

---

27:45–56: Mk 15:33–41; Lk 23:44–54; Jn 19:28–30. **27:46:** Ps 22:1. **27:48:** Ps 69:21. **27:51:** Heb 9:8; 10:19; Ex 26:31–35; Mt 28:2. **27:54:** Mt 3:17; 17:5. **27:56:** Lk 24:10. **27:57–61:** Mk 15:42–47; Lk 23:50–56; Jn 19:38–42; Acts 13:29. **27:63:** Mt 16:21; 17:23; 20:19. **27:66:** Mt 27:60; 28:11–15. **28:1–8:** Mk 16:1–8; Lk 24:1–9; Jn 20:1–2. **28:1:** Lk 8:2; Mt 27:56 **28:2:** Mt 27:51, 60.

27:45 sixth hour . . . ninth hour: i.e., from noon until 3 P.M. See note on 20:1. • The phenomena surrounding the Crucifixion recall Amos 8:8–9. In context, Amos prophesies the day of the Lord, when God would judge his enemies and the sinners of his people. On this day, the land would "tremble", the sun would "go down at noon", and there would be "lamentation" like the "mourning for an only son". • *Symbolically* (St. Cyprian, *De bono patientiae*, 7), the disturbances of Good Friday signify creation's distress over the death of its Creator. The sun in particular withdraws its rays to look away, lest it be forced to gaze upon the crime of Jesus' enemies.

27:46 Eli, Eli: A mixed Hebrew and Aramaic quotation of Ps 22:1. Matthew elsewhere alludes to the psalm in 27:35 (Ps 22:18), 27:39 (Ps 22:7), and 27:43 (Ps 22:8). • In context, Ps 22 depicts the plight of a righteous sufferer. Although innocent, he is mocked and abused by the ungodly. He thus turns to God in his distress and petitions God for deliverance. By citing the psalm's opening line, Jesus expresses his agony as he experiences the full brunt of rejection. This evokes the entire plot of Ps 22, where the sufferer's humiliation gives way to his vindication. Thus Jesus does not consider his Passion meaningless or a mark of failure; still less does he succumb to a sin of despair. Rather, he "trusts in God" (27:43) and surrenders his spirit to the Father (Lk 23:46). Like the innocent suf-

ferer of Ps 22, he is confident that God will turn his misery into victory (cf. Lk 23:43).

27:51 curtain of the temple: Hung between the Temple's two holiest chambers, the holy place and the most holy place (Ex 26:31–34). The veil was a sign that God's infinite holiness could not be approached by sinners (cf. Heb 9:8). With Jesus' saving death, forgiveness is secured for man, and access to heaven is reopened (Eph 2:18; Heb 10:19–22). This is announced by God himself, who tears the veil **from top to bottom**. See note on Mk 15:38.

27:52 saints . . . were raised: Apart from Matthew's Gospel, history is silent regarding this event and the OT personalities involved. No indication is given as to *who* was raised, how long they remained, or what *kind of body* these saints possessed; yet there would be no reason for Matthew to record it, except that witnesses from Jerusalem verified the facts (27:53). Theologically, it is essential to note that these OT saints were raised "after" (27:53) Easter morning, since Jesus was the first to be resurrected in glory (Col 1:18).

27:65 a guard of soldiers: Probably Roman military personnel, since they sought refuge with the Jerusalem priests after verifying the empty tomb (28:11). This was to keep them "out of trouble" with Pilate (28:14). The consequences of Jesus' disappearance for these soldiers would have likely involved capital punishment (cf. Acts 12:19; 16:27).

28:1 first day of the week: Sunday, the day following the Jewish Sabbath. To commemorate Christ's Resurrection, the early Christians called it the "Lord's day" (Rev 1:10) and designated it a day for sacred assembly, eucharistic worship, and prayer (Acts 20:7; CCC 2174).

---

m Or *earth.*
n Other ancient authorities insert *And another took a spear and pierced his side, and out came water and blood.*
x Or *a son.* *o* Or *Take a guard.* *p* Greek *know.*

of the Lord descended from heaven and came and rolled back the stone, and sat upon it. ³His appearance was like lightning, and his clothing white as snow. ⁴And for fear of him the guards trembled and became like dead men. ⁵But the angel said to the women, "Do not be afraid; for I know that you seek Jesus who was crucified. ⁶He is not here; for he has risen, as he said. Come, see the place where he *q* lay. ⁷Then go quickly and tell his disciples that he has risen from the dead, and behold, he is going before you to Galilee; there you will see him. Behold, I have told you." ⁸So they departed quickly from the tomb with fear and great joy, and ran to tell his disciples. ⁹And behold, Jesus met them and said, "Hail!" And they came up and took hold of his feet and worshiped him. ¹⁰Then Jesus said to them, "Do not be afraid; go and tell my brethren to go to Galilee, and there they will see me."

The Report of the Guard

11 While they were going, behold, some of the guard went into the city and told the chief priests all that had taken place. ¹²And when they had assembled with the elders and taken counsel, they gave a sum of money to the soldiers ¹³and said, "Tell people, 'His disciples came by night and stole him away while we were asleep.' ¹⁴And if this comes to the governor's ears, we will satisfy him and keep you out of trouble." ¹⁵So they took the money and did as they were directed; and this story has been spread among the Jews to this day.

28:4: Mt 27:62–66.   **28:7:** Mt 26:32; 28:16; Jn 21:1–23.   **28:9:** Jn 20:14–18.   **28:11:** Mt 27:62–66.

28:6 he has risen, as he said: Jesus predicted his Resurrection six times in Matthew (12:40; 16:21; 17:9, 23; 20:19; 26:32). Historically, the miraculous fact of Jesus' Resurrection is central to the Christian faith and provides the ultimate proof of his divinity (Jn 10:17–18). The event is not a mere resuscitation of Jesus' body but a glorification of his humanity, body and soul. Christ's Resurrection anticipates the general resurrection of all people before the Last Judgment (cf. Jn 5:28, 29; 1 Cor 15:20–24; Rev 1:5; CCC 638).

28:15 this story: A desperate fabrication by the Jerusalem leaders. Their bribe of the Roman soldiers illustrates how willful blindness hardens the heart to resist uncomfortable truths, even in the face of evidence (cf. Rom 1:18–21).

---

q Other ancient authorities read *the Lord.*

28:18 All authority: The Father vindicates Jesus at his Resurrection and gives him full dominion over creation (cf. Dan 7:13, 14; Eph 1:19–22). Jesus confers his authority on the apostles to preach the gospel and "make disciples" (27:19) as witnesses of his Resurrection (cf. Lk 10:16; Acts 2:32). See note on 24:30.

28:19 Go therefore: Christ's commission to evangelize and catechize the world fulfills God's covenant oath to Abraham that "all the nations" would be blessed (Gen 22:18; Gal 3:8). His outline for the Church's mission is threefold: (1) Evangelizing **all nations** involves more than winning individuals; it entails the conversion of entire cultures. Every area of life must be brought under the Lordship of Christ and in line with the gospel. (2) The administration of the sacraments is essential to the Church's mission and our response. **Baptizing**

The Appearances of the Risen Christ

Central to Christian faith is the bodily resurrection of Jesus. By recording the resurrection appearances, the New Testament leaves no doubt about this event.

IN OR NEAR JERUSALEM
To Mary Magdalene
Mk 16:9; Jn 20:11–18
To other women
Mt 28:8–10
To Peter
Lk 24:34
To ten disciples
Lk 24:36–43; Jn 20:19–25
To the Eleven, including Thomas
Mk 16:14; Jn 20:26–29
At his Ascension
Mk 16:19, 20; Lk 24:50–53; Acts 1:4–12

OTHER APPEARANCES
To the disciples on the Emmaus road
Mk 16:12, 13; Lk 24:13–35
In Galilee
Mt 28:16–20; Jn 21:1–24
To 500 people
1 Cor 15:6
To James and the other apostles
1 Cor 15:7
To Paul on the road to Damascus
Acts 9:1–6; 22:1–10; 26:12–18; 1 Cor 15:8

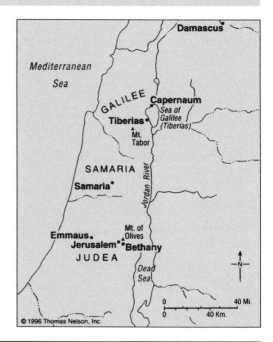

© 1996 Thomas Nelson, Inc.

The Commissioning of the Disciples

16 Now the eleven disciples went to Galilee, to the mountain to which Jesus had directed them. [17] And when they saw him they worshiped him; but some doubted. [18] And Jesus came and said to them, "All authority in heaven and on earth has been given to me. [19] Go therefore and make disciples of all nations, baptizing them in the name of the Father and of the Son and of the Holy Spirit, [20] teaching them to observe all that I have commanded you; and behold, I am with you always, to the close of the age."

28:16–17: 1 Cor 15:5; Jn 21:1–23.   **28:18:** Mt 11:27; Lk 10:22; Philemon 2:9; Eph 1:20–22.   **28:19:** Lk 24:47; Acts 1:8.
28:20: Mt 13:39, 49; 24:3; 18:20; Acts 18:10.

---

new converts is the first step in a long process of sanctification and participation in the life of the Church. **(3)** The transmission of **all** that Christ taught necessitates the assistance of the Holy Spirit, who guides the Church to proclaim the gospel infallibly (cf. Jn 14:26). See note on Jn 16:13. ● The Sacrament of Baptism incorporates Christians into the divine family of the Trinity as children of God (cf. Gal 3:26, 27). The single **name** of the **Father, Son,** and **Spirit** reveals the unity of God's inner life and the oneness of his nature. This expression has become the normative baptismal formula for the Church (CCC 849, 1122, 1257). See note on 3:11.

28:20 I am with you always: Jesus' parting words further elucidate Isaiah's prophetic name for the Messiah, "Emmanuel . . . God with us" (1:23). The risen Christ's ongoing presence in the Church is both ecclesial (18:20) and eucharistic (26:26–28); he thus directs and empowers the worldwide mission of the Church throughout history (CCC 860, 2743).

STUDY QUESTIONS

Chapter 1

For understanding
1. **1:2–17.** What is the purpose of Matthew's genealogy of Jesus? What does it mean to say that this background is "foundational"?
2. **1:16.** Even though Joseph is not the biological father of the Child Jesus, he has responsibilities and exercises certain paternal rights when Jesus is born. What are these?
3. **1:23.** Matthew quotes Isaiah 7:14 and applies it to Jesus. Whose birth was Isaiah referring to? How has the name Emmanuel been fulfilled in Jesus?
4. **1:25.** In the statement that Joseph "knew her not until she had borne a son", what does the word "until" mean?

For application
1. **1:1–17.** Matthew's genealogy is intended to build the reader's faith in Jesus the Messiah. As you study this list of names, what about it helps to build up your faith in him?
2. **1:20.** Joseph had already been committed to Mary when the angel in the dream encouraged him not to "fear to take Mary your wife". How has God addressed fears you may have had about your state-in-life decisions?
3. **1:24.** What is the importance of the detail that Joseph "woke from sleep" as he was considering his relationship with Mary? What events in your life have entailed a similar "waking from sleep"? What happened as a result?
4. **1:25.** Matthew says that Joseph (not Mary) named the child and that he knew the meaning of the name. Who named you, and why? What does your name mean to you? What does it mean to God?

Chapter 2

For understanding
1. **2:1–3.** What were the origins of Herod the Great? What Old Testament prophecy caused Herod to be "troubled"?
2. **2:11.** The three gifts of the Magi have been understood as having symbolic and spiritual significance. On an allegorical level, how does St. Irenaeus understand these gifts? On a moral level, how does St. Gregory the Great understand their meaning?
3. **2:15.** Matthew quotes Hosea 11:1 with reference to the Holy Family's return from Egypt to Palestine. What is the link that Matthew is making between that event and Israelite history?
4. **Topical Essay: Is Matthew's Infancy Narrative Historical?** What are the five reasons given for defending the historical trustworthiness of Matthew's infancy narrative?

For application
1. **2:6.** Following St. Gregory's moral interpretation of the Magi's three gifts, how has your behavior reflected wisdom, worship, and sacrifice?
2. **2:16–18.** God did not prevent Herod from killing innocent children in his effort to destroy Jesus. What effects have tragedies involving innocent persons had on your own or others' faith? How have you dealt with them?
3. **2:19–23.** Consider how God led Joseph to care for the Holy Family and protect them from dangers. How have you noticed the Holy Spirit guiding your life? How sure of his guidance have you been? Despite uncertainty, how have you followed his guidance?

Study Questions

Chapter 3

For understanding

1. **3:2.** Why does Matthew prefer the expression "the kingdom of heaven" over the expression "the kingdom of God"?
2. **3:6.** Which two Old Testament events in the Jordan River prefigure the saving power of Baptism?
3. **3:15.** Although Jesus is sinless and has no need to be baptized for repentance, he submits to John's baptism. Why?
4. **3:15. Word Study: Righteousness.** What does it mean to say that God is righteous? What does righteousness mean for us? How is this word used in Scripture?

For application

1. **3:1–2.** Assume that John the Baptist is speaking to you personally about repenting because "the kingdom of heaven is at hand". What repentance do you think God has in mind for you to do?
2. **3:7.** Suppose further that John addressed you as one of the "brood of vipers". How might that figure apply to you? How would you respond to John's accusation?
3. **3:7, 10.** Compare John's warning with John 15:2, 6. When the Baptist speaks of the "wrath to come" and fruitless trees being burned with fire, how is his teaching similar to that of Jesus? What kind of fruit does the Baptist expect of you?
4. **3:15.** What kind of righteousness does God have in mind for you? What does he want the outcome to be in your life?

Chapter 4

For understanding

1. **4:1–11.** Look up the passages referred to in the note from Deuteronomy 6 through 8. In what ways does the temptation of Jesus in the desert, as Matthew recounts it, fulfill Deuteronomy? What virtue does the Church see in Jesus' behavior? How?
2. **4:1.** Inasmuch as Jesus, as a divine Person, could not sin, what was the point of tempting him?
3. **4:12–16.** Since most prophets were reputed to come out of Judea, why did Jesus choose Galilee as the focus of his early ministry?
4. **4:23.** Matthew says that Jesus taught in synagogues. What was the importance of the synagogue for Jews, as distinct from that of the Temple in Jerusalem?

For application

1. **4:1.** Matthew says, "Jesus was led up by the Spirit into the wilderness to be tempted by the devil." What spiritual *benefit* can be gained through temptation, and why would the Holy Spirit lead you (or allow you to go) where you would have to face it?
2. **4:6.** Satan quotes Psalm 91 out of context, and Jesus immediately places it back into context. How have you tested God or presumed on his care for you? What was the result? What does Jesus' reply to Satan tell you about the attitude you should foster toward God's care?
3. **4:17.** Jesus opens his public ministry with the same message as that of John the Baptist, his cousin. If Jesus were to appear to you and reveal his plans for your life, what do you think his first words would be? Why?
4. **4:20, 22.** Matthew emphasizes that the fishermen immediately left their family business to become Jesus' disciples. How has Jesus' call on your life affected your relationships with your family, specifically parents and older relatives?

Chapter 5

For understanding
1. **5:3–12.** How do the first seven beatitudes correspond to the seven gifts of the Holy Spirit (Is 11:2), according to St. Augustine? What about the eighth beatitude?
2. **5:17.** If the Old Covenant has not been abolished, what does the New Covenant do? Why are the laws of animal sacrifice no longer followed? What happened to the Old Covenant version of the moral law?
3. **5:21–30.** What new dimension does Jesus add to the commands not to kill and not to commit adultery?
4. **5:38–42.** What point does Jesus make about the law of retaliation ("an eye for an eye")? What was the purpose of that law? What is Jesus' response to it?

For application
1. **5:1–11.** Examine each of the eight beatitudes for the way it applies to your life, starting with spiritual poverty. How have the sufferings mentioned in the beatitudes manifested themselves in your life? Even though the promised blessings are fully realized in heaven, how are they being realized on earth?
2. **5:19–20.** What attitude do you think Jesus wants you to take regarding the observance of his law? How can your righteousness exceed that of the scribes and the Pharisees?
3. **5:27–30.** In an age when sexual expression is not only approved but promoted, how can you avoid looking lustfully at another person? What do Jesus' warnings in verses 29–30 tell you about the importance of self-control?
4. **5:43–48.** What enemies has God given you to love? How can you love them? Why does he command you to love them?

Chapter 6

For understanding
1. **6:7–8.** If Jesus is not condemning memorized and repeated prayer, what is he condemning?
2. **6:9–13.** Consider the structure of the Lord's Prayer. Why is it called the "model of prayer"?
3. **6:22–23.** Read the annotation for these verses. How do the verses fit into Jesus' remarks on attitudes toward money?
4. **6:28–30.** In using this rabbinic mode of arguing, what point is Jesus making? What is the anagogical significance of this passage?

For application
1. **6:1–18.** In your own prayer, fasting, and almsgiving, what elements of hypocrisy (a pretense of being better than you are) have you discerned? What have you done to remove the hypocrisy?
2. **6:12, 14–15.** When you pray the Lord's Prayer, how do you respond to verse 12? Whom do you need to forgive? If you refuse to forgive, what (in effect) are you asking God to do to you?
3. **6:24.** What is your attitude toward your possessions? your estate? your career? whatever you hold valuable? How are you "serving" these things? How does that attitude compare with what Jesus says in 5:3?
4. **6:31–34.** Jesus often warns his disciples not to be anxious, because anxiety contradicts the attitude he is promoting here. What are you most commonly anxious about? How does Jesus propose that you deal with your anxiety?

Chapter 7

For understanding
1. **7:1–6.** What kind of judgment does Jesus forbid in this passage? According to the note, what kind of judgment does he require elsewhere in this chapter?
2. **7:13–14.** On what is the comparison of the wide vs. narrow gate based? What was the significance of the gates in the Temple?
3. **7:21–23.** If working signs and wonders in Jesus' name is not itself a safeguard against his condemnation, what is? What is the relationship of sanctifying grace to this passage?
4. **7:24–27.** When this passage is understood from a moral perspective, how does the wise man build and maintain the house of his soul? How does the foolish man fail to build and maintain his?

For application
1. **7:1–5.** Jesus addresses the human tendency to view others' faults as worse than one's own. Of whom are you most critical, or with whom do you compare yourself favorably? What prompts your criticism or comparison? What "log" do you need to remove from yourself?
2. **7:7–12.** What does verse 12 have to do with persevering prayer? What links have you noticed between prayer for yourself or others and the way you treat others?
3. **7:21–23.** How have your natural talents or charismatic gifts contributed to your own growth in holiness? How might they be hindering it?
4. **7:24–27.** How often do you make use of the normal means of sanctification, particularly prayer and the sacraments of Reconciliation and Eucharist?

Chapter 8

For understanding
1. **8:4.** How is mortal sin like leprosy? What is the role of the priest in the restoration process?
2. **8:11–12.** How are Abraham, Isaac, and Jacob linked with the Gentile nations who come from the east and the west to the kingdom of God?
3. **8:22.** What does Jesus mean by saying, "Leave the dead to bury their own dead"? What point is he trying to make?
4. **8:32.** What is the significance of driving the swine into the Sea of Galilee?

For application
1. **8:8.** At Mass we repeat the words of the centurion before receiving the Eucharist. How often do you really pay attention to what you are saying? How well do you mean these words?
2. **8:18–22.** How are creature comforts and family commitments affecting your willingness to follow Jesus? How likely is it that others who know you would agree with your assessment?
3. **8:26.** When have you cried out to God for safety because you were afraid? How did your faith in Jesus calm the fears?
4. **8:33–34.** Did the citizens of Gadara pay more attention to the fate of the demoniacs or of the swine? If God's action causes a change in the direction of your life or that of an acquaintance, on which are you more likely to focus, the change of life or God, who changed your life or that of your acquaintance?

Chapter 9

For understanding
1. **9:3.** Why did the scribes accuse Jesus of blasphemy when he forgave the sins of the paralytic?
2. **9:13.** What prompted Jesus to quote Hosea 6:6, "I desire mercy, and not sacrifice"? What is the significance of the Hosea passage?
3. **9:16-17.** What point is Jesus making about the relationship between the New Covenant and the Old in these two verses?
4. **9:36.** What is the significance of the sheep/shepherd imagery in the Old Testament?

For application
1. **9:8.** Matthew suggests that, seeing Jesus forgive the sins of the paralytic and then heal him, the crowd was afraid of the God who gives such power to men. Recall a time when God acted powerfully in your experience. What reaction toward God did the event cause in you?
2. **9:9-13.** What is the proper sort of company for Christians? How do you respond when the "wrong" sort attempts to join your parish or community?
3. **9:17.** The Holy Spirit has been compared to new wine, and the self to a wineskin. How does the Holy Spirit cause you to "stretch" when he acts in your life?
4. **9:14-15.** How much a part of your religious life is fasting? What are your reasons for fasting or not fasting?

Chapter 10

For understanding
1. **10:2.** Why did Jesus choose 12 apostles, rather than 10 or 14?
2. **10:5.** Why did Jesus tell the apostles to "go nowhere among the Gentiles"?
3. **10:28.** If the disciples are not to fear "those who kill the body but cannot kill the soul", whom *should* they fear, and why?
4. **10:42.** Who are the "little ones" in this verse?

For application
1. **10:9-10.** How have you been called on to exercise the faith to which this passage invites you? How have you been called on to give the sort of hospitality that the passage implies?
2. **10:24-25.** How much like your master are you when persecutions, disagreements, and misunderstandings arise against you or what you stand for?
3. **10:34-39.** What kinds of divisions has Jesus caused in your life? What would you do if Jesus asked you to turn away from or leave those you love most?
4. **10:39.** How has the paradox of this verse worked itself out in your life? If you do not know, what might "losing your life" for Jesus' sake mean for you?

Study Questions

Chapter 11

For understanding
1. **11:11.** What does Jesus mean by saying "among those born of woman, there has arisen no one greater than John the Baptist", then adding that the "least in the kingdom of heaven is greater than he"? Does Jesus criticize the saintliness of his cousin in this verse?
2. **11:12.** What does Jesus mean by saying that men of violence take the kingdom of heaven by force?
3. **11:23–24.** Why does Jesus compare Capernaum unfavorably with Sodom?
4. **11:25–27.** Look up the passages from John's Gospel cited in the note. Which is most like these verses from Matthew? How so? What do they mean?

For application
1. **11:2–6.** When you ask Jesus a question, does he answer with words, or does he point to his deeds in your life? How have these deeds provided the answer you were looking for?
2. **11:16–19.** Do you tend to measure how the Gospel should be lived against the standards of religious or social practice around you? Or do you measure religious or social practice around you based on the standards of the Gospel? Which is harder to do?
3. **11:25.** How has your level of education helped or hindered your response to the words and deeds of Jesus? Would you consider yourself one of the "wise and learned" or one of the "infants"? Which should you be?
4. **11:29.** The word "yoke" connotes drudging, plodding work, yet Jesus is offering rest. What is the difference between his yoke and the heavy burden he is inviting you to lay down?

Chapter 12

For understanding
1. **12:18.** Why does Matthew quote Isaiah 42:1–4 here?
2. **12:31.** What is "blasphemy against the Spirit"? Why can it not be forgiven?
3. **12:46.** What four observations support the Church's tradition that Mary was a perpetual virgin and that Jesus had no siblings?
4. **Chart: Jesus and the Old Testament.** What is typology? Why is it important for the understanding of Scripture?

For application
1. **12:9–14.** Read the note on this passage. What kinds of works do you engage in on the Christian Sabbath, the Lord's Day? How do you use the day of rest? What do you think Jesus would make of the way you use it?
2. **12:36–37.** How carefully do you think before you speak? What does this passage suggest to you regarding casual talk that is critical of others?
3. **12:43–45.** After you receive forgiveness of sin, do you respond by growing in virtue? Are you leaving your soul open to the return of old, sinful habits or to the grace of God?
4. **12:50.** How would you recognize a brother or sister of Jesus today?

Chapter 13

For understanding
1. **13:11.** How does Jesus' private instruction of the disciples reflect his intention to arrange the Church hierarchically?
2. **13:33.** How is the image of leaven used here? How is it often used in Scripture?
3. **Word Study: Parables.** How many ways are parables used in the Old Testament? For what purposes does Jesus use parables?
4. **13:52.** How does Matthew's ministry reflect the role of the "scribe who has been trained for the kingdom of heaven"?

For application
1. **13:3–9.** Jesus compares how you receive the word of God with the type of ground it falls on. Which type of ground most closely matches how *you* respond to his word? What makes you think so?
2. **13:24–30.** How do you answer criticisms that the Catholic Church is "dead" or "lifeless"? Where do you see signs that the wheat is growing?
3. **13:44–45.** Of what worth is the kingdom of heaven to you? Examine how you spend your time and ask yourself what you would sacrifice for heaven?
4. **13:54–57.** Have you had a relative or close friend evangelize you? What was your reaction? How close did the experience come to reflecting Jesus' remark in verse 57?

Chapter 14

For understanding
1. **14:1–12.** What two points does this narrative make? What does it suggest about the fate of the committed Christian?
2. **14:4.** What is the biblical reason John the Baptist cites for condemning the desire of Herod Antipas for Herodias?
3. **14:13–21.** How does the feeding of the five thousand in Matthew's Gospel reflect eucharistic language? What Old Testament event is similar?
4. **14:19.** How does their function of distributing the loaves and fishes point to the disciples' priesthood?

For application
1. **14:4.** What is your attitude toward unlawful sexual or marital unions within your family or church community? How have you sought God's wisdom in responding to such unions?
2. **14:13–21.** When did God ask you to do something you had no resources for? How did you know he was asking that? How did you respond? What was the result?
3. **14:12–13, 23.** How do you respond spiritually to grief? What is your prayer like when you are bereaved?
4. **14:28–31.** When have you asked God to let you do something you had no resources for? What was the result? How might Jesus' question to Peter apply to you?

Chapter 15

For understanding
1. **15:1–20.** In what way were the Pharisees, who advocated a strict observance of God's commandments, actually transgressing the law?
2. **15:19.** What is real defilement in religion? From where does it arise?
3. **15:26.** On a moral level, what sort of person does the Canaanite woman represent? How can such a person receive physical or spiritual healing?
4. **15:32–39.** What are the differences and similarities between this multiplication of food and that of 14:13–21?

For application
1. **15:3–6.** How may your religious attitudes and practices have substituted for, or taken the place of, the genuine care you owe your family, particularly your parents?
2. **15:8–9.** Which of your religious attitudes and practices are actually derived from personal preferences, local or family custom, or ethnic or national traditions? How might Jesus judge their effect on heartfelt worship of God?
3. **15:13.** Which religious attitudes and practices did you once hold and now hold no longer? What happened to them? Does their disappearance from your life illustrate this passage, or should you reconsider them?
4. **15:22–27.** What happens to your faith when God appears not to answer? Do you give up, or do you persist?

Chapter 16

For understanding
1. **16:13–20.** What are some of the key concepts and images used in this passage, and what is their Old Testament significance? How did the First Vatican Council view the importance of this passage?
2. **16:17.** What are some of the parallels between Genesis and Matthew's Gospel in this passage?
3. **16:19.** What is the importance of the metaphor of the keys? What does Peter's authority to bind and loose signify?
4. **Word Study: Peter.** What Greek word translates the Aramaic word *kepha*? What do both words mean? Why is the change of Simon's name to Peter significant, aside from the meaning of the name itself?

For application
1. **16:8–11.** How often do you forget the ways God shows his loving care in your life? How does he remind you of his concern for you?
2. **16:6.** In what ways may your own ideas about Christianity and Catholicism have been influenced by the "leaven" of dissent in the Church? What have you done to heed Jesus' warning?
3. **16:15.** In terms of the practical matters of everyday life, how do you answer Jesus' question to Peter for yourself?
4. **16:24–26.** In what ways has your commitment to Jesus and his Church entailed a denial of yourself? How have you "lost your life" by denying yourself? How does that compare with what you have gained by taking up your cross?

Chapter 17

For understanding

1. **17:1–8.** What is the Old Testament background for the Transfiguration of Jesus? What are the main points of comparison?
2. **17:5.** Whom do Moses and Elijah represent? Why is their presence on the Mount of Transfiguration important?
3. **17:20.** What seems to be the real problem Matthew sees in the "little faith" of the disciples who cannot exorcise the demon?
4. **17:27.** What is the significance of Jesus telling Peter to pay the Temple tax for them both?

For application

1. **17:5.** What do you do to obey the command of the Father to listen to his Son?
2. **17:7–8.** In what ways are you afraid of God? How might looking only at Jesus help you to overcome this fear?
3. **17:19–21.** When have you asked God why you were unable to perform a task you know you have the ability or responsibility to perform? What might too little faith have to do with your inability?
4. **17:24–27.** How generous are you in your financial support of the Church? What is your attitude toward that support?

Chapter 18

For understanding

1. **18:10.** What does this verse have to do with the Catholic belief in guardian angels? What do angels do?
2. **18:15–20.** Outline Jesus' three-step procedure for Church discipline.
3. **18:18.** Compare this passage with Mt. 16:19. What is the difference between them, in terms of authority? What is the connection between this verse and the priestly power to forgive sins?
4. **18:22.** What does the number Jesus gives (seventy times seven) imply regarding forgiveness of others? How does this number compare and contrast with the number used by Lamech in Genesis 4:24?

For application

1. **18:7–9.** Have you ever knowingly tried to induce someone to sin? What have you done to repair that damage? How close to Jesus' abhorrence to such inducements does your own attitude come?
2. **18:15–17.** How do you handle disagreements or wrongs done to you by others, especially by family? What pattern do you follow? How close to the model presented in this passage is your method of handling problems?
3. **18:21–22.** What are the limits of your own willingness to forgive others? Do you forgive readily, do you wait for the offenders to ask for forgiveness, or do you look on forgiving others as a sign of weakness? What should the limit of your willingness be?
4. **18:23–35.** Multiply your gross annual salary by 20, then multiply that amount by 10,000. Now multiply how much you earn in a single day by 100. Compare the two amounts. The difference between the two figures is comparable to the difference between what the servant owed the king in the parable and what the servant himself was owed by his fellow servant. What does the difference between the two amounts tell you about God's willingness to forgive you and about your willingness to forgive others?

Study Questions

Chapter 19

For understanding

1. **Topical Essay: Jesus on Marriage and Divorce.** How does Jesus' teaching on the permanence of marriage compare with that legislated by Moses in Deuteronomy 24:1–4? Why did God permit divorce and remarriage in the first place?
2. **Topical Essay: Jesus on Marriage and Divorce.** Summarize the three approaches taken by Catholic scholars to clarify the meaning of Jesus' "except for unchastity" clause. How would each view reinforce the Catholic Church's teaching on the indissolubility of marriage?
3. **19:14.** What is the connection between Jesus' blessing of the children and his previous discussion on divorce?
4. **19:28.** What is the meaning of Jesus' promise to the disciples that they will sit on twelve thrones and judge the twelve tribes of Israel?

For application

1. **19:3–9.** Compare the attitudes toward marriage current in our culture with the attitude of Jesus in these verses. Is your attitude toward marriage more like the culture's or like that of Jesus?
2. **19:10–12.** What is your personal attitude toward celibacy? Do you regard it as an opportunity to serve the kingdom of heaven or as an impossible burden rendered unnecessary in the modern age? If you are not married, what consideration have you given to a possible vocation to a celibate way of life?
3. **19:21–22.** What does poverty have to do with perfection? What renunciation does Jesus ask of you by way of following him? How has your response been like that of the rich young man?
4. **19:27–30.** When have you asked Jesus the question Peter asks here? How would you react to the answer Jesus gives him?

Chapter 20

For understanding

1. **20:1–16.** Why is God not being unjust to Israel by including Gentiles in the New Covenant?
2. **20:17–19.** What is the main difference between this prediction of the Passion and others in Matthew's Gospel?
3. **20:22.** What is the "cup" to which Jesus refers? How is it fulfilled in reference to the sons of Zebedee?
4. **20:30.** What belief might the title "Son of David" in this passage reflect?

For application

1. **20:1–16.** Using the hours of the day in the parable as an analogy for the time in your life when you first responded to Jesus Christ, where do you think you would fit? The parable talks about what the workers get paid; what is Jesus offering you?
2. **20:11.** When have you ever grumbled at God because of his generosity toward others?
3. **20:21–22.** Have you ever asked God for something, only to realize on hindsight that you did not know the full extent of what you were asking for? What was the request? What happened as a result? What do you now think of the result?
4. **20:25–28.** Considering that the Son of Man came not to be served but to serve, why are you here?

Chapter 21

For understanding
1. **21:1–11.** How does Jesus' triumphal entry into Jerusalem recall Solomon's coronation as king of Israel?
2. **21:13.** The selling of animals in the Temple was a service to pilgrims. What was wrong with it? What is the significance of Jesus' quotation from Isaiah 56 as the passage applies to Gentiles?
3. **21:19.** Why did Jesus curse the fig tree?
4. **21:42.** How does Jesus apply Psalm 118 to himself? How else does the New Testament use this psalm?

For application
1. **21:12–13.** Since you are the temple of the Holy Spirit, what "robbers" do you think Jesus wants to drive out?
2. **21:28–32.** Are you more like the first son or like the second one? In what ways?
3. **21:33–43.** How have you responded to people who have tried to evangelize you? If you were offended, what offended you? How much evangelism do you now think you need? Why do you think so?
4. **21:23.** What do you do when you disagree with the exercise of authority in the Church? Do you question it, challenge it, or submit to it? How do you see the authority of Jesus in it?

Chapter 22

For understanding
1. **22:11.** What is the "wedding garment" that the guest has failed to wear?
2. **22:15–22.** What is the malice in the collaboration between Pharisees and Herodians in asking Jesus the question about paying taxes?
3. **22:32.** How does Jesus tailor his answer to the Sadducees and their acceptance of only the first five books of the Hebrew Bible? What conclusions is Jesus drawing from the text?
4. **22:45.** What point is Jesus making to the Pharisees about Psalm 110 that they seem to have missed in their understanding of it?

For application
1. **22:4–5.** Are you a Sunday Christian? In the light of your everyday life, how are you responding to the invitation of God to his feast?
2. **22:21.** How honest are you in paying taxes to the local, state, and federal governments? What excuses do you make to yourself to avoid paying taxes? How generous are you in contributing to the financial support of the Church?
3. **22:37.** What does it mean to you to love God with your whole heart, soul, and mind? What do you do to demonstrate that love?
4. **22:39.** What does it mean to love your neighbor as you do yourself? How do you love yourself? How does that apply to the way you love your neighbor?

Chapter 23

For understanding
1. **23:9.** What does Jesus mean when he tells his disciples and the crowds to "call no man your father on earth"? How does this passage compare with other New Testament passages where the title "father" is used of the apostles themselves?
2. **23:35.** Who are the prophets Jesus alludes to in this passage? How is Jesus comparing his fate to theirs?
3. **23:37.** What Old Testament images does the simile of the hen echo? How does this image apply to the Church's Magisterium?
4. **23:38.** Look up Ezekiel 10:18 and 11:23. How does Jesus' departure from the Temple at this point recall Ezekiel's vision?

For application
1. **23:2-3.** What kind of trust have you placed in your religious teachers? If you are a parent, catechist, or religious teacher, how well do you practice what you preach?
2. **23:12.** What are some stories from your life that illustrate the truth of this passage for yourself? How have you been humbled? What did you learn from these events?
3. **23:16-22.** How often do you use sayings, expressions, or epithets in private conversation to proclaim your honesty, such as "I swear to God"? Why should you avoid these?
4. **23:23-24.** How would Jesus' condemnation of the scribes and Pharisees in these verses apply to your practice of Catholic devotions? For example, how does scrupulous observance of your favorite devotion compare with how you practice charity to others?

Chapter 24

For understanding
1. **24:1-46.** On what two basic levels is Jesus speaking in this sermon?
2. **Topical essay: End of the World?** In what ways are the Temple and the world linked in the Bible and in ancient Jewish tradition? What does the fate of the Temple have to do with the fate of the cosmos? What does this have to do with the modern Church?
3. **24:15.** What is the "desolating sacrilege" referred to in this verse? How does Jesus use the image?
4. **24:29.** What does the graphic imagery of the falling of the sun, moon, and stars usually refer to in the Old Testament? How does Jesus redirect it?
5. **24:36.** How does Christian tradition understand Jesus' apparent ignorance of his Second Coming?

For application
1. **24:12.** In your experience, how has the "multiplication of wickedness" in your environment or even in your own life caused your love for God to cool? What can heat it up again?
2. **24:23-26.** What has been your response to invitations to join lifestyles, new (or newly rediscovered) movements, or religious practices that promise peace, serenity, self-fulfillment, or inner harmony but are different from or inconsistent with the Christian message?
3. **24:36-44.** How does the admonition of Jesus to be watchful apply to how you live your life? How might your surroundings be distracting you? What do you need to do to prepare for the Lord's coming?

Chapter 25

For understanding
1. **25:1–13.** What Jewish marital custom is this parable based on? What moral interpretation do the early Church Fathers (Origen, Hilary) give this parable?
2. **25:26.** Why is the servant who hid the talent dealt with so harshly for his laziness?
3. **25:31–46.** At what two historical levels does the parable of the judgment of the nations operate?
4. **25:40.** Why does Jesus say that by serving others as they do, they serve (or fail to serve) Jesus himself?

For application
1. **25:1–13.** What preparations have you been making for the coming of the Bridegroom?
2. **25:14–30.** How faithful have you been over what God has given you to work with? How might you be hiding your talent?
3. **25:31–40.** Of all the corporal and spiritual works of mercy listed here, which have you done? Which have been the most fruitful for you or others?
4. **25:41–46.** Of all the corporal and spiritual works of mercy listed here, which have you failed to do even though you had opportunity or perhaps even an invitation from God to do them?

Chapter 26

For understanding
1. **26–29.** What aspects of the Last Supper does Matthew's account highlight? What Old Testament practices or imagery does the account incorporate?
2. **26:39.** Why does Jesus pray to let the cup of suffering pass him by? How does the Church traditionally view the Gethsemane event?
3. **26:64.** Why does Jesus break his silence before Caiaphas? What is the significance of Jesus' response to Caiaphas as the High Priest?
4. **26:74.** What interpretation do the saints give to the crowing of the cock after Peter's denials?

For application
1. **26:10–13.** What has been your response to persons who seem to "waste" their lives on Jesus (for example, by entering seminaries or convents when they could have married)? When have you "wasted" your own resources on him?
2. **26:30–35.** Have you ever wanted to be a martyr? Why or why not? If you once did and now no longer do, what has changed your mind?
3. **26:39.** How have you handled the major hardships of your state in life? What does resignation to God's will mean to you? How similar to Jesus' obedience is your own?
4. **26:63.** What has been your response to accusation and slander over your practice of your faith? Do you keep silent before your accusers, or do you respond in kind?

Study Questions

Chapter 27

For understanding
1. **27:8–10.** What is the Old Testament background of the potter's field? What is the geographical focus of the Old Testament passages and their New Testament application?
2. **27:46.** Why, besides the obvious reference to his own suffering in the opening lines, does Jesus quote Psalm 22 from the cross?
3. **27:51.** What is the significance of the rending of the Temple veil?
4. **27:52.** How are we to understand the raising of the saints following Jesus' Resurrection.

For application
1. **27:4–5.** When have you felt stinging remorse over something you did? Was your remorse like that of Judas (without hope) or like that of Peter in 26:75? What has been the result?
2. **27:24.** Pilate's symbolic act has resulted in a proverbial expression: "to wash one's hands" of a matter is to quit responsibility for it. For what situations have you "washed your hands" of responsibility, even though responsibility was placed on you? What did your conscience tell you about that action?
3. **27:25.** Some Christians have (wrongly) used this verse to justify their anti-Semitism. What is your attitude toward Jews and Judaism? How has that attitude changed over the years? How much do you know about the Jewish origins of Christianity?
4. **27:46.** When have you felt abandoned by God? What was the occasion? What effect did it have on your faith?

Chapter 28

For understanding
1. **28:8.** What kind of event is the Resurrection of Jesus? What event does it anticipate?
2. **Map: Appearances of the Risen Christ.** How many appearances to his disciples did Jesus make as recorded in the New Testament? In round numbers, how many people did Jesus appear to? Why so many?
3. **28:19.** What is Jesus' threefold outline for the Church's mission?
4. **28:20.** In what manner is Jesus with the Church always?

For application
1. **28:9.** If Jesus took the initiative in your life and met you before you sought him, what would be your response? Can you recall such a time? If not, how would you recognize him if he did meet you?
2. **28:19.** What is your experience with evangelizing? What is your attitude toward doing it? What do you think Jesus wants you to do about any fears you may have?
3. **28:20.** How do you recognize the ongoing presence of Jesus in your life? What do you do to encourage his presence there?

NOTES

NOTES

NOTES

NOTES

NOTES

NOTES

NOTES

NOTES